HIDDEN TAPESTRY

HIDDEN TAPESTRY

JAN YOORS, HIS TWO WIVES, AND THE WAR THAT MADE THEM ONE

DEBRA DEAN

Northwestern University Press
Evanston, Illinois

Northwestern University Press
www.nupress.northwestern.edu

Frontispiece: Annabert, Jan, and Marianne Yoors. Courtesy of the Yoors Family
Partnership.

Printed in the United States of America

10   9   8   7   6   5   4   3   2   1

Library of Congress Cataloging-in-Publication Data

Names: Dean, Debra, 1957– author.
Title: Hidden tapestry : Jan Yoors, his two wives, and the war that made them
    one / Debra Dean.
Description: Evanston, Illinois : Northwestern University Press, 2018. | Includes
    bibliographical references and index.
Identifiers: LCCN 2017043920 | ISBN 9780810136830 (pbk. : alk. paper) | ISBN
    9780810136847 (ebook)
Subjects: LCSH: Yoors, Jan. | Yoors, Jan—Relations with women. | Textile artists—
    Belgium—Biography. | Textile artists—New York (State)—New York—Biography.
Classification: LCC NK3055.A3 Y6633 2018 | DDC 746.392—dc23 LC record available
    at https://lccn.loc.gov/2017043920

For Marianne and Kore

CONTENTS

PART ONE: WAR

PART TWO: UTOPIA

PART ONE WAR

1 Pingola

A child will forever remember a certain happening in his or
her life and one cannot explain why—yet those memories
are always with them. And so it was that summer, when
I was seven years old, away from home, staying with my
father's friends and meeting Jan Yoors.
—FROM ANNABERT'S DIARIES

It was the summer of 1935, and Annabert van Wettum had been sent
to the resort town of Zeist in the Netherlands to spend a few weeks at a
vacation camp for children. All the way from The Hague, three hours by
car, she had been brave, but that night, alone in a strange bed, she was
overwhelmed with loneliness. She wrapped the hem of her flannel nightgown around her feet to protect them and tried to picture her guardian
angel, but it was no good. She wept, heartbroken.

She had not been apart from her father since her mother ran off with
the architect three years earlier. At a loss, her father had placed his two
children with neighbors. Annabert's earliest memories were of waking
up at night, the other children in the house pinching her toes. She curled
into herself, both figuratively and literally, and stopped eating. Twice a
day for nearly a year, her father came to the house and spoon-fed her
lunch and dinner, until at last they were reunited in a house by the sea
that her regal, white-haired grandmother, Omie, had built for this purpose. Now, her father had sent her away again.

Daughters adore fathers, but Annabert's propensity to worship was
unusual, and to understand the rest of the story one must first know a little something about Anthroposophy. Annabert's father, Jan van Wettum,
was an ardent disciple of a movement that emerged in the spiritualist craze

of the late nineteenth century, a religion blending teachings of Christianity, Buddhism, Rosicrucianism, and Goethe's mystical writings, along with original occult doctrine. The movement's followers believed that over time human beings had become too attached to the material world and thus blinded to reality which was, they said, largely spiritual. Anthroposophy promised to redevelop their innate spiritual perception.

Anthroposophy's founder, Rudolf Steiner, had a particular interest in childhood education, and it's here that his reach is felt even today: the thousands of schools and kindergartens worldwide known as Waldorf schools are grounded in the principles of Anthroposophy. Annabert's father taught at one of the first of these, the Vrije School den Haag (Free School of The Hague), which Annabert attended alongside her best friend, Marianne. Here the children listened to their teachers recite Germanic fairy tales and myths and were encouraged to understand their own lives in these same romantic terms.

Steiner's followers had also founded a school, called Zonnehuis, House of the Sun, to serve the needs of developmentally disabled children. In the summers, they added a camp for the children of Anthroposophists.

Her first morning at Zonnehuis, Annabert peered out the window of her room and saw a blond boy waving at her from an upper window of an ivy-covered stone house across the way. She waved back. For timid Annabert, it was a hugely significant moment, and she began to recast the narrative in her head. He was a fairy-tale prince, and the stone mansion was a dark and somber castle where lived strange people from the underworld.

The next day, she and the other campers were exploring a nearby wooded park and discovered a clearing with a large oak tree at its center and a little makeshift dugout. All at once, they were startled by whooping cries, and the boy—her prince—sprang out from behind the oak tree. The boy was costumed in a makeshift American Indian costume—his wide-collared white shirt opened to the waist and a blanket thrown over one shoulder—and he was armed with a real bow. He shook a lock of hair out of his eyes, a carefree gesture that devastated the young Annabert. Then he dove into the dugout and reemerged with a bar of chocolate to share.

Tall, slender, and flaxen-haired, twelve-year-old Jan Yoors possessed a confidence that mesmerized not only Annabert but the other campers as well, more of whom gathered around him each day. Like a Pied Piper, he enlisted their help to build a village of huts, which he decided to call Pingola. They would all be Indians, he proposed, peaceful and brave, and he would be their chief, Woega. Another girl, Esther, quickly volunteered to be the chief's wife, and he named her Woeganda. He designated Annabert their daughter and christened her Chikita.

She followed Jan about, shy to the point of wordlessness but continually at his elbow. Unlike the other boys, who were coarse and rambunctious, Jan always spoke to her gently. One day, they fashioned a rope swing for the big oak tree and were taking turns swinging in it. It was wonderful, she wrote later, swinging higher and higher, her head in the leaves, then past the ground and up again, into the heavens. Suddenly, the rope broke. She fell and blacked out. When she came to, Jan was bent over her.

Did you hurt yourself? he asked.

She saw the tender concern in his expression and forgot her pain. He lifted her up in his arms and carried her to her house. Trained by Anthroposophy to recognize the hand of destiny, Annabert knew she'd found her soul's mate. She might only be seven, but it was a conviction she would carry for the rest of her life.

Annabert van Wettum, circa 1936. Courtesy of the Yoors Family Partnership.

*Jan Yoors, circa 1936. Courtesy
of the Yoors Family Partnership.*

In Pingola, time stopped, but outside it ticked forward. After two weeks had passed, Annabert was scheduled to visit her mother, who had married the architect. Jan was to return home to Antwerp, Belgium. They pledged to write each other, but Annabert was bereft. Jan gently reassured her: Esther might be his pretend Indian wife, but someday when they were big, he would come back to the Netherlands and take Annabert as his real wife. As she was being driven away in her stepfather's car, he ran alongside, waving. She waved back frantically until he was lost to view.

The Hague 3 October '35

Dear Jan,

How is everything with your wrist? I like it so much that your letter came right on my birthday. I got twelve presents. I got a photo album, and now I can put your photos in it.

Merry Christmas from Annabert

18 December 1935

Dear Annabert:

*How are you? You have to excuse me that I didn't write to you earlier,
but don't think that I have forgotten you. I have been very busy with
examinations and I am very well graduated. I was one of the first three
of eleven in Latin, Greek, Netherlands, French, German, and the
first in Drawing. I wish very much to come to The Hague. My wrist is
totally healed and you cannot see anything anymore, and I can use it
just as well as the other one. When I can, I will bring you the bracelet
that I bought in Malang. During the last vacation I was in Gistroux,
Malang. There my father has sugar, corn, banana, and cassava plantations, that I went to visit.*

*My father has enormous pampas near Tuantepec where hundreds of
horses and buffaloes are. I think I told you about that in Zeist. As soon
as I see you, I will tell you about my travels and show you beautiful
photos from there. Thank you very much for your photos. You are all
looking very well.*

With many greetings from Jan

*Detail of letter written from Jan to Annabert, 1935. Courtesy of the Yoors
Family Partnership.*

In truth, the thirteen-year-old boy boasting about his academic successes had been attending school only sporadically. And though he'd been traveling continually, he had never stepped foot off the continent, much less to Malang in East Java or Tehuantepec in Mexico. His father had no plantations, no herds of horses and buffalo. In short, there would be no photos forthcoming. In lieu of these, Jan had illustrated his letter with tiny pencil drawings of a bracelet; a temple topped by a half moon; two hunters, one with a ten-gallon hat, the other in native garb; and at the bottom of the page, next to his signature, a little sketch of two Indians in feather headdresses sharing a pipe at a campfire. Nearby was a group of teepees shaded by, of all things, a palm tree.

Most likely the wrist injury was a guise to explain the lapse on his side of their correspondence. Even so, the inventions contained threads of truth. His mother had some American Indian blood and was descended from a prominent shipbuilding family that had come to Antwerp a generation earlier, following a slave revolt on their plantation in Cuba. It's reasonable to think they may have raised sugar, cassava, corn, or bananas, and that this bit of family lore trickled into Jan's fabrications, along with the palm trees. And while he was doing poorly in more subjects than he was excelling, he did possess an unusual gift for languages and had gotten good marks in those classes. At home, he spoke French with his mother, Spanish with his father, and German with the exchange students who helped in the household. When in school, he conversed in Flemish. When not in school, he was gaining fluency in yet another language, Romani.

He had also earned that first in drawing. His father, Eugeen Yoors, was a painter and stained glass artist, and many of Jan's idyllic early memories were set in the skylit studio on the top floor of their house. His mother, a social reformer, traveled frequently, and in her absence his father would sit him down in a sunny corner with paints and charcoal and drawing paper to keep him occupied. As a reward for working quietly, his father told him tales from Greek, Finnish, and Indian mythology as well as reminiscences of the Gitanos, the Spanish Gypsies from Eugeen Yoors' own childhood in Andalusia. He recited the deeds of Old Testament heroes, and the Catholic saints and martyrs who were the subjects of the church windows he was designing. It's no surprise that when Jan first met Annabert, he was playing at being an American Indian or that his subsequent letters to her invoked fantasies of faraway lands and wild peoples. No, the surprise is that his fibs to Annabert were cover for a real-life adventure every bit as improbable as the lies.

2 The Gypsies

I was probably 6 years old when I first heard about gypsies. I was lying down on my stomach in the middle of the
floor of my father's large atelier and I was drawing. . . .
My father spoke of a little gypsy girl that he met on the El
Rocío pilgrimage. From the portrait that my father told us
about the little bohemian, she was extraordinarily pretty,
intelligent also, and she was only six years old, the same age
as my father at the time. What caught my attention was that
she was exactly the same age as I; that, above all, brought
me closer to her. And then her foreign name, "Pepita," and
also that my father discussed gypsies a lot that night. He
told thousands of stories.

   That night I dreamed of gypsies. I was ignorant about
what they were, but I imagined that they must be extraordinary beings of beauty and intelligence, almost superhuman
and close to angels.

—JAN YOORS

Just as Annabert's life was set on its course by a chance meeting in childhood, so too was Jan's. When he was twelve years old, the spring after he
met Annabert and her friends, he happened upon another group of children. An extended family of Gypsies, called a *kumpania*, had made camp
on the outskirts of his hometown of Antwerp, and he was lured there
one afternoon by the chance to see real, live incarnations of his father's
stories. A caravan of about fifteen covered wagons was drawn into a
semicircle, and from inside rose thin plumes of campfire smoke. Several
men lounged in the shade of a tree, and the women, dressed in long,

flowing skirts and with gold coins for jewelry, tended the fires. Children, naked or in dirty rags, ran about the camp, shrieking and tossing sticks for wildly barking dogs. They were quite different from the Gypsies his father had described, "who were ethereal, mythical, and above all imaginary." These people were earthy and exuberant, laughing and shouting. They had an animal magnetism that pulled Jan closer to the fire. The older Gypsies paid him no mind, but a few of the boys ran to meet him.

Jan addressed them in Spanish, the language of his father's Gypsies. The boys didn't know Spanish and tried answering in broken German. However, their mutual curiosity overcame the challenges of language, and soon the boys were showing Jan the tribe's horses, tethered at the edge of the camp. Then they showed him a string of small, dead animals hung on a line. One of the boys, Nanosh, explained that they had caught these, that they were hedgehogs and were a great delicacy. He promised to show Jan how to hunt them next time he visited.

Suddenly, an ancient, leather-skinned woman appeared and began hurling abuse at Jan, yelling at him to go home. Jan was unnerved, but behind her back the boys grinned and gestured that he shouldn't pay her any mind. Old Lyuba wouldn't really hurt him. They all disliked strangers, of course, but Lyuba was in the habit of expressing her dislike very loudly.

Rom—Nanosh pointed proudly to his own chest—was the word for themselves. He hesitated and then pointed at Jan: *Gaje* was the word for everyone else. Jan saw, to his surprise, that the word was not a compliment. Not only did the Rom not feel themselves inferior, they had as many prejudices against the Gaje as the Gaje had against them.

The Gypsy boys were barefoot, and trying to fit in, Jan took off his shoes. First one boy tried on the shoes, then another took a turn. He then passed the shoes to the older boys whose feet were too large, a problem they solved by lopping off the toes of the shoes. Briefly, Jan wondered how he was going to explain this to his parents, but only briefly. He was having too much fun.

The boys invited Jan to stay for dinner. Sitting with Nanosh, he listened to the Gypsies telling stories and singing around the blazing campfire. Though he couldn't understand a word, he was entranced. Before he knew it, the sky had darkened, the Gypsies were spreading eiderdown quilts on the ground, and Nanosh was inviting him to share a makeshift bed with him and his little brothers. It was already so late and Jan was without shoes. Without reasoning any further than this, he spent the night.

He awoke early the next morning to the hysterical barking of the dogs, voices yelling, and a bedlam of frenzied activity. The police were raiding the camp, forcing the Gypsies on their way. Bedding was being pulled up, and pots and pans thrown into the wagons. The men unchained the horses and hitched them to wagons. Putzina hurriedly directed Jan into his family's wagon, and Nanosh helped hide him under a pile of quilts. The wagon began to rock and move. Jan peeked out from under the quilts and saw policemen at a crossroads shouting directions, sending one wagon this way, another that, in order to break up the large group. When Jan finally dared to come out from under the quilts, he was on an unfamiliar road, in a small caravan of wagons.

"I just stayed from one day to the other," he later explained, "and eventually I stayed away for six or seven months. It was not running away in a rebellious sense; it was not a planned thing. It just kind of happened. You see, the longer I stayed with them the more difficult it was to go back home. After one night, I might have, but after the second night, I couldn't have anymore. And with the third night, it was impossible."

Had he been any older, he might never have been able to insinuate himself into the closed Romani culture. But with the facility of a child and his own innate charm, he slipped under the fence. He adapted rapidly, learning the language of his hosts and aping their practices. He ate with his fingers and afterwards wiped the grease on them through his hair for shine. He learned which buckets were for wash water, which were for drinking, and all the observances and civilities that allowed the Gypsies to live in close quarters without privacy. The tribe he had joined, headed by Putzina's father, Pulika, was called the Lowara, and they were horse traders, so he learned how to tend to the animals.

The Rom were always on the move. In a sense, this was enforced—no community tolerated their staying in one place for more than a few days—but even had they been allowed, they were too restless to settle anywhere. To be alive and free was to be on a journey. The journey had no timetable and no known destination, but that isn't to say it was without purpose. Jan learned to read the subtle signs called *vurma*—broken twigs or a bit of colored thread tied to a tree that the Rom left along the sides of the road like maps pointing the way for each other. Gypsies traveled in order to meet up with other Gypsies, and as if by magic, hundreds of wagons might converge in one place over the space of a few days, arriving from every compass point. These meetings were cause for celebration, feasts, and an exchange of stories. And then after an indeterminate period, the groups would break apart again and move on, but never in exactly the same configurations in which they had come together. Jan likened the Rom to quicksilver, "joining and splitting and joining, not with the same group, but joining with other groups and splitting again. It's completely different. Nothing is ever static."

As winter approached—a miserable time for the Gypsies because they had to hole up inside their cramped wagons—Jan was told one day that they would be passing close to his hometown. Pulika, a gentle father with intelligent eyes and an impressive drooping moustache, gave him change for a bus and then pulled him into a hug, saying that certainly they'd meet again. Jan said his goodbyes to his friend Putzina, to Putzina's sister Keja, and his brother Kore, to Pulika's wife, Rupa, and the various members of the extended family. And then he made his way back to his parents.

As though waking from a dream, he walked back into the house in Antwerp, filthy and dressed in the rags of the clothes he'd been wearing when he left six or seven months before. His parents were entertaining guests at dinner, fellow writers and artists; when they saw him, they affected a calm manner and simply sent him upstairs to clean up. He obeyed and then waited in his bedroom, braced for the punishment that was surely coming, but they never reproved him. Astonishingly, they said only that they loved him and though they had hoped he might follow in his father's footsteps and become an artist, the decision was entirely his: if he preferred to live as a nomad, they wouldn't stand in his way.

For their part, Eugeen Yoors and Magda Yoors-Peeters must surely have been frantic when their son disappeared, and perhaps even instigated the police raid that had unwittingly sent their son on the road—but that side of the story is lost. Jan told a radio interviewer in 1966: "It was something we never talked about and even today they don't. It's a subject that's kept in mythical haze. . . . My parents just kept it vague and mysterious, and I think it's much nicer that way. One shouldn't know the truth."

The truth, it seems, was not nice. In Jan's memoirs and in countless interviews, he portrayed his running off with the Gypsies as a romantic, boyish whim. However, there is an undated entry in Annabert's 1978 diary that suggests a darker explanation. Addressing herself to Jan, Annabert wrote about the influences that had shaped him. "And I think of you, your life. How your Pappy gave you such books to read, when you were a growing boy—so you knew many things about life, but seen from the sad side of unfaithfulness, intrigues between lovers, friendships between women in the unnatural sense. How you were molested by your priest teacher in school. Then your involvement in the war. And next to this the positive influence of Pulika and his family."

It is a single line—*How you were molested by your priest teacher in school*—but it casts a long shadow across Jan's story, recasting his adventure as an escape. It also helps to explain why the devout altar boy who drew pictures of the Virgin Mary in his father's studio would eventually reject the Catholic Church and its teachings, and invent a new utopia in its place, one dedicated to art and harmony.

In the spring, the Gypsies returned and Jan once again left with them. "I was drawn to the Gypsies as by a magnet," he explained, "and felt strangely unable to shake off their spell." So began his double life and a pattern he would follow for the next seven years: leaving his parents' house in the spring to seek out the Gypsies, and returning to Antwerp for a few months each winter.

3 The Belgian Bohemians

It makes a certain sense that a boy would act out the then-common fantasy of running away with Gypsies, even more so if he were fleeing sexual abuse, but what kind of parents would respond with such leniency?

Jan's mother, Magda, told a story about his first attempt to leave home when he was two or three years old. He announced to her that he was going out, and began to dress, putting on his mittens, his shoes, and his coat. She responded that she, too, would get ready. No, he answered solemnly, I'm going alone. They lived on a quiet, untrafficked street in Antwerp with a small plaza, so Magda opened the door and bade her little son goodbye. Watching through the front window, she and her husband saw him walk out into the street and then stop. He stood for some minutes looking around, and then abruptly turned and came back up the walk. He knocked on the door. When they answered, he said, I am still too small.

The anecdote portrays Jan as a child consciously preparing for his life's journey, but it also suggests that his parents viewed their own role as only very lightly custodial. In keeping with their larger social views on emancipation, they regarded Jan as an autonomous and equal person capable of charting his own destiny.

One neighbor recalled that Magda was always barefoot or in sandals and that Eugeen never wore a tie, leading the neighborhood to conclude that they must be communists, anarchists, or vegetarians. They were correct only in the last supposition: the Yoors had become vegetarian under the twin influences of Mahatma Gandhi and their sensitive young boy. Jan persisted, night after night, in asking the origins of the meat on the table before it was killed. Upon being told, he would then earnestly inquire if this little chicken or cow or rabbit or pig had been so naughty that it had to die. The strain of this nightly inquisition led the Yoors to give up meat, and eventually they went a step further and became among the first practitioners of macrobiotics. As artists, political activists, and freethinkers in the bohemian tradition, they were no doubt quite the curiosity in conservative Antwerp.

Eugeen and Magda had first met at the house of a mutual acquaintance: Eugeen, a thirty-five-year-old artist, and Magda, a poet and suffragette thirteen years his junior. The acquaintance had commissioned Eugeen to paint him, but before he could do more than a few preliminary sketches, World War I broke out. Yoors enlisted in the Belgian Army and very shortly ended up in an internment camp in the Netherlands, not as a prisoner of war but as one of more than 33,000 Belgian soldiers who had fled from the Germans across the border only to be disarmed by their neutral Dutch neighbors and forced to sit out the war. They were housed in overcrowded barracks and tents at Amersfoort, Camp Zeist.

To improve morale, Yoors and a couple of fellow internees persuaded camp directors to allow them to set up a little art studio. Using the materials at hand—chalk, butcher paper, and charcoal—Yoors drew portraits of hundreds of his uniformed comrades, as well as landscapes of their blighted surroundings.

When the city of Antwerp fell to the Germans in October 1914, and an estimated one million Belgian civilians flooded over the Dutch border, Magda Peeters was among them. Somehow, in that mass of refugees, the two found each other and renewed their acquaintance. On July 6, 1918, they were married in the little wooden chapel of the camp.

One winter afternoon, the two were returning from a day spent caring for other Belgian refugees. They were walking on a road near the Dutch-German border and saw something lying in the mud up ahead. Upon closer inspection, they saw it was a German soldier. His bloodied feet showed through broken shoes, and he was delirious with cold and hunger, unaware even that he had crossed the border. They hated the Germans—in fact, Magda had taken an active hand in disseminating that hatred through magazine and newspaper articles—but they were also devout Catholics and couldn't leave a man to die. They sneaked him into their landlady's house, and Magda knelt down and washed his bloody feet. In that moment, she later wrote, "something fell from my eyes, and I saw that he was a brother. A German was my brother."

She began working with the Quakers, and when she returned to Brussels she founded a Flemish branch of the International Fellowship of Reconciliation and testified on behalf of Flemish conscientious objectors. She had a radio program on which she pressed for women's rights and tackled Flemish cultural and political issues. She argued for legislation against the common practice among farmers of watering down their milk. Through the International Fellowship of Independence, she met Gandhi in 1931 and subsequently went to India in support of its independence movement. Later she would speak out on the air against the growing threat of Nazism. In 1938, with her friend Betsie Hollants, a journalist with the Catholic newspaper *De Morganpost*, she went to Germany to lecture and participate in an anti-Nazi protest. Betsie sent a postcard back to Belgium with their itinerary and closed by saying, "And if we cannot be found at these places, just ask Hitler [where we are]."

Dear Woega,

Thank you for your letters and postcards. Forgive me that I let you wait so long for an answer, but I write you now after your last letter for my birthday. I'm happy that you thought about my birthday. I'm now eleven years old. You ask me what I want the most from you. Well, I will tell you. I should like that bracelet you brought back from Mexico, and that you would bring it over the weekend, but if that is not possible you can send it to me. I got so many presents that if you don't have the bracelet anymore, I don't have to have anything, but I would like it very much.

Many greetings,

Chikita

Dearest Chikita,

I cannot come this vacation because I am on the seaside with my father who suffers again from "balula" since he came back from our colonies. It will probably be another time, maybe at Pentecost.

*With a lot of greetings from Woega
who loves you very much.*

Jan became more Gypsy in his ways, more Vanya, his Gypsy name, than Jan, though his long limbs, blond hair, and delicate, pale features still set him apart. More than once, some well-meaning Gajo tried to rescue him, in the certainty that he had been abducted.

The Rom thought this was hilarious: why would Gypsies steal children? Didn't they already have enough mouths to feed? But count on the Gaje to get it all wrong; they were an endless source of amusement. The boys peppered Jan with questions about the inscrutable mysteries of Gaje culture: why, for instance, did they save their "nose dirt" in handkerchiefs? Bathrooms and bathtubs were another puzzle. The Rom preferred to clean themselves in running water, and found disgusting the notion of soaking both their private parts and their hands in the same warm, still water. They were also more discreet in their toilet habits. A man might casually suggest that he was going to check on the horses, and other men would join him on this errand. How, the Gypsies wondered, could one avoid the mutual embarrassment of letting members of the opposite sex know that you were relieving yourself if you had to use a room in the house expressly for that purpose?

Beyond such trivial differences was a wider gulf, with fear, scorn, and distrust on both sides. The onset of the Great Depression had only exacerbated the tensions. Underemployed locals increasingly viewed Rom who were itinerant workers—musicians, tinkers, woodworkers, or the like—as competition. The rest were assumed to be thieves. When the Rom rode into town, the local peasants ostentatiously took their clothes off the line and drove their cows and horses into the barn. If something went missing, from a chicken to a pie plate or a ball of twine, and Gypsies were anywhere in the vicinity, it went without saying that they had stolen it. Local police routinely raided Gypsy camps, disemboweling wagons and slitting open feather beds in search of stolen property, and making arrests.

In their defense, Yoors later pointed out that had the Gypsies committed even half the thefts of which they were accused, they wouldn't have been able to travel under the great mountain of their booty. They were nomads with compact wagons, and their material needs were few. More to the point, though, they didn't place any value on possessions. To them, the Gaje's attachment to property was just one more enigma.

Nevertheless, Yoors admitted, Gypsies would beg or steal for today, if not for tomorrow. Because the men of the Lowara tribe traded horses and the women told fortunes, they were less reliant on pilfering than some other tribes, but even so, they supplemented these earnings by helping themselves to a few chickens or a bushel of apples as needed.

In the second year that Jan was traveling with Pulika's family, the always-smoldering hostility between Rom and Gaje flared into the open, with dire consequences. One night Jan, with a group of the boys and girls, decided to go to a dance being held at a country fair. Even before they went inside the fairground tent, Jan heard muttered remarks around them about the *barakkenvolk*, a word that translated literally as "people living in covered wagons" but was generally understood to mean scum of the earth. Inside, girls, both Gypsy and peasant, danced to the mechanical strains of a barrel organ. In both groups, it wasn't considered proper to dance with a young man unless he was a cousin or a fiancé, so mostly the boys stood around the periphery of the tent and watched. They watched

Jan Yoors (second from left) with the Gypsies, circa 1930s. Courtesy of the Yoors Family Partnership.

the girls, but they also cast glowering looks at one other. When a few of the Gypsy boys directed appreciative remarks at the local girls, the tension in the air sparked. Suddenly there was a scuffle that spilled out into the night. Gypsies and farm boys pummeled each other in the dark, and then Jan saw the glitter of knife blades. Putzina's brother, Kore, yelled at them to scatter. Putzina and Jan ran into the road, almost simultaneously but not quite. Jan saw headlights and a dark, rumbling mass, and then his friend lay dead on the road behind him.

The Gypsies' grief was loud and intense. Though quieter in expression, Jan's distress over the loss of Putzina equaled theirs, and this shared grief sealed the bond between Jan and the boy's family. One evening Lyuba, the old woman who had once tried to frighten Jan away from the Gypsy camp, called him over to her. In a primitive gesture of affection, she began searching his scalp for fleas. Now you are Pulika's son, she said.

Pulika and the other Rom began to call Jan *Putzina o jovinda*, the live one. Eventually it was shortened to just Putzi.

April 12, 1937

Dearest Chikita,

. . . I am here alone with my father who is ill and who is lying on his campstool on the beach, and then I have to stay with him and help him and take care of him. But today for my birthday he got up for the first time and celebrated me with a pair of his Indian cabin boys who otherwise stay on the deck of my yacht. And that was a big surprise. Next to my plate was a package from Holland, and from who else but you, with that beautiful portrait of my dearest, dearest Chikita. If you knew what a pleasure that was for me. Do you still remember Pingola and all the huts that we built and the little snake that I caught and showed you that time you came with your uncle with the car back in Zeist? And the time that you fell from the swing . . . yes, I remember everything very, very well, everything that concerns you. I don't know if you remember all that but I know that you haven't forgotten me and because of that I am very, very happy. I stay here for another few days with my father and then I'm going back to Antwerp because I have to go back to

school, but as soon as I see a possibility to come to The Hague I will do it. Be sure about that. Again, many, many thanks for your beautiful portrait and many, many greetings from my father and from me.

Woega, who loves you very much

Annabert's letters to Jan, forwarded from Antwerp to addresses and post offices around Europe, were belatedly answered. Their plotted reunions were deferred from season to season and then from year to year. Finally, in 1937, three years after they had met, the two made plans for Jan to visit on his way to the World Scout Jamboree in the Netherlands that August. Annabert eagerly anticipated his visit: with the help of her friends, they would build huts and re-create their beloved Pingola on the dunes behind her grandmother's house. And this time they would be under the same roof, so they could be together every minute. When Omie scotched the notion that Jan would sleep with her, Annabert was pliant but mystified: when her friend Marianne spent the night, they always shared her bed. Omie blushed, but the wellborn daughter of the former governor of Dutch Borneo couldn't bring herself to explain the difference to her granddaughter.

It turned out to be an unneeded precaution. On the day of his scheduled arrival, Jan didn't show. After a few days, they wired an inquiring telegram to Antwerp, but there was no response. The summer passed, and a little bit of Annabert's dream died. Eventually a profuse apology arrived: his parents had gone on vacation in July, Jan said, and he'd been sent to his aunt Mimisse's. She had opened Annabert's letter and forbade him to go. It had all been a misunderstanding.

Annabert didn't question the explanation and instantly forgave him everything. They resumed their correspondence, but it would be nine more years before she saw him, except in the photograph that sat on the dresser next to her bed.

IN ROMANI CULTURE, marriage made a man of a boy, a woman of a girl. There was no category for bachelors; if you weren't a married man, you were still a child. As for their female counterparts, the Romani word for "girl" was the same as that for virgin; no distinction was thought needed. Strict codes of behavior curtailed contact between the sexes—no talking, much less flirting—and as Jan learned, albeit slowly, even looking too intently at a Gypsy girl was forbidden.

There was one girl in particular whom he struggled ineffectively not to look at. Her name was Dijidi, and Jan found her intoxicating. When the extended Lowara family gathered together for their annual meeting, called the *kris*, he devised reasons to be in her company, talking with another boy perhaps but keeping her in his peripheral vision. His attraction to her didn't go unobserved. One day Jan's adopted sister Kaje found him alone and took it upon herself to chastise him.

Our father has seen the looks you give Dijidi, she scolded, and he has chosen her for your wife. But you're not a Rom. If you marry her, you'll end up regretting the wife and children that keep you with us. Or you'll leave them behind and return to the Gaje world. And what will become of Dijidi then? Have you considered that?

He hadn't. Pulika's plans for him came as a complete surprise. It was traditional for the father to select a bride for his son and negotiate the bridal price with her father. The arranging of marriages was a traditional culmination of the annual *kris*, one of the main reasons the far-flung families came together. But his sister was right: he hadn't seen this coming because he still had one foot in the world of his birth. He loved people on both sides, but he didn't fit completely into either world. When one place started to chafe, he'd flee to the other until longing pulled him back again. Years before, Pulika's wife, Rupe, had called him a *vadni ratsa*, wild goose, due to his sudden departures and returns. At the time, it had amused him to think that the Rom found *him* wild, but now he saw the truth of it. As moved as he was by Pulika's fatherly consideration, as attracted as he was to Dijidi, he couldn't marry her.

He dreaded telling Pulika, and not only because the thing was done and to undo it would, inevitably, be awkward. With this act, he would be rejecting a future life among the Rom. Still, it couldn't be otherwise. He went to his adoptive father, but before he could force out the words, Pulika sensed the boy's agony and embraced him tenderly.

A short time later, he arranged for Jan to accompany a small delegation that was traveling to Paris on some mysterious business with fellow Rom.

Much later, Jan would learn that the trip to Paris had been a last-ditch attempt on the part of Pulika to secure papers for his family to travel *perdal l paya*, beyond the waters, to the Americas. His younger brother had brought his *kumpania* west, fleeing the looming peril in Germany, but the two brothers agreed that with war coming, safety lay even further west. Such a journey, crossing an ocean, had always been difficult for Gypsies to arrange; now, however, it turned out no longer to be possible.

Jan returned from Paris to the Lowara, happy to be in their midst, though he detected an ineffable change, an awareness perhaps only on his part that he wasn't entirely one of them.

On the morning of May 10, 1940, they were camped in a peaceful wood just north of the French-Belgian border. The night had been warm, and they were sleeping in the open under eiderdowns. He woke to a pleasant humming sound, which grew steadily louder and more ominous. The horses began to spook, and suddenly the air was screaming, and the sky filled with bombers. They flew slowly over the camp, and then tilted their wings one by one to release their payload farther on. The sound of thunder was followed by columns of black smoke in the distance and the wail of sirens.

Though unharmed, the Gypsies were terrified. Naked children ran for cover under the wagons, and their mothers shrieked and keened in an orgy of grief, just as they did at funerals. Old Lyuba raised her withered arms to the sky and yelled out that the end of the world had come. It was more prophetic than even an old fortune-teller could know.

4 The Best Friend

For their first years in prewar Holland, Marianne Citroen and Annabert van Wettum lived in a peaceful and affluent suburb of The Hague. In the compact geography of childhood, their world was circumscribed by the dunes behind Annabert's house and by Marianne's house across the street, the farm next door, and their schoolhouse at the end of the street. They gravitated to one another, each girl wordlessly recognizing a sympathetic spirit. After school, the two friends pushed their baby dolls around in Marianne's doll carriage, or played contentedly together in the large sandbox under the fir trees behind Annabert's house. The girls dressed and undressed their dolls, the size of real toddlers, in little outfits the Citroens' seamstress had made and then fed them imaginary cakes before tucking them into their beds and covering them with blankets of sand. They sang lullabies to their babies and dreamed of becoming real mothers someday.

When Marianne was nine or ten, Henri Citroen, a prosperous businessman (though no relation to the automobile magnate), moved his wife and four children to a larger house. Marianne and Annabert continued to see each other at school and on occasional sleepovers, but after school Marianne returned to her new home on the edge of the Haagse Bos, the forested park in The Hague. Cautioned not to disturb her mother, who lay sick with another migraine in her darkened room, Marianne and her little sister, Anneke, would quietly amuse themselves for hours in their playroom. At night, they fell asleep holding hands across the gap of their twin pull-down beds.

Then, in March 1939, when she was twelve years old, the bottom of Marianne's world dropped open like a trapdoor. It was the most ordinary of mornings, with Henri Citroen getting dressed for work, the servant clearing breakfast, and the children grabbing book bags and rushing

27

Marianne Citroen, circa 1936. Courtesy of the Yoors Family Partnership.

out the door to their various schools. In the hubbub, Anneke missed the neighbor who was to walk her to school that morning. Her two older brothers had already left, but someone was found to accompany her across the road and through the Haagse Bos. Marianne still had to walk her dog Queenie before she could bicycle to her school. She snapped the leash onto her little terrier's collar, opened the front door, and let Queenie tug her out into the sunshine and down the front walk.

On the far side of the highway, her sister was calling to her from atop the little bridge over the canal. Marianne will take me, Anneke informed the young woman with her. Already she was trotting toward Marianne, down the bridge and back across the tram tracks. As Marianne watched, her little sister stepped out into the road and was struck down by a car.

Marianne stood on the far side of the road, frozen in shock. At some point, an ambulance came and then left again. Her uncle ran after it and jumped in. Other things may have happened, Marianne didn't know, she was gone from her body. When she came back, two old people, supported on the arms of neighbors, were being led into her house, and Queenie was tugging the leash to follow them. She let the dog lead her back up the walk like a blind person and into the house, where she found the two old people seated in the front room, slumped into each other like a pair of rag dolls. They were her mother and father.

Some indeterminate time later, she was ushered into her parents' room, where her mother was propped up in the bed. Most likely she'd been given a tranquilizer, because her eyes were empty and she was eerily calm. She said, Anneke has died. And your sister is now a little angel.

Can she come back? Marianne wanted to know.

No.

Can I go and tell Fiena?

Yes.

She went downstairs to the kitchen where the German maid, Fiena, was sitting with the nurse and the woman who came in once a week to do the heavy work. She joined them at the kitchen table and announced that Anneke had died.

Yes, we know, they said. And that was that. Later, a neighbor lady took Marianne to a store to buy burial clothes for Anneke: woolen stockings and winter clothes so that she wouldn't get cold in the earth.

The family left that house almost immediately; it would have been too painful to stay. They moved a few miles to the seaside resort of Scheveningen, to a lovely house covered entirely in yellow tea roses and with a huge cherry tree that shed drifts of blossoms onto the back lawn. That summer, the family went for a few weeks to a grand old hotel in the countryside. Her parents had bought Marianne a small box camera to occupy her, and she used it to take a photo of them. The couple sat side by side on wicker deck chairs, and Ellie Citroen raised herself up and allowed Marianne to pose Queenie on her lap. Though Henri Citroen attempted a genial expression for the camera, his wife could not manage it. Both parents' lips were pressed thin, their eyes hooded in shadow. It was a portrait of forbearance and exhaustion.

That summer of 1939, the outside world looked increasingly dark as well. Every measure to appease or forestall German aggression seemed to be failing, and Europe was now nervously rearming and choosing up sides. The Netherlands intended to remain on the sidelines, as it had for the last war. They had a long history of neutrality, and prided themselves on being a peace-loving people who were above the fray of political turmoil. There were also less high-minded reasons to remain neutral. Henri Citroen's business was emblematic of these: he was a dealer of German and English office machinery, and a pact with either country would have severed his business with the other. At the national level, it was much the same: if the Netherlands aligned themselves with Germany, they risked losing the Dutch West Indies to the British; if, on the other hand, they threw in their lot with England, Germany might be sorely tempted to cross their shared border in a preemptive strike.

Inside the Citroen house, it was all Marianne's parents could do to hold themselves together. Her mother, Ellie Citroen, was dying of cancer and had probably been sick for many years. Nothing was said of this to the children, but more and more frequently Ellie was sequestered in her room. Finally a woman, Mrs. Blomsma, was brought in to run the house in her stead.

Marianne, naive but highly intuitive, understood in a deep, animal way long before she could make any logical sense of it. It came in a moment, inexplicable and powerful as a dream: she was standing outside the door of her parents' room where she was not allowed to enter. The door was ajar. She couldn't see her mother, though she sensed vaguely that she was inside and lying on the bed, but through the sliver of the open door she saw her handsome father's profile. He was standing next to the gramophone, and husband and wife were listening to a violin concerto by Max Bruch, the music slow and achingly romantic. Her father's gaze rested on some invisible distance, and in that moment Marianne perceived that her mother was going away.

Ellie Citroen remained at home long enough to celebrate her daughter's thirteenth birthday at the end of October 1939; the following day, she went into the hospital. Marianne didn't see her for two months until one day her father picked her up from school at lunchtime and drove her to the hospital. They went into a bare room with a single bed so high that Marianne was compelled to climb onto a bench in order to see her mother. The sight horrified her: her mother had transformed into someone nearly unrecognizable, her face yellow, swollen, and covered in large lumps.

Ellie Citroen searched her daughter's face and said, Oh, *Kindje*—my child—do I look so bad? She sat up, reached for a little hand mirror, and looked at her reflection. Then she closed her eyes.

In the car driving back, her father said, Mama is not coming back. Mama is going to die.

A week into the new year, Mrs. Blomsma woke her and told her to come downstairs. The hospital had called her father to come because the end was near. With her two brothers, Marianne sat at the table in the too-bright dining room and waited. Sometime later, the phone rang again, there was a brief murmured exchange, and Mrs. Blomsma came into the dining room and told the children that their mother had passed away. As she had at the time of her sister's death, Marianne felt the need to tell someone. She asked Mrs. Blomsma if she could call her friend, Gerdie. The housekeeper said yes, perhaps not realizing that the girl didn't intend to wait until morning. Marianne went out to the phone in the front room and woke up Gerdie's family with her news.

On the morning of the funeral, her mother was laid out in the front room. People crowded into the house, aunts and uncles and friends, to view Mrs. Citroen, but Marianne wouldn't make the mistake of looking on her mother's countenance again. When everyone had said their goodbyes, her father kept the children in the front room with him, just the four of them, and led them in a little farewell speech to their mother. They promised her that they would stay together and take care of each other. Then they went to the cemetery. Marianne trailed her father and two brothers behind the coffin. Who is next? she thought, and she began to cry. Her brother Hans turned around and sharply admonished her. She stopped.

One Sunday afternoon not so long after the funeral, Tante Alice and Om Dick came from Amsterdam to visit. They weren't really her aunt and uncle but the best friends of Marianne's parents, a wealthy, child-less couple who fascinated the Citroen children because they employed lace-collared maids and a butler, and Tante Alice's upstairs rooms were decorated entirely in white, with even a white-lacquered grand piano. That afternoon, everyone sat in the Citroens' living room. The grown-ups were listening intently to a man on the radio. Marianne couldn't understand what the man was saying because he spoke German, but he was shouting and sounded very angry. After the man on the radio had finished talking, Om Dick announced that he and Tante Alice were leaving Holland. They were going to Canada, he said, and they implored Henri to come with them. Marianne's father shook his head. He wouldn't consider it. My wife and daughter are buried here in Holland, he said. For better or worse, we will remain here with them.

On the 10th of May, 1940, Marianne had stayed at Gerdie's house for a sleepover. The two girls were awoken at three in the morning by a lot of noise. They went into the parents' bedroom. The family lived in the woods, in a large, modern house, and the bedroom was like a treehouse, with huge panes of glass from floor to ceiling. Through the trees, Marianne saw airplanes coming toward the windows, coming over the treetops and releasing bombs.

Still in their nightclothes, she and the family all went running through the trees to a nearby house. Marianne heard the dull thud of bombs and, closer, another sound like popping corn. Inside, they were taken downstairs to a shelter in the basement. Someone at this house phoned her father and then told her that he was coming to fetch her home. She waited for what seemed like hours, increasingly fearful. Eventually her father arrived. It had taken so long, he said, because the road that led directly there was bombed out, and he had had to come in a roundabout way.

When they reached home, Marianne saw her brother and a group of his friends standing outside on the street corner, looking up and out toward the sea. The whole sky was filled with airplanes and parachutes. In wave after wave, the chutes burst open like great white poisonous mushrooms and fell slowly to earth.

5 The Occupation

After Hitler marched into Poland in September 1939, France and Britain had responded by declaring war. However, they hesitated to follow words with decisive action, leading to a tense eight-month stalemate variously dubbed the Phony War, the Bore War, or the Twilight War. Then Hitler forced their hand.

In the early hours of May 10, 1940, he launched a massive, coordinated attack on Belgium, the Netherlands, and Luxembourg. In a matter of hours, war was no longer an abstraction. In The Hague, the Dutch woke in the night to the thunder of German planes passing overhead, apparently headed across the North Sea toward England. Then the planes circled back. Roaring in low over the city, they began to drop bombs. As the first light of day made them visible, wave after wave of planes continued to come, like a plague of locusts darkening the sky. Now they were releasing paratroopers, thousands of white chutes drifting down and dropping softly onto the dunes. It was the first large-scale paratroop assault in history, the first time the enemy had come by air.

For the Dutch in The Hague, their city was suddenly and shockingly a battlefield, and the chaotic nature of the paratroop landings lent the impression that the Germans were everywhere. Some 350 German troops landed in the dunes, and others were making their way through The Hague on foot and confiscating private automobiles.

Only in retrospect can one sort out the jumble of memories and line them up alongside facts: what Marianne had witnessed early that morning was the bombing of military barracks directly behind her friend Gerdie's house and, later, the paratroop landings in the dunes around Valkenberg airfield, a few miles from her family's house.

In the moment, though, the experience was one of random and unexplained terror. Marianne and her family huddled inside, hearing gunshots and antiaircraft fire but not knowing what was happening. After she watched from her bedroom window a plane shot and spiraling like a corkscrew, down, down, down, down, Marianne was too frightened to be alone and slept in her father's room.

There was someone else at the house, a pretty blonde woman, a friend of her father's named Lidi. Marianne didn't know her and couldn't guess at the time why this young woman had taken refuge with her family, but she recalls helping Lidi boil potatoes in the kitchen, how she held the colander over the sink while Lidi poured out the steaming potatoes, and how Marianne accidentally scalded her arm, how the skin curled up like a glove and the young woman took handfuls of butter from the barrel next to the sink and gently smoothed the butter over her arm. In the same muddle of images is black smoke rising off in the distance and filling the sky. The city of Rotterdam was burning.

Goering had allotted five days to take the Netherlands, and to the shock of the Dutch five days turned out to be sufficient. The German offensive was begun on Friday morning, and by the end of the weekend, it looked dire enough that Prince Bernhard, Princess Juliana, and their two young children decamped to safety in London. On Monday morning, Queen Wilhelmina and the Dutch cabinet followed. They left behind instructions to keep fighting and to surrender only when further resistance was pointless, vague wording that proved disastrous. On Tuesday morning at 10:30, a German messenger came to the Dutch military command with an ultimatum demanding immediate surrender and threatening the destruction of Rotterdam otherwise. The Dutch, fearing a ruse, asked for confirmation: a new document with a clearer signature. However, by the time the Germans got the counterproposal, their bombers were already in the air and had pulled up the trailing aerials that permitted radio contact. The Germans tried to call off their aerial attack on Rotterdam by firing flares, but only one squadron saw them; the rest headed to Rotterdam and dropped a combined payload of 107 tons of bombs on the city. The center of Rotterdam was almost entirely destroyed. The Netherlands capitulated, and within hours German soldiers were marching into Holland's cities.

A few of these soldiers came and stood outside the Citroens' front door. They were there to see the maid, Fiena. Perhaps she had a brother or a friend among them; the girl did not say, but only grabbed her coat and hat and left in the company of the soldiers. Much later in the evening she returned to the house, again without explanation.

Marianne packed up her doll's clothes, all the little handmade outfits that the seamstress had created, and gave them to the clothing drive, for the babies in Rotterdam. Her childhood was over.

UNDER THE NAZIS, daily life changed, but the genius of the German occupation was that initially it changed in slow increments, a blood-letting that happened one drip at a time, not enough to stir widespread panic or revolt. A few, however, saw the coming evil. In the first weeks, a little more than two hundred Dutch Jews took their own lives while others made desperate attempts to escape to England or Spain. But most persisted in the belief that the persecution of Jews in Nazi Germany wouldn't be repeated in the Netherlands.

Germany, which regarded the non-Jewish Dutch as Aryan brothers, had hopes to bring them into the fold, and so was careful to avoid alienating the general population. Dutch civil servants were left in place, lending the appearance of self-rule, and the disenfranchisement of the Jews from society was conducted gradually and quietly. Though stunned by their defeat, many Dutch were thus able to believe for a while that the new regime might be tolerable.

One day, Mrs. Blomsma took Marianne to a three-story house in an unfamiliar neighborhood. They were admitted by a small-statured man with warm eyes encircled by black-rimmed spectacles. He introduced himself to Marianne as Dr. Kalker. Marianne remembered him— years earlier he had been called to her bedside after she'd stepped on a needle, but he wasn't their regular family doctor. Dr. Kalker and Mrs. Blomsma led her upstairs to the third floor and opened a door: inside was her bedroom, re-created in every detail. All her mother's furniture had been brought there, the two little armchairs and the oriental rugs, her bed and her desk, even Marianne's dog, Queenie, and her cat.

You are going to stay here for a while, Mrs. Blomsma said. There was no further explanation. The housekeeper exchanged a few words with the doctor's wife and then left.

Somehow, Marianne intuited that questions were off-limits, because she didn't ask why she was there or where her father was. She cried herself to sleep at night, but otherwise suffered dumbly the confusion and pain of abandonment. One by one, each member of her family had been taken from her. In less than a year, her sister had been killed before her eyes, then her mother had died. War had come. And now, in spite of the pledge made on the day of her mother's funeral that they would stay together and take care of each other, she had been separated from the remaining members of her family.

Her father was a Jew and had gone into hiding, but Marianne knew nothing of this, neither that he was Jewish nor what this meant. For all she knew he was still living in their house. Her ignorance of his whereabouts was most likely a harsh but necessary precaution. If she knew nothing, she could divulge nothing, and not only she and her father but also unnamed others would be safer.

ONE OF THE contentious questions in Holocaust studies is why the Netherlands had one of the highest percentages of Jewish mortality in Western Europe, higher than Germany itself. The Dutch were noted for their religious tolerance; in fact, they were the only occupied peoples who staged protests at the treatment of the Jews. Following the registration of Dutch Jews in January 1941, rising tensions resulted in first a skirmish between Jewish students in Amsterdam and German police, and then a retaliatory pogrom. The non-Jewish population countered with a general strike that shut down Amsterdam and spread to the cities of Utrecht and Hilversum. Another protest came when the Jews were required to wear the star of David.

The Germans responded to both incidents with brutal harshness, meting out to anyone who stood alongside the Jews the same punishment: the concentration camps. As a result, the protests quickly fizzled and may have even backfired by generating a retaliatory sadism on the part of the occupiers.

Unlike the other occupied European countries, the Netherlands was run by the more oppressive SS rather than the Wehrmacht. And the man appointed to run the civil government, Reichkommissar Artur Seyss-Inquart, was regarded, even by his fellow Nazis, as a peculiarly callous and brutal man. He was zealous in his persecution of Jews. "The Jews for us are not Dutchmen," he wrote. "They are those enemies with whom we can come neither to an armistice nor to a peace."

Another factor that most certainly contributed to the widespread genocide was the problem of geography. The Netherlands is a flat and highly cultivated landscape; unlike the other occupied countries, there is very little forested area, and it's hard to hide in a field of tulips. Compounding the problem, most of the Jewish population lived in Amsterdam, and that concentration meant proportionally fewer places to hide than if they'd been more spread out.

There was also the way in which Dutch society was organized, in pillars. Jews lived harmoniously alongside Catholics, Protestants, and those with no religious affiliation, but the groups didn't mix. Each group had its own political and social institutions, its own trade unions and schools and newspapers and banks. Right before the war, Dutch authorities had required citizens to register their religious affiliation for the purposes of calculating church taxes. As a result, when the Nazis came it was that much easier to identify Jews and isolate them from their neighbors.

True, all of it, yet one can't fully account for the rate of genocide in the Netherlands without acknowledging the complicity of so many of its Gentile citizens. Only one quarter of those Dutch whom the Nazis defined as "full" Jews survived the war; of these, nearly a third had Christian spouses. That her mother hadn't been Jewish turned out to be critical to Marianne's survival. In Germany, there was a dispensation for the Jewish spouses of Aryans and for their offspring, *Halbjuden* as the Nazis called them, "half-Jews." This was a work-around in answer to the problem of several thousand German soldiers who had some Jewish blood, a quarter or an eighth, and who might have qualms about enforcing anti-Jewish policies if they identified with their victims. As Goebbels wrote in his diary in 1942, the problem of intermarried couples and their children raised "a gazillion questions of extraordinary delicacy." It was a temporary measure, a wartime exigency on the way to the Final Solution, but as Germany conquered its neighbors the exemption was extended to the occupied countries. In January 1941, all Dutch Jews were required to register and were issued identity cards. Marianne's card noted two Jewish grandparents, but it didn't have the "J" on it that would have marked her as a Jew. She wasn't obliged to observe the increasing restrictions: the curfew and banishment of Jews from public transportation, theaters, and libraries, the confiscation of bicycles and, eventually, the mark of the yellow star. She had inherited her mother's fair, pink-cheeked complexion—she looked like one of the poster children for the Hitler Youth—and this allowed her to move among her Aryan neighbors without inviting suspicion.

However, though the majority of "half" and "quarter" Jews survived, Marianne's status was more precarious than she knew at the time. In the Netherlands, the loopholes for the Jewish relations of Aryans weren't so uniformly observed as in other countries. After the general strike, children of mixed marriages were among those the Germans chose to make examples of by sending them to the concentration camps and torturing them to death. Eichmann later sent instructions that the *Halbjuden* were to be sterilized to prevent them from procreating—a half-measure until a more thorough genocidal cleanup could be undertaken. Timing was everything.

As for Marianne's father, Henri Citroen's late wife could offer him no protection from the grave. One of the first anti-Jewish directives after the occupation had been to confiscate all Jewish businesses. Mr. Citroen had been able to get around this by passing ownership to his youngest brother, who was married to a Christian. (All four Citroen brothers had married Christian women; of these, only Henri was forced into hiding due to the misfortune of being widowed.)

Lidi, the pretty young blond friend of her father whom Marianne first met during the five-day war, came to the rescue and hid Henri at her parents' home. Lidi's father was a very poor cobbler who worked in a shed behind their ground-floor dwelling near the railroad station. Seeing a chance to improve his fortunes, he had joined the Dutch Nazi Party, the NSB. However, when he came home wearing his natty new uniform, his wife, a feisty Belgian woman, had refused to let him set foot inside the apartment until he took it off. It's illustrative of the many ambiguities of the Dutch occupation that while Lidi's father didn't forswear his affiliation with the Nazis, he risked his life to hide a Jew in his apartment. Henri Citroen stayed there for six months until the risk of discovery forced him and Lidi to move on.

Marianne knew none of this. She was living with the Kalkers. Though she didn't feel welcomed by the wife, in Dr. Kalker she found a kindly father figure. At night, he would come upstairs to bid goodnight to Marianne and his two children, a son and a daughter, also named Marion, who shared the room next to hers. He would lie down beside each of his children for a few minutes while they settled in to sleep, and then he would come in and do the same with Marianne. He didn't touch her or kiss her goodnight, but he showed a gentle, wordless compassion. Sometimes he took her with him on the back of his motorcycle when he went to visit his patients in the Jewish quarters. By this time, his practice was restricted to fellow Jews. When they rode into the quarter, everyone on the street knew him. Their faces lit up with happiness and he answered their affection.

One day, Mrs. Kalker sent Marianne down to the butcher at the end of the block to get some cold cuts. As she was returning, she saw a small crowd of people had gathered in the street, among them Dr. Kalker and his houseman. Drawing closer, she saw a small, bloody animal in the street: her dog, Queenie, had been run over by a German truck. She must have left the door ajar when she left. She dropped the package of cold cuts and went running to her dog, but Dr. Kalker put his arm around her and gently drew her away. He stroked the top of her head and tried to calm her sobs. A policeman saw this and came over and spoke harshly to Dr. Kalker.

It was her dog, the doctor explained.

The policeman scowled. But what does she have to do with you? he asked.

Marianne felt a terrible tension buzzing in the air, so heavy that it was hard to breathe.

Dr. Kalker gave some answer—she is staying with us—that clearly did not pacify the policeman. He studied the two of them for a long moment, then turned and walked away. Dr. Kalker's houseman wrapped Queenie in an old shirt and carried her home across the street. They buried her in a corner of the back garden, and then Dr. Kalker said a few words over the grave. We will make a little stone for her, he promised.

At lunch, Marianne was too upset to eat. Dr. Kalker tried to console her, but Mrs. Kalker had had enough. Oh, leave her alone, she snapped. Put her food in the closet. Pretty soon, she will get hungry, she will eat.

Marianne didn't recognize then what she sees now: the menace of the policeman's question and the incalculable stresses and fears that might have caused Mrs. Kalker to treat her harshly. Only in retrospect does she see clearly what was happening all around her.

IT WAS OCTOBER 1941, and she was walking down the street with a friend. Her fifteenth birthday was coming, and Marianne spontaneously decided to have a party for herself and invited the girl to come. They couldn't have a cake, but she could make *Haagse Bluf.* This was a dessert made of egg whites whipped with red currant juice and lots of sugar until it was a sweet foamy pink cloud. The name was a joking reference to the residents of The Hague, who were thought by the rest of the country to be puffed up and arrogant, all full of air. There was no white sugar left in the stores, and no eggs either, but Marianne could buy little packets of gelatin, and she could whip it with grated sugar beet.

The two of them stood on a street corner planning what they would do and whom else they would invite. It wouldn't be a celebration like those Marianne had known when she was younger, just a few girls invited up to her room—as parties go, it would be *Haagse Bluf* both literally and figuratively—but she was excited nonetheless.

On the far side of the divided avenue, a young German soldier bicycled past. Marianne said to the girl, Should we invite him? and they laughed. Two minutes later, the soldier had circled back around the street and stood in front of them. He slapped the other girl hard in the face and said, I don't want to be laughed at.

The girl was scared to death. Even after the soldier had gone, she kept glancing about as though he might come back again.

He's gone now, Marianne said. Let's just go home.

But the girl was afraid to.

Marianne didn't understand.

The soldier might follow her. The girl's eyes were dark with terror. He might see where she lived.

Marianne was still baffled.

He might come for me and my family, she said.

AT SOME POINT, Marianne learned that her father was alive. Lidi came to the Kalkers' and invited her to dinner. She brought Marianne to a modest little worker's row house in an unfamiliar neighborhood on the outskirts of The Hague. It was early spring; the earth behind the house had been turned up to make a garden. They went inside, and there were Marianne's father and her two older brothers, who apparently were not living there but had also been brought for this family dinner. For Marianne, it was a confusing, strained evening, heavy with the unspoken. Her brothers talked over her head and seemed to know more than she did, and this increased her sense of having been put out to the curb, rejected by her father for reasons she couldn't fathom. When one of her brothers teased her about something, she burst into tears and asked to go back to the Kalkers.

As it turned out, Lidi and Henri Citroen didn't have time enough to plant a garden. Just after dawn one morning, Lidi showed up at Dr. Kalker's front door to fetch Marianne. The house where she and Marianne's father were living had been betrayed, she said. They had escaped in time, but Lidi needed to go back and get a few things, and she asked Marianne to bring her bicycle and come with her.

At the house, the Germans had put a paper seal with official stamps across the door. *Ist Verboten*, it warned in large black letters. While Marianne stood watch, Lidi broke the seal and went inside. It was still early, just past dawn on a placid spring morning. No one stirred from the row of workers' houses, no curtains parted. Across the street were only meadows. Marianne stood and waited as nonchalantly as one might on an empty road at daybreak, until at last Lidi emerged carrying a large leather suitcase. They heaved it up onto the bicycle and walked away. That was the last she saw of Lidi or her father for more than a year.

The wolves were closing in. In mid July 1942, the Germans began calling up Dutch Jews for mass deportations to the east. A few weeks later, the Kalkers, too, decided to go into hiding. Marianne couldn't come with them, Dr. Kalker explained, but a place had been found for her with her tutor. When she asked the Kalkers if she could take her furniture with her to Leen's, they told her no. Were anyone to see furniture being moved from the house, it might raise suspicions. But then Dr. Kalker relented: perhaps their neighbor would help. And so in the middle of the night, Marianne and the Kalkers' houseman hefted her furniture over the wall that separated the Kalkers' house from their neighbor's. The next morning, Marianne rented a pushcart and piled her belongings onto it—her mother's two rugs and the little boudoir chairs, her desk and her clothing, even her cat, all but the bed, which was too heavy. She left the Kalkers by way of the neighbor's front gate, and—pushing the cart, stopping to rest, pushing again—she made her slow way to her new home.

6 The Operative

The bombs that fell on the first morning of the war panicked Jan's Gypsy family, but only momentarily. Even as church bells in the surrounding villages began to toll the alarm of war, the Rom gathered up their horses and returned to their peaceful routines, like birds briefly startled from a branch.

For Jan, though, the outbreak of war induced an urgent desire to go home to Antwerp and his parents. He had tried in vain to suppress the truth that Keja had spoken aloud, but it surfaced again: he wasn't fully a Rom. The ties to the world of his birth were too strong.

He went to bid Pulika goodbye, aware that it might well be for the last time. He asked his adoptive father for a photograph to keep.

Why do you want my photograph? Pulika asked.

To remember you by, Jan answered.

Pulika's eyes grew sorrowful. At last he said to Jan, If you need a photograph to remember me, it is better that you should forget.

JAN FOUND HIS parents and younger sister, Bixie, at home, but they were making preparations to leave. If Antwerp fell to the Germans, Magda's life would be in danger. On her radio show, she had been vocal in her criticism of Hitler, and from the mid-1930s she had been helping Jews to escape from Austria and Germany. One man, a doctor, and his family had stayed in their house for a year before they got their papers to go to America. The Yoors' best hope was to find a way to England, where they had contacts and family.

So Eugeen and Magda Yoors, together with their son and daughter, joined a mass exodus, some eight million French and Belgians heading south and west, away from the approaching German Army. Overnight, roads that the Rom had previously traveled more or less alone were choked with every manner of truck, bus, and car. Refugees on foot pushed wheelbarrows and carts piled high with their belongings, while others carried suitcases. Swept along in the crowds were peasant and upper crust alike, the latter complaining indignantly when their customary privileges were not recognized. Jan observed a clutch of orphans being shepherded along by nuns, and the inmates of an insane asylum being led by their guards. Orthodox Jews in their long black caftans and black hats stayed apart, moving forward with a particular urgency. Prostitutes, too, stood out in the crowds, though they had tried to make themselves inconspicuous by throwing shawls over their garish costumes. Weaving through the foot traffic were young conscripts on bicycles heading south to induction centers.

At first, stations were set up along the way in churches and schools and town halls to shelter the crowds, and towns provided soup and coffee to those that passed through. But the numbers kept growing and soon overwhelmed even the resources of the National Guard and other authorities. Blistered, hungry, and sunburnt, the crowds were driven on by hysteria. As the days passed, more and more cars that had run out of gasoline were abandoned in ditches by the side of the road, along with furniture, mattresses, and suitcases—flotsam discarded as people became too tired to carry it any further. Profiteers and crooks took advantage of the growing desperation, and vandals wantonly ransacked abandoned homes along the way. And all the while, the Luftwaffe bombed and strafed the roads; at night, the skies were red. Always, there was the smell of burning, and, increasingly, the smells of death and rot.

The family reached the Somme River in northern France only to find that retreating British and French troops had destroyed most of the bridges in their wake. The Germans caught up to them near Abbeville, and Jan was separated from his family.

Here the threads of the story are thin and difficult to untangle. According to Marianne, Jan was put into a barracks with other fighting-age men. That night, Eugeen and Magda and Bixie saw the barracks destroyed by firebombs and believed that their son must be dead. They made their way to the coast and were evacuated with the retreating British soldiers over the Channel and to safety in England. It would be a year before they learned that Jan had survived the bombing.

In fact, because he was fluent in both French and German, he had persuaded the German army to keep him on as an interpreter for one of the advance troops. His goal was to get to Spain, and from there to England, where he hoped to reunite with his family. Riding the Germans' tail to Paris seemed as quick a way to get there as any. The troops were stalled at Abbeville for about three weeks but then marched straight into Paris on June 5, 1940, with Jan in their company.

Once in the city, Jan slipped away from the Germans and went to see a friend of his mother's, the prioress of a convent across from the infamous La Santé Prison. The sister who answered the door informed him that the prioress was not in residence and wouldn't return for some time, but welcomed Jan to stay the night.

The next morning, he returned to *la Zone*, the neighborhood around the Porte de Clignancourt where he'd met the Kalderash Gypsies only a few months earlier. He needed to obtain forged documents or, better yet, stolen identification that would allow him to cross the border into Spain, and he hoped that the Kalderash might be able to help him. He also went to nearby St.-Denis, a run-down district populated by Spanish refugees from the Civil War. His fluency in Spanish and his father's Andalusian heritage allowed him a certain entrée, and he was able to eavesdrop and to join conversations. If any conversation happened to turn in the direction of passports, he'd subtly try to move it forward. More than once, someone bragged of being able to procure papers, but further discussion of the transaction became mired in vagueness, the prices for such services varied wildly, and the shifty manner of the go-betweens didn't inspire confidence. Jan would be staking his life on the authentic appearance of these papers, and he didn't know whom to trust.

Day after day he followed this routine, in the evening slipping back to the convent before curfew and being admitted by the nun who watched the door. After he had returned to his room, he sometimes heard whispers and quick footsteps in the corridors, the rustle of habits or the distant melancholy chanting of the choir, but except for the impassive nun who opened the door to him each evening, the sisters were invisible as ghosts. He was eighteen years old and unused to being on his own—with the Gypsies, one was never alone, not even for a moment—and now, lying

The Operative 45

in the dark on the narrow convent bed, he was overcome with a sense of his isolation and vulnerability.

One evening when he returned, a stranger was waiting for him in his room. Jan wondered briefly why the sister had admitted this man and then hadn't bothered to mention his presence, but the man's calm, scholarly manner set him immediately at ease.

Without introducing himself, the man came straight to the point: he wished Jan to act as a liaison operative between "them" and the Rom, with the purpose of recruiting the Gypsies into anti-German resistance. Jan understood without question that the unnamed party was British intelligence, though the man never said as much and spoke with a light accent that Jan thought might be regional French.

Their interest in the Gypsies was practical: here was a group already well practiced in the skills of evasion and subterfuge. They knew how to survive in the forest and to cross borders without detection. And they were by this time the only group still moving. As for the Gypsies, they would be serving their own interests as well as the Allies': the Nazis had declared Gypsies to be *Artsremdes Blut*, "alien blood," and had begun arresting them in Germany as early as 1936. The writing was on the wall.

The man didn't actually offer Jan the chance to refuse, but neither did Jan wish to. On the one hand, he felt wracking guilt for having left the Gypsies. Conversely, he was eager to prove that his years of wanderlust had had some purpose after all. He had in him an almost painful excess of youthful idealism and fervor waiting only to be channeled. This man was offering him a raison d'être.

So began Jan's indoctrination into the shadowy world of the Resistance. The man returned at unannounced intervals, and the two of them would sit together in Jan's room for long hours at a time while the man schooled him in the theory of dissent. The ruthless pragmatism of his words belied his low-key manner, as he patiently encouraged Jan to accept his assignment unconditionally.

The times, he said, call on us to turn our back on the old morality, on tenderness and pity. We should renounce life out of our love for life, in order to prevent it from becoming a blasphemy.

There were no specific plans laid out, no personal information exchanged, but the man hinted at what "they" expected and hoped for. Jan understood that he was committing himself to do violence, and that the recognition password they had chosen for him—*Mortem servituti antepone*, death before slavery—was as much a prediction as a code of honor.

After a few more days, the man showed up and, after handing Jan papers and a large sum of cash, instructed him to leave in the morning and return to the Gypsies; he was to do everything in his power to incite them to join the fight, and when he had secured the necessary assurances, he should simply return to the convent and wait there to be contacted. Jan looked over the documents in his hands: French identity papers, employment records, demobilization papers, letters of recommendation. According to all of them, he was now Henri Vandries.

False passport identifying Jan as Henri Vercamerton, circa 1940–44.
Courtesy of the Yoors Family Partnership.

Dear Woega,

Are you still alive? We have not heard from each other in such a long time. We were evacuated because bombs fell behind our house. And now I am in Bennekon in a camp with my class. The mother of a girl in our class rented a barn and a garage, and we made them into living quarters. Upstairs, in the garage, the girls sleep. In the barn, the boys. On the ground floor are the dining room and bathrooms.

We went swimming in the Waal and after that we picked cherries. We also went to Grebbeberg, where there was such terrible fighting. Now after the vacation, I will go to the Mulo [a lower-level academic school] *because our school had to be closed. And since I am not interested in studying, I want to go to the K.N.O. for child care and teaching. Father and the other teachers are now without work. Now I don't have anything more to write. Will you write back soon?*

Greetings from Annabert

P.S. How is your father? Annabert, I mean Chikita

Jan followed the *vurma*, signs the Gypsies had left along the road for one another, and eventually found Pulika and his *kumpania*. At first glance, they seemed to have sidestepped the war entirely, but Jan noticed subtle changes. Like chameleons, the Rom had changed their skin to make themselves less conspicuous. They were traveling in smaller groups and meeting with other groups less often. When outside the privacy of their camp, the young men and women stayed out of sight entirely, and the older women refrained from fortune-telling and from wearing the bright clothing and jewelry that marked them as Gypsies. The skills they had formerly used to improve the appearance of their horses were now employed to opposite effect, so that the animals might not be confiscated. Whereas formerly they had built blazing campfires, now they tended a few small flames and embers and were always ready to douse these at the first distant murmur of a plane.

Still, in contrast to the deprivation and oppression in Paris, Jan felt a familiar peace here. He was home, and like the prodigal son he was welcomed back without questions. More than he'd expected, he was stirred by love and nostalgia for the uncomplicated happiness that had so recently been his. It was tempting to dismiss his intense exchanges with the intelligence agent as morbid fantasy. How could he have contemplated betraying the Rom to the agencies of the Gaje? And yet, in the back of his mind, he knew that this calm was illusory, at best a temporary respite.

Pulika got up to go check on the horses, and Jan and Kore went with him. Jan was trying to think how to broach with Pulika the reason for his return, when Pulika wordlessly fell back and allowed Kore to go on ahead so that Jan might speak to the older man privately. Jan began to ramble on about his mission. It now sounded absurd in his ears.

Pulika lit a cigarette and listened calmly, and then he began to talk about the dangers of believing in fortune-telling. At first Jan could make no sense of this segue, but as it gradually unfolded, he saw that Pulika wasn't calling into question the proposal to become saboteurs, but Jan's motive.

In fortune-telling, Pulika opined, there is no gain at all, but you lose insight into yourself in a vain search for magical solutions to problems, especially since the problems are caused by an unwillingness to face life as it is.

He reminded Jan of an incident when an old farmer had shot at Jan and Kore, how Jan had chafed at the injustice and wanted to take revenge. His anger had eaten him up. In these times, Pulika continued, a man should resist being seduced by death. He should not face the sun as if it were already night! Heroism is to stay alive in the face of danger and to dare to love.

The two of them smoked and watched black clouds sweep across the luminous night sky. Whatever conviction Jan had felt was gone. He had never heard Pulika speak so passionately.

Courage about death, Pulika continued, often disguises cowardice about life. He took a long, thoughtful drag on his cigarette. Leave to others the quest for eternal certainties. Learn to accept that there are questions that have no answers.

But then, inexplicably and without explanation, he instructed Jan to go back to Paris and give his assent. For his part, he would present Jan's proposal to the tribes.

JAN RETURNED TO the convent in Paris and was met, as promised, by his former contact, Monsieur Henri as he was called, the French equivalent of John Doe or Mr. Smith. This Monsieur Henri took Jan to a large basement hideout in another part of the city for what amounted to basic training. To Jan's boyish disappointment, he was escorted past a shooting range lined with sandbags. Because he'd be serving as a liaison rather than in the field, he wouldn't be allowed to carry a gun, lest he be picked up by the Germans. He was led past another young man practicing knife throwing. Finally, he was delivered to an instructor called Tonkin, an unimpressive Asian man of slight build, dressed in what appeared to be dirty pajamas. Tonkin motioned him over to where he stood, an area of the basement covered by padded matting, and Jan noted that his left hand hung lame and immobile at his side. Jan assumed that the man must be a wrestling or boxing coach, and since he'd taken classes in both arts, he sauntered over with what must've been visible condescension. The next thing he knew, he was thrown sprawling across the mat. Humiliated and angry, he stood up and approached Tonkin, expecting some kind of explanation or apology, only to be thrown down again and pinned painfully to the floor. He tried to retaliate and was brutalized again, over and over, Jan flailing in his fury and Tonkin easily evading his jabs and sending him back to the mat. Then, suddenly, the man held up his good hand like a traffic cop, signaling Jan to stop. Mesmerized, he did. Tonkin bowed briefly, and with surprising affection addressed Jan as *mon petit*. That was lesson number one.

He learned from Tonkin how to fight with the empty hand, a martial art that, in keeping with the rest of his training, was at least as much mental as physical. Much of his training was directed at learning to control his emotions, so that neither fear nor anger would weaken him. He and his fellow trainees also learned how to create and maintain their false identities, how to evade notice, and how to respond if interrogated.

One evening, this training was put to the test. As Jan was leaving the building, several young men waylaid him. They shoved him against a wall and searched him at gunpoint. They found his documents, but these were false, they said, they knew who he was. Taking him around a corner, they took turns roughing him up, insulting him, and threatening him with graphic injuries. This was the end, he thought. He despaired at the thought that he might just disappear, and no one, not his parents or Pulika, would ever know what had become of him. However, though he was terrified and humiliated, he stuck to his story, partly because he didn't know what else to do. His history of living a double life and telling elaborate white lies was finally being put to good use.

Like a guardian angel, Monsieur Henri walked up and with a calm half smile called off the thugs. In his confusion, Jan thought at first that he'd been rescued; it dawned on him only slowly that Monsieur Henri had staged the attack.

Despite understanding the necessity of such tests, he was stubborn and prideful. On another occasion, armed men speaking German stopped him in the streets. This time, the ruse was even more elaborate and included other victims beside him. He was indignant: enough was enough, he protested, had he not long since proved his mettle? He was answered with a punch in the mouth. He continued to answer their interrogations with impatience and threatened to report them to their mutual superior. The threat seemed to work, because he was left behind while the others were dragged off to headquarters for further questioning. It was only after the fact, alone in the street, that he realized this had been the real thing and he had narrowly escaped a German dragnet.

7 Rom Underground

In a letter dated February 14, 1942, Jan wished Annabert a happy new year. He was taking courses in art and architecture, he said, and was sculpting, modeling in clay and blue stone, and learning to make his own chisels. *So you see*, he continued, *my days are filled, and because of that I don't have much time to think of my parents and my little sister who you saw in Zeist and of whom I have no more news.* He inquired after the well-being of Annabert's younger brother, Erik, who'd been getting into some trouble. Just as there had never been any mention in his letters of Gypsies, there was no suggestion here that he was anything but an art student. He promised to come to The Hague as soon as it was possible; what he did not say was that this wouldn't happen anytime soon. So long as he continued his work in the Resistance, to visit her would be to put her life at risk.

FOOD WAS STILL more plentiful in the countryside than in the cities, but to obtain anything that required manufacturing or processing—salt, coffee, tobacco, shoes, or clothing—one needed to register for ration stamps. Together with a net of roadblocks, the system of rations made it simple for the Germans to identify and track the movements of individuals, and to isolate and starve out those who tried to hide. Initially, the Rom held out, but eventually they registered. And then they registered again in the next town, and in the next, using their mobility and multiple passports to advantage. Their surplus stamps for soap or textiles they traded with farmers for food that in the past they might have stolen.

After he and Jan spoke, Pulika had sent out the word to convene a *kris* in order to discuss the question of joining the Gaje in their war. With Germans patrolling everywhere, it was no longer possible to gather hundreds of wagons together for a traditional *kris*, so instead the various leaders met in a French tavern. Even coming together in such numbers was cause for suspicion, so they disguised the gathering as a funeral, explaining to the authorities that they were laying to rest the esteemed old Gypsy Bengesico Niamso: in Romani, "Cursed German."

It was a long and drawn-out discussion—never had the Gypsies practiced warfare, it was against their beliefs—but Pulika eventually won them over to the understanding that everything had changed now, and their own survival would depend on engaging in this conflict.

In a sense, the Gypsies had practiced resistance long before the war. Over the course of their history, they had cultivated the skills of stealth and subterfuge that allowed them to survive in opposition to the enemy in power, the Gaje. Now, because they shared a common oppressor, these same Gaje who had reviled them had become allies. The farmers and the Rom warned each other of impending raids and, even before they gave Jan the go-ahead to offer their cooperation to British intelligence, the Rom had begun to transport individuals who needed to escape the Germans. They would hide the fugitive in the storage box that hung between the wheels of every Gypsy wagon and carry him to the next point on his escape route. Perhaps it was their natural sympathy for a fleeing man; perhaps it was merely self-interest to strengthen their network of allegiances. Either way, they were naturals for covert operatives.

The Gypsies agreed to aid Monsieur Henri and his compatriots by providing them with ration coupons to feed those in hiding. Later, they also began to pick up and transport supplies dropped by British planes. Given notice of a planned drop by means of a coded message on BBC radio, they'd go to the relayed coordinates and wait in the dark. When they heard the throb of an approaching British plane, they'd quickly light a triangle of little fires to signal the pilot where to drop his cargo, and then just as quickly extinguish them to avoid alerting the Nazis. The plane would come in very low, release its cargo, and leave. Sometimes the parachutes floating to earth in the moonlight carried containers of small arms and ammunition; they'd quickly stash the parachutes and then hide the containers away to be retrieved later, after the risk of detection had lessened. At other times the parachutes carried "friends" rather than "parcels."

It wasn't only the men who participated in the work of the Resistance. Once, when they were caught up in an SS raid, the Gypsy women approached the officers with great friendliness, speaking German and claiming to be very glad to see them because, you see, the whole tribe had become infested by scabies, which they had picked up in this filthy country. And they were so, so happy the Germans had come and would cure them. All the while, they were scratching themselves furiously as they approached. Horrified, the SS officers held up their hands and said, Please, please, please, stay where you are. By this means the Gypsies avoided inspection. The women were hiding weapons and ammunition under their layered skirts, which a simple search would have revealed. Even the children had parts to play: the story goes that they once crawled underneath a train bound for Germany that was carrying grain. They drilled small holes into the floors of the boxcars so that the grain would slowly leak out onto the tracks and the train would arrive in Germany empty.

Jan, his Gypsy brother, Kore, and some of the other young men in the Lowara and Tshurara tribes gradually moved from supporting roles to more active work in the Resistance. They recruited and trained other Gypsy youths, and as the war progressed and the numbers of those in hiding grew, they were responsible for acquiring increasingly large numbers of ration coupons needed to feed the movement. It was no longer sufficient to simply register under different names, and so they began to stage armed holdups of the coupon distribution centers. As Monsieur Henri had warned, violence became necessary to achieve their ends, and they killed German guards and workers in these raids.

The initial misgivings of Pulika and the other Rom turned out to be prophetic. In spite of Pulika's warning against being seduced by violence, Jan could feel himself falling under its spell. His idealistic notions of heroism and social justice had fallen away and been replaced by hardened efficiency and a single-minded addiction to the adrenaline of war. Jan persuaded Monsieur Henri to send them on more active missions, and they were assigned as support to a demolitions expert. The first time they blew up a train carrying armaments, this son of pacifists was seized by what he described as a "sense of fierce exultation, a frighteningly unsuspected rapture of destruction, a drunkenness strangely more satisfying than that of wine. We too now possessed the power to terrify and destroy."

Over an unspecified period of months, they derailed trains and blew up bridges. In his memoirs, Jan glosses over the particulars of these actions, noting only that their small organization participated in far-flung operations all over the occupied territories. A few of these actions stand apart because they went awry. Once, Jan's left arm was severely injured when they were detonating a bridge. On another occasion, following a successful demolition, the Germans netted Jan and his crew, along with many others, in a large-scale sweep. In typical fashion, the Gypsy women and children followed the arrested men.

One child, five or six years old, came up alongside Jan and tugged at his sleeve. She had a story to tell him. Perhaps she had been sent by a mother or father because she was small and wouldn't be stopped. She was insistent and began to walk alongside Jan and to tell him the story of the two frogs. The first frog jumped in a pail and found that it was half full of milk. The sides of the pail were too steep to climb out. Treading in the milk, he could not touch the bottom with his feet, and so he could not jump high enough to leap out. He was a very rational and intelligent frog. He quickly saw that there was no hope of escape, and so he gave up and drowned. The next day a second frog also jumped into the pail of milk. This frog was not so smart as the first one, but he was stubborn and determined. He began to jump, and even though he could not leap high enough, he jumped and jumped for hours on end. Eventually, his jumping legs churned the milk into solid butter, and the determined frog was saved.

There might be no way out, but there could also be no giving up.

At the station, Jan was held for hours, but in the end the Germans released him and his fellow saboteurs, in part because they could find no evidence against them, but also because the women and children, acting as a diversionary force, created such an unpleasant disturbance at the station, howling and heckling the police and refusing to leave, that the police were eventually eager to be rid of them all.

After that first arrest, Jan carried the story of the frog with him like a talisman, reminding him to keep jumping and never to give up hope. He would have need of the lesson again in the months to come.

LIKE THE JEWS, the Gypsies were official enemies of the Reich. In 1937, the Nuremburg Laws that had been directed against the Jews were amended to include Gypsies as well. Those arrested were sent to the Jewish ghettos in Poland or to concentration camps, but in contrast to the Jews, they weren't yet being systematically hunted down; arrests and deportations were random and left to the discretion of the local SS.

In November 1942, Jan wrote letters to Queen Elizabeth of Belgium, the Ministry of Justice, the assistant to the head of State Security, and anyone else he could think of, seeking asylum for the Rom, but he was diplomatically rebuffed by government officials who continued to serve only by collaborating with the Germans. The best remaining strategy, then, was for the Rom to make themselves inconspicuous and avoid detection for as long as possible. They had long since given up their colorful wagons for more discreet covered farm wagons, but when the Germans confiscated their last remaining horses they stopped traveling entirely.

In the immediate aftermath of a covert operation, the men working with Jan would lie low in various hiding places stocked with a few supplies. It wasn't safe for Jan to return to his family home in Antwerp, but he had a key to the Yoors family mausoleum, and on at least one occasion he and Kore camped there among the graves.

In Brussels he sometimes stayed with one of his honorary aunts, the progressive Catholic journalist Betsie Hollants. This was the same woman who had gone to the anti-Nazi rally in Germany with Magda Yoors a few years earlier. She worked in the Resistance and was likely the person responsible for Jan's first meeting Monsieur Henri. In the back of her garden, she had a furnished room disguised as a coal shed where Jan periodically stayed. At the end of 1942, he wrote her a letter in which he made a veiled reference to their arrangements. *I cannot come today because I went to Deinze with the leader and that is why I sent you one of the group. . . . Here among the Rom important events also happen daily, and if I didn't feel guilty toward you I would be satisfied. Several times already I was in your neighborhood but I didn't dare to come. Now that I have reached so far it would be a pity to give up, and that is also why I didn't dare come to you.*

Farther south, he and the Gypsies often stayed at a hunting lodge in the Ardennes mountains with a group of Gaje partisans and their leader, a man identified by Jan only by his nom de guerre, Le Capitaine Lothar. They left the women and children in a forest hideaway, a necessary precaution but problematic because the miserable women seemed

False passport identifying Jan as Jean Baptiste Janssens, circa 1940–44.
Courtesy of the Yoors Family Partnership.

constitutionally incapable of remaining quiet and sedentary and were continually going out and jeopardizing their safety. The men, too, were unhappy to be separated from their families and, like fish out of water in the Gaje world, couldn't adjust to sleeping in beds and eating unfamiliar foods. Ironically, the way of life they were fighting to preserve was dying in the effort.

They were doomed one way or another, but the end, when it came, was hastened by their own missteps.

The Lowara had always regarded the Tshurara branch of the Rom as a nuisance, like trashy cousins one couldn't disown because they were family. Recklessly stealing and brawling, the Tshurara tended to leave a wake of ill will that the Lowara then paid for if they happened to follow them into a region. Now, the Tshurara Resistance members were hanging out with the many unsavory criminal types that the Resistance relied upon to carry out its work. Taking advantage of the Rom's access to extra ration coupons, the Tshurara operatives dressed loudly, went out to establishments that could only be afforded by black market profiteers, and ate, drank, and tipped extravagantly, inviting unwanted attention from the authorities as well as resentment from the impoverished locals. Jan and the rest of the Lowara couldn't restrain them, but rather than simply abandon them to their fate Jan continued to intervene and cover for them when they got into trouble.

He and Kore were in their company at a Paris café one afternoon. As they were about to leave, the bartender uncharacteristically offered to stand them to another brandy. Moments later, black cars pulled up in front, and swarms of Germans burst inside. They searched all the restaurants' patrons, but Jan alone was beaten, handcuffed, and then dragged outside to a waiting van. He passed a man he knew who was being held up on either side by Germans because his bare feet were too swollen to support him. The man hid his face, and from this Jan intuited that the man had been tortured to betray him.

8 The Prison Window

At the time of his arrest in February 1943, Jan was twenty years old.

After an initial interrogation during which he declined to give up the names of his comrades, he was transferred in the night to the Begijnen-straat Prison in Antwerp. He was thrown into a dark cell where he could see nothing, but his other senses were uncomfortably heightened. He lay on a hard, foul-smelling pallet and listened to the hollow silence of the prison, a silence broken now and then by the screams of prisoners somewhere else in the building. He was assaulted by overpowering smells—human feces, stale urine, rusting iron, and something else, something sweet, which he later learned was carbolic acid. When injected directly into the heart, carbolic acid caused instant death. The Nazis used this method of execution throughout the war, especially at Auschwitz because though not efficient for mass exterminations, it was more economical than Zyklon B.

Jan's fatigued mind circled like a trapped animal, replaying the scene of his capture and worrying about the fate of Kore and the rest of his family. He cursed himself for having put them in danger by his association with the Tshurara. Alone in the dark, he lost any sense of time. Then in the quiet, a voice cried out in the Romani language. He didn't recognize the voice, didn't know whether it was Lowara or Tshurara. The voice addressed the other Rom within hearing and reminded them that they were all one, all Rom.

I forgive you, the voice called out, and may God forgive you, too. The sound echoed off of the concrete walls and then there was silence again. Listening to it brought up, Jan later wrote, "a clear and strong vision of a long line of Gypsy wagons and horses moving relentlessly toward the horizon. It was a vision of a floating world in a moment of timeless, spaceless quiet."

He awoke to dim light filtering down into the cell from a tiny window high above. The window was barred and made of frosted glass, providing no view but only the suggestion that dawn was breaking in the outside world. If the night had had the quality of a nightmare, daylight brought to Jan the bleak reality of his new circumstances. Sounds of approaching boots, slamming doors, and curses announced a succession of morning transactions: first, the exchange of a full slop bucket for an empty one, then wash water, then a thin slice of black bread and a cup of lukewarm liquid made with acorns and passed off as coffee. After that, the heavy silence returned and forced him to contemplate his future. He would be tortured, there was no question. What had formerly been an abstract possibility now rose up in his imagination in harrowing images and stories—everything he'd ever heard about the history of torture. Worse than death, he feared the prospect of prolonged, unendurable pain. He also questioned his ability to avoid the final dishonor and humiliation of giving up his friends. The only way out was suicide, but the Germans had taken his belt and shoelaces. Desperate, he began slamming his head against the concrete wall in order to kill himself, but he only passed out and woke up again later, still painfully alive.

His fears weren't unfounded. The Geheime Feldpolizei, the secret police known as the Gestapo, began the work of interrogation and torture by bringing him to a room where he might first observe his future: an emaciated, naked man lay face down on a rack, babbling and whimpering. The room was no stone-walled dungeon; quite the opposite, it was well-lit and heated, with linoleum on the floor, an ordinary-looking office. Opposite the naked prisoner, young and neatly dressed German men sat around a table, sipping beer and chatting among themselves about girls, behaving no differently from any other group of bored civil servants.

When the prisoner was unstrapped and hauled limply to his feet, he let loose his bladder. Some of the young men grinned, a little embarrassed, but another one ordered him, Keep it in! Keep it in!, all the while hitting the prisoner on the head with a book as though he were training a puppy. The prisoner only gurgled and laughed insanely. As he was led past Jan and out the door, Jan saw that the man's eyes were glassy and empty of anything but animal fear. His own fear exploded in his gut.

The officer in charge leafed through Jan's impressively thick file and asked him a few routine questions. He didn't appear cruel—in fact, Jan judged him to be well educated, reasonable, even sentimental. He assured Jan that he disliked this whole business of torture and would much prefer that they work together. If Jan cooperated, he said, they might avoid all *that*. He waved his fingers dismissively toward the other side of the room. But of course he had a job to do—here he smiled at Jan as though they were sharing a little joke—and he had no desire to be sent to the Eastern front for shirking his duties.

As the officer continued to talk, Jan formulated a strategy. He couldn't stay silent and stay alive. He must try to wipe clean his own memory, to forget his history as an agent and invent a new history and new stories. He determined to adapt the techniques of the Gypsy fortune-tellers: he would tell the listener the lies he wished to hear, disguising the vagueness with specific dates and trivial details. By these means he might buy a few more hours or days of life.

Jan became like Scheherazade. His days were taken up by interrogation, during which he'd weave his stories and embroider on whatever came to mind, throwing in just enough plausible matter that his interrogating officer couldn't afford to disregard him. He would invent, for instance, a meeting with a Resistance agent and then say that the man had worn a green necktie and might have been from Lourdes. The meeting place was a café on the Avenue Hoche. Or was it Foch? Near the Arc de Triomphe, anyway. No, he couldn't remember the name, but they served an excellent roast chicken.

Jan and his interrogator had pleasant conversations and found they had many shared interests and areas of knowledge; for long stretches, their talk would resemble that between two educated and sophisticated peers. But the purpose of these exchanges couldn't be indefinitely disregarded. Sometimes the officer would merely threaten torture; periodically he'd make good on the threat. There was no more apparent thought given to this than to ordering coffee or cognac after a meal, a whim tossed off with a feeble joke.

Jan was waterboarded, an experience that made him realize for the first time how much he wanted to live. They also attached electrodes under his arms and to his penis. This was different from pain, more like an intense sensation, more intense by several powers than anything else he had ever felt, agonizing and intolerable.

"The trouble with Germans," he wrote, "just as with all really enthusiastic torturers, was that by the time they got you to where you'd have talked, they were too engrossed in their work to notice it. Then the moment passed, and you were too close to pain and blood and death to have anything left to say."

Stoic by training, he initially endured the torture in silence until an old-timer in the prison counseled him emphatically against this approach. The only way to keep the torture lighter, he told Jan, was to yell and scream. And so Jan did.

Afterwards, he was returned to the grueling monotony of his cell, where there was nothing to distract him from his physical miseries—the gnawing hunger, the damp cold, the bruises and lacerations that never healed. He could feel himself withering. But each morning when he woke, he knew that he'd been granted reprieve for another day because those who were to be executed were customarily removed before dawn.

In a state of starvation, he would call up in detail meals he had eaten—the spiced and garlicky stews in the Gypsy camp, the bitterness of a draft beer, the spongy lightness of fresh bread. However, when he had relived every meal he could recall, he'd finish feeling even hungrier than he'd been before.

His imagination, he learned, must be strictly controlled; harnessed and directed, though, it provided escapes that kept him on the right side of sanity. Left alone in his cell at night, he talked in his mind to Pulika and Kore as though they were sitting there beside him. He unburdened himself of the horrors of the day and mourned the waste of his life, that he'd made no mark on the world and would leave nothing behind when he died, no work, no wife, no children. As an answer, he seemed to hear again Pulika's challenge to him not to let the knowledge of death stand between him and joy. He recalled a sideways glimpse of the beautiful young girl that Pulika had chosen for him, Dijido, her body loosely concealed by her long skirts. Images of other Gypsy women followed: Yojo's wife nursing an infant at her breast, her belly swollen with another child; the matriarch Lyuba leaning over to tuck his feet back under the quilt at night; in the morning, his sister Keja gently blowing the embers of a fire back to life. They were the reason to keep living.

Dear Woega:

Will you write me as soon as you get this letter? Because Father, Omi, and Eric, we are very tense to hear how it is with you and with your family. But maybe you have to carry a great sorrow, and we are really thinking of you. From now on I will run every day to the mailbox to see if there is a letter from you. And I painted this flower for you. I hope that you got my letter for your birthday. I wish you all the best and a beautiful Easter.

With all the best wishes from Chikita.

P.S. I was in Zeist on Sunday, but the garden from a long time ago in Zonnehuis is not beautiful at all. I visited Bea and we remembered all the things from Pingola. You were so clever.

Hours and days and weeks bled together, abstractions marked by the subtle dimming and fading of the blank pane of glass above Jan's head. He didn't know how long he had been imprisoned, but the bitter cold in the cell had begun to recede and the light stayed in the window incrementally longer each day, by which he deduced it must be spring. He had been arrested in February.

One night, overcome by a loneliness so wrenching that his imagination could no longer divert him, he took a risk. He made the sound of the screech owl and then waited for a Rom to answer. Instead, a guard came running. The overhead bulb in his cell snapped on and flooded the cell with blinding light. The guard wrenched his arm painfully behind his back and yelled for others, who came running. He was beaten and then yanked from his cell, marched down long corridors, and thrown into another cell. The door clanged shut.

It was dark, even darker and more silent than his former cell. Feeling about in the blackness, he found no pallet, no blanket, only the stinking metal slop bucket. When exhaustion overtook him, he succumbed to sleep, awaking in pain and with the cold stiffening his bones, and then drifting off again. He had no idea how much time had passed—there was no window here, nothing but blackness—but it seemed that it might have been days. He realized that he was probably underground. He remembered visiting a gorgeous chateau once that had a small underground cell, really just a hole with a trapdoor in the ceiling where enemies were left to die. It was called an *oubliette*. As a child, he had been impressed in an abstract way but had not fully imagined the plight of the prisoner. Now, he could not stop thinking about it. He tried to quell his rising panic by calling on Pulika, but the escape dreams wouldn't come. The Gypsy women were gone. When he could bear it no more, he found the metal door and began to bang on it and yell. This was strictly forbidden and would probably lead to more beatings, but he was beyond caring.

No one came.

He began to count. A count of sixty equaled a minute, and then another sixty and another. He reached an hour and kept going. Some hours later, he was still counting though he'd lost track of his tally. His best guess was that he'd been in the hole for several days. Unexpectedly, there were footsteps and the clanking of keys. With the screech of metal came a sliver of light. Bread and water were shoved into the cell, and then the dark closed over him again.

Jan broke the bread into pieces so that he might ration it, and began a routine wherein he'd try to estimate the time between breakfast and lunch, and then between lunch and supper. After supper, he'd sleep. When he awoke in the dark, he called it morning and would begin his next day by eating a piece of bread.

Then one day, the guard let him out. To his disbelief, he was told that his imprisonment in the hole had totaled a mere four days.

He was returned to his old cell, grateful for the comparative luxury. The watery soup was wonderfully hot and the daylight filled him with joy. He looked up at the pane of opaque glass and inexplicably it was a square of the most intense blue, the deep hue of a Maxfield Parrish sky. Then this blue wavered and was replaced by a lighter but no less lovely hue, the blue of a cornflower. This in turn shifted to another shade and another, the colors of warm Mediterranean waters and pale blue eyes.

He attempted to manipulate the hallucination, to shift it to reds, which he liked better. At first, the vision snapped back to the dirty window, but slowly the reds began to appear. Here was a bloody red, which made him wince, and then another red, this one the ugly burning red of war, the color of the fires he had set over previous months. Gradually, this moderated to the happy red of field poppies blooming in late summer. And then clear wine reds, burgundies and bordeaux and clarets. Then the coarser red of the bullfighter's cape. He remembered the *arena de toros* in Madrid, the harsh sunlight, the noise, the trumpets and pageantry. The bull, angry and snorting. And again, the red of blood. Always blood and more blood. He forced the image away and what came to him next was the vibrant stained glass of the cathedral of Chartres, the way the red in those windows glowed in the dark cavern of stone, the color quietly singing, deep as prayer.

He remembered his father taking him to the cathedral in Antwerp for the first time, with its forest of gray pillars and the colored light streaming down from high windows. And in the studio, watching his father design and execute windows for the churches and monasteries in Belgium. His father's large hands measuring and then drawing the lines for the lead, choosing the pieces of glass that would fill each shape, a pirate's treasure chest of precious jewels—rubies and emeralds and sapphires. And all the other gem colors, turquoise and the delicate yellow of citron, the fresh green of peridot. Smoky topaz and the exquisite, vibrating orange of the fire opal.

This became his daily reprieve, calling up different colors and their attendant images. One day he might devote to yellows, the next day to greens, transforming his cramped cell into a vast cathedral of color. Just as Eugeen Yoors had drawn portraits to keep up his spirits while in a World War I internment camp, so his son Jan stepped into his birthright as an artist while in a prison cell.

9 The Sardine Letters

Jan was given a mock trial in prison and sentenced to death. Lying in his cell and awaiting his execution, what haunted him most was that when he died, he would leave nothing behind. He was twenty-one and his life seemed to have had no purpose. It had all been a waste. Then he heard steps coming down the dark corridor. Just as expected, they stopped at his door.

Instead of being taken to his death, though, he was given a roommate, a Russian named Ivan. Over the next days, Ivan insisted on teaching Jan Russian, as preparation for when the Red Guard arrived. The man's incessant talk made Jan's reveries impossible, and he resented the intrusion. Then two more prisoners were thrown into the cell, and later another two. They brought with them rumors of Allied advances and German losses, but Jan couldn't share in the excitement. His solitude was replaced by the discomfort and bickering that came of having to share a few square meters of space with five others, and at night, the new prisoners took to banging on their doors for hours.

Perhaps hoping to gain information, Jan's captors decided to allow him to communicate with the outside world. He wrote to and received letters from friends staying in the Yoors' house in Antwerp and from Betsie Hollants in Brussels, and they in turn served as conduits to his family in England.

In a letter dated June 18, 1943, Betsie insisted that he needed a lawyer to defend him and offered to hire one. In cryptic fashion, she then rambled on about four boxes of sardines received from Portugal—*Bixie has sent them via the Red Cross as an answer from you*—and about a dearth of butter and sugar, though she might ask Aunt Jeanne for some. *I was in Limburg*, she continued, *and I hope to hear something in connection with your understanding of etymological connection. But I don't want to bore*

Jan Yoors and Betsie Hollants, winter 1943. Courtesy of KADOC Archive.

you with that now. . . . Moeky [Jan's grandmother] *always thinks that it is you who rings the bell at unexpected hours. Do you know that many of your acquaintances such as Luc are working in the Arbeidsdienst* [the obligatory labor force in the Netherlands] *or they are working in the factories in Germany?* She concluded the letter with more discussion of food and recipes, summer pears and white cabbage, and then signed off under an alias, *a warm kiss that I have never given you, Lisette.*

It's irresistibly tempting to think coded messages are embedded here, especially given that other letters from Betsie to recipients in England and Lisbon show a peculiar obsession with numbered shipments of sardines. The Resistance organizations that helped downed airmen, Jews, and others escape Hitler often referred to the escapees in their care as "packages," and the delivery point for these packages was most often Lisbon. Furthermore, as Jan explained in an interview years later, they often got their forged documents through connections with Swedes in the Red Cross.

Jan's reply seems intended to deflect any curiosity on the part of his torturers by feigning confusion. *The first sentences from Moeky gave me a lot of pleasure, that she is healthy and courageous. The rest of the letter I didn't understand too well.* He went on to insist that she not waste her money on a lawyer, that it couldn't really help him. But there was a fellow prisoner, a Gypsy with no family, who really needed fifty pounds if she could spare it.

It must be so beautiful outside now, he went on. *If I am not out on the 29th of July will you remember that it is Binnie's birthday? Will you give my greetings to everybody: my dear old Moeky, and Gigi, and Michel Wailea and his cousin, Luis DeSchilde.*

One day, a guard came to the cell, crooked his finger at Jan, and called him out by a name that wasn't his own. Jan didn't contradict or correct him, but just did as he was told. He was taken on an unfamiliar route through the prison to an office that he had never seen. They sat him down at a desk, put a sheaf of forms in front of him and told him to sign them. Here and here and here. Fear made his hands so shaky that he could barely scrawl a signature, much less read what he was signing. His own death warrant, he assumed, perhaps false confessions. When he was finished, they handed him someone else's effects—a wedding ring, this man's papers, and photos of his wife and children—and then quickly escorted him down a busy hall. Then, as if in a dream, the prison gate was unlocked for him. Outside, trees that he had last seen gray and leafless were a lush green. Ordinary Belgians walked past the open gate, men and women and children going about their daily lives.

He assumed that this was a final, sadistic bit of fun for his captors—give the prisoner a glimpse of freedom and then shoot him in the back when he makes a move to grasp it—but he knew that he would rather die on the outside, and so he ran. He ran down the street as fast as his atrophied legs would carry him, waiting to feel the impact of the bullet. When it didn't come, and when he had put a little distance between himself and the gate, he slowed his pace and tried to blend in with the civilians on the sidewalk. People stared at him. A prostitute put a comforting arm around his shoulder. Expertly, she slipped a roll of money into his pants pocket, and then wordlessly sent him along his way.

Was he being set up to lead the Germans to other members of the Resistance or had the Resistance itself somehow orchestrated his escape? Or, equally as likely, had there simply been an administrative mistake that, once his absence was noticed, would result in his being hunted down? He felt a wave of fear at the prospect of returning to the world, stronger even than his former longing for freedom.

He found himself heading to the poorest section of town, where his ragged clothes and emaciated appearance would be less noticed. Turning into a street, he came upon a small neighborhood café and was overwhelmed by the remembered smells of cooking, of sausages and garlic. He asked for a table in the corner and ordered food and drink, just enough so as not to call attention to himself. Sitting with his back to the wall and one eye on the door, he scanned the people in the café: the waiter coming and going from the kitchen, a man and woman intently flirting, a child being helped to cut her meat, a priest reading a book at the table nearest the kitchen. He vacillated between the fear that at any moment he might be discovered and a lightheaded, almost effervescent delight at the humanity around him. It was as though he had never seen human beings before—they were endlessly fascinating and wonderful.

UPON HIS RELEASE, Jan sent a tender letter to Annabert, assuring her that he was alive and "still as happy and healthy as before." This couldn't have been farther from the truth—he was emaciated, weak, and suffering from unexplained fevers—but he didn't want Annabert's innocence tainted by more worry for him. He asked after her family and friends, urged his "little sister" to write, and closed the letter with encouragement to "stay honest, sweet, and straight."

He wandered aimlessly, traveling first back to Brussels. He went to the Marolles, the poor medieval quarter where the Sinti Gypsies lived.

How long since you have eaten? they asked him, a standard form of greeting among the Gypsies. Eating in the outside world, amongst the Gaje, didn't count.

It had been a very long time, he replied, six months. He was hungry, in all senses of the word. They brought him potato pancakes, sauerkraut, and a pig's stomach so delicious that it nearly brought tears to his eyes. Later, he felt the greasy heaviness like stones in his atrophied stomach.

After they had shared a meal, the Sinti told him of the massive roundup of the Tshurara and Lowara tribes. The men had been arrested at various meeting sites, signaling beyond any doubt that they'd been betrayed by an insider. Then the Germans had raided their camps. They had beaten the women, the old people, and the children, and then hauled them away like cattle in open trucks. They had set fire to the Gypsies' wagons, making it clear that there would be no coming back.

The Sinti, because they were sedentary city dwellers and uninvolved in Resistance activity, weren't under suspicion. Still, Jan worried that by staying with them he exposed them to danger. He couldn't take the risk. The Sinti arranged a meeting with some smugglers who were trafficking saccharine from Spain, and they agreed to get Jan out of occupied Europe. He was given a false passport, and by a circuitous route made his way to Madrid.

He stayed in Spain for only a few days. Eating and drinking to excess with friends in intelligence and other expatriates, he tried to numb his wracking grief and guilt. Never mind that Hitler had targeted the Rom for extinction, it was Jan who had introduced his extended family into the Resistance, and he felt responsible for their imprisonment and probable deaths at the hands of the enemy. He couldn't stomach remaining in safety with the rest of the "half-conscious world," and so with the help of local Gypsies, he arranged to cross back over the Pyrenees and traveled to Paris.

Once there, he went to the bar where he had been arrested. Peering through the front window, he saw the same bartender who had offered him a complimentary brandy on the day of his arrest. When the man caught sight of Jan in the window, his face drained to the color of ashes. Holding his hand inside his jacket pocket, Jan mimed pointing a concealed gun at him. He held the man's gaze meaningfully, then smirked and walked away. This was the best possible revenge, he decided: the bartender would spend the rest of his life wondering when Jan would return to kill him.

Back in France, he learned in more detail about the wrenching, ugly fates of Kore, his other family members, and scores of the Tshurara. Most had been arrested and carted away to death camps by the Germans. Those who were too slow to move were clubbed to death on the spot. Some had disappeared—his sister Keja and her husband, Yayal, and Paprika, and Nanosh—but it was impossible to hide large family groups, and the Gypsies couldn't conceive of going it alone. The few individuals left would be lost outside the community that had provided them with their entire identity.

A childhood friend, Jan Daelemans, offered him a haven at his family's country estate in the Ardennes, where he would be safe because the father was known to be unsympathetic to the Resistance. Jan Daelemans was a law student about to marry a sweet, curly-headed girl named Roosje, and was living a comfortable life that Jan envied but couldn't reconcile with the hemorrhaging world beyond their forested sanctuary. The Allied bombings that Jan had heard with increasing frequency while he was in prison seemed to signal that the war might soon be over, and in the days that Jan stayed with his friend, the two young men talked about the future. Yoors persuaded his friend that he must not wait another moment: he must take a stand now and join the Resistance. Too many had died on their behalf. Even in the twelfth hour, he argued passionately, this action would spare Daelemans a lifetime of regret that he hadn't acted on the side of right.

Jan stayed there for ten days, sleeping and bathing and looking at art books, trying to find his way back to his old self, but it was no use. The boy that he had been was dead, and the haggard, gray-haired stranger in the mirror couldn't rest. Though still sick and feverish, he left abruptly and returned again to Spain.

In a café in Madrid, he found what he was seeking. He was approached by an intelligence officer who said that they'd been watching his movements. They wanted him to set up an escape route between occupied France and Spain. He would be provided with plenty of money, and they would ask that he run the route for no more than a few months, after which time he could go to England. Jan accepted the assignment with fatalistic relief.

10 Death and the Gardener

Jan responded to the massacre of his Gypsy family with a rash disregard for his personal safety. Marianne suffered her own traumas and losses—it was a bond that would draw them to each other after the war—but to opposite effect. She became paralyzed by timidity and nerves. While living with the Kalkers, she'd hardly been able to work up the courage to leave the house alone, not even to fetch stamps from the post office next door. Now when her tutor, Leen, asked her to bring the inkwell to the table at the start of her lessons one day, she dared not comply for fear she would drop it.

After Leen's husband, Henk, left for work each day, Marianne and Leen would wash up the breakfast dishes, do their calisthenics, and then sit down at the dining table to work on the day's lessons. She practiced her handwriting in a copybook. One of the pieces that Leen had her write out and illustrate was a well-known Dutch poem titled "Death and the Gardener," the theme of which was the futility of trying to escape death when one's time has come. It might seem an odd choice of poetry to assign a traumatized young orphan, but death was very much on the tutor's mind.

If the weather was fine, the two of them would have lunch on the apartment's little stone balcony. Afterwards Leen would disappear, leaving Marianne alone in the house for long hours at a time. One afternoon, the doorbell rang. When Marianne pressed the buzzer, heavy footsteps rushed up the stairs and two men burst into the apartment.

Where is Leen Cost Budde? they demanded.

She had no idea; she had never asked where Leen went in the afternoons. They searched all the rooms and then came back to where Marianne still stood in the front hall. They ordered her to remain in the house. She wasn't to use the phone or go to the windows. The house was surrounded, they said, and she was to stay put. And with that, they stormed out again.

She stood staring at the black telephone on the front hall table, trying to decide whether to defy her orders. She might call Leen's husband, but what if someone were listening on the line? She couldn't say that the Nazis were there. She couldn't call them SS or NSB or collaborators. She tried to think of a message that wouldn't incriminate them. She picked up the phone and dialed.

When Henk answered, she said, The *Gendarme* were here, and then hung up.

Henk came home and walked Marianne out to the corner of their avenue. If Leen passed this way, he said, Marianne must stop her and warn her against returning to the house. She did as she was told and stood watch for hours, but nobody came. Just before curfew, Henk retrieved her.

You can come home now, he said.

They went back to the house. Leen wasn't there. Henk made dinner for the two of them, which they ate without conversation, and she went to bed.

The next morning, Henk put Marianne on an eastbound train to Lunteren, the geographical center of the Netherlands, where Leen's parents lived on a farm. Like the Kalkers before her, Leen Cost Budde had gone into hiding, and Marianne would have to move on.

IN THE SPRING OF 1943, the momentum of the war was turning against Germany. They responded with increasingly draconian measures, siphoning off labor from the occupied civilian populations and stepping up the deportation of Jews. In May, Germany issued an order for all Dutch young men to register for *Arbeitseinsatz*, forced employment in the east. And overnight, thousands of male students went into hiding, a number that would eventually swell to roughly 300,000 so-called *onderduikers*, or "divers." Even during the daytime, the streets felt strangely quiet and empty. By the end of the year, there were no Jews to be seen. Of an estimated prewar Jewish population of 140,000, some 25,000 had gone into hiding, but the vast majority had registered and then been picked up for deportation to so-called labor camps.

With hindsight, one might wonder why more Jews didn't hide. However, the Dutch Resistance cells came late to the aid of Jews, so the chance to hide depended on the luck of finding a protector among your neighbors and friends. With few exceptions, it was an expensive proposition because food for those in hiding had to be obtained on the black market. Even if you could afford the cost, it was risky to put your life in the hands of someone who might just as easily take the money and then turn you in for a reward as risk his own life to protect you. Against this gamble, registration for what was termed "forced employment" often seemed the safer course. What sane person could imagine Auschwitz?

Marianne's father, Henri Citroen, had been doubly fortunate: he was well-heeled enough to hide and was beloved by a young woman willing to risk everything to keep him safe. However, his luck had run out in December 1942, when he was discovered hiding with Lidi in Rotterdam. He was sent to Westerbork, the transit camp in the northeastern Netherlands where Dutch Jews and Rom were processed. Nearly every Tuesday morning from July 1942 on, transport trains left Westerbork carrying Jews to the extermination camps in Poland: more than 103,000 by the time the last cattle cars rolled out in September 1944.

Westerbork was divided into strata of privilege. For most, it was a brief way station on the way to their deaths, but by comparison with the transit camps in Eastern Europe the accommodations were deceptively tolerable and gave no hint of what was to come. A school, hairdressers, and a post office lent the suggestion of a small town; a theater even offered entertainments on Tuesday nights for those who had survived that day's selection for deportation.

However, those who'd been caught hiding rather than given themselves up voluntarily were deemed "convict Jews" and were treated accordingly. Guards shaved their heads and confiscated their clothing, issuing them blue overalls and clogs. They were assigned to separate barracks and given the punishing work of stripping dead batteries. They were also generally the first to be put on the transport trains.

On the top rung of the social ladder were the "permanent" residents, a group comprised almost entirely of Jews who for one reason or another were exempt from deportation. These residents were given health care and encouraged to pursue a "normal life"; if they had money, they might even buy luxuries no longer available in the rest of Holland. Some of these persons were privileged by virtue of being members of the Jewish Council or being married to a Christian. Others, mostly German Jews, earned their stay of execution by running the camp, though for most their service only forestalled the inevitable. At the peak of the camp's activity, 6,035 people were employed at Westerbork. Other than the camp commandant, not a Nazi was among them.

Henri Citroen might logically have fallen into the category of convict Jew, but it seems he was instead granted permanent residence. He remained at Westerbork for five months, until an evening in May 1943, when he was summoned into the main hall. Alongside 102 other inmates, all from "mixed" marriages with children, he was given a choice: be deported to Auschwitz or undergo "voluntary" sterilization. He had half an hour in which to decide.

WHEN HENRI CITROEN went into the hospital for surgery to sterilize him, Lidi fetched Marianne from the farm where she was living with her tutor's parents. The two of them went to Amsterdam. As a Christian woman, Lidi was forbidden from having a relationship with a Jewish man, so Marianne would have to be the one to get permission from the authorities to visit the hospital. They went to the Reich's headquarters, a formidable building with German guards posted at the entrance, and Lidi waited outside while Marianne went inside alone. Later, Lidi admitted that when she saw Marianne going up the stone steps, she feared she might never come out again.

Afterwards, visitor permits in hand, they walked across the city to the Portuguese Israelite Hospital in the Jewish ghetto. When they arrived, though, a raid was under way. This was an increasingly frequent occurrence: the Germans would surround a section of the city and search, house to house, for Jews and conscription-aged men, and take them away. Under these circumstances, Marianne and Lidi didn't dare enter a Jewish hospital, but Lidi tipped someone at the entrance to go upstairs and tell the patient Henri Citroen that they were there. As they stood on the street, he came to a window, high up, and waved at them. Just then, German trucks rumbled into the street, and that was the end of their visit.

Marianne (front), Lidi, Hans, and Henri Citroen, taken after Henri was released from Westerbork, circa 1943–44. Courtesy of the Yoors Family Partnership.

After his surgery—a mutilation for which he most probably was compelled to pay—Henri Citroen was freed to live out in the open again. He couldn't go back to his home—the previous spring, Germans had forcibly evacuated the local residents from up and down the coasts of France, the Netherlands, and Belgium—but he and Lidi found an apartment farther inland, in the city of Utrecht, and collected his three children, who were scattered here and there. For almost a year, their lives regained a semblance of normalcy, albeit a wartime version of normalcy with its attendant curfews, rations, and shortages. Marianne's father found her a place in a vocational school, where she learned domestic skills, including how to care for children, cook, make beds, and iron a man's shirt without any creases. She even acquired a boyfriend.

Then, in August 1944, Henri Citroen received a summons from German headquarters to come to The Hague and register. His elder son, Hans, warned him against going and argued that he should go back into hiding instead. Henri rebuffed his son's fears. After all, he had struck his bargain with the Germans and he had the papers to prove it. He got on a train and left.

A day or two after he had gone, there was a knock on the door. Marianne answered. Two men in German uniforms asked for Lidi Kraus. Marianne answered that she was not at home, but just as she did, Lidi opened the kitchen door and walked out, practically into their arms.

They took her from the house. Marianne and her boyfriend followed at a discreet distance, until they came to a big house on a tree-lined street. Lidi was taken inside and then a short while later brought back out and escorted on foot to the train station, with Marianne and her boyfriend again trailing behind. The two German men walked Lidi up the platform and onto a train.

Marianne ran up to the train and took a few steps inside. She saw Lidi being walked down the narrow passage by the two men. Helpless to do anything else, Marianne called out, Everything is all right! It was a ridiculous thing to say, everything was far from all right, but she wanted somehow to console her. Lidi and the two men turned around in surprise and, at the end of her courage, Marianne fled the train.

After she had gone, the men asked Lidi, Is that his daughter?

LIDI WAS RETURNED to the house the next day. There was nothing more she could do for Henri; she had already broken the law by cohabiting with a Jew. Marianne's two brothers were similarly constrained, as by now they were in hiding. It was left to Marianne to go to The Hague to plead for her father's life. Perhaps a pretty, Aryan-looking daughter could coax some mercy from the Germans. Lidi gave her directions to the Reichskommissar's headquarters, but Marianne knew the way: five years ago—in another life—she had lived in that very neighborhood. She had walked her dog Queenie down that same pleasant lane bordered by trees. It ran for miles before ending at the Clingendael Palace, though she had never used to come this far. Now, though, she was passing through the iron gates of the palace and down the double avenue of ancient beeches to the graceful brick and white manor at the end, the residence of the Reichskommissar of occupied Holland, Artur Seyss-Inquart. She was admitted and when she had explained the reason for her visit she was told to wait in the wood-paneled foyer, where a fire burned in the fireplace.

After a wait, she was let into his office. The Reichskommissar sat behind a large desk. He was a stern man with a receding hairline and thick glasses that magnified his fish-like gaze. He gestured Marianne to sit in the chair opposite.

She spoke very little German and stumbled trying to explain her situation.

Meine Mutter . . . Ich habe keine Mutter. I have no mother. *Nur ein Vater.* Only a father. She could think of nothing to add.

He looked her over with no expression whatsoever, then bent over and opened the file cabinet of his desk, rifled through it, and removed a folder. He studied its contents, running his finger down a page until he found what he was looking for.

Ah, he is already on the train to Auschwitz.

So far as he was concerned, that concluded the matter, and Marianne saw herself out.

11 The Hunger Winter

On June 6, 1944—D-Day—160,000 Allied troops landed on the beaches of Normandy, the largest invasion by sea in the history of the world. By the end of the day, 9,000 Allied soldiers had lost their lives or been wounded, but more than 100,000 began the march north and east toward Germany. On August 25, Allied forces liberated Paris, and in the first few days of September they took back Brussels and then Antwerp.

On Monday night, September 4, Radio Oranje, the voice of the Free Dutch, broadcast from London that the Allies had crossed the Belgian-Dutch border. People went to bed on Monday night expecting to be liberated the next day. On what would become known as Mad Tuesday, some 65,000 Dutch Nazis, the NSB, made a frantic break for Germany. Ironically, many of them stopped over at Westerbork, where the last transport train had left for Auschwitz the previous day. Meanwhile, the Dutch eagerly awaited the arrival of the Allied troops with flowers and flags.

Nobody came. The liberators turned out to be one British patrol that had accidentally crossed the border. The rest of the Allies were stuck in Brussels; they had advanced so quickly that they had essentially outrun their supply chain and had to wait for reinforcements.

On September 15 the Allies finally pushed across the Dutch border and freed much of the southern territory of the Netherlands up to the Rhine. However, the country's major cities and most of the population were to the north and remained under German control. Then on the 17th, in what must have appeared to the Dutch like a fitting bookend to the war, a massive airborne invasion filled their skies: more than 40,000 British, American, and Polish soldiers, along with jeeps, artillery, and equipment, were dropped into the Netherlands behind enemy lines. Their intent was to capture several strategic bridges so that the Allies could force their way into Germany over the Lower Rhine and end the war by Christmas.

The plan, dubbed Operation Market Garden, went spectacularly awry. Fog in England delayed the second wave of paratroopers who were supposed to bring in supplies, with the result that those already behind enemy lines were short on water, food, and ammunition from the beginning. A ground offensive that was to have linked up with the paratroopers—the "Garden" half of the plan—bogged down in the soggy Dutch soil and had to ford dike after dike, each time exposed like ducks in a shooting gallery. Meanwhile, the paratroopers were stranded and left to fight it out alone for nine days against unexpectedly robust German divisions, a story of courage and defeat dramatized in the film *A Bridge Too Far*. In the end, the Allies' losses totaled between 15,000 and 18,000 killed, wounded, or captured.

The Netherlands north of the Rhine would have to wait another eight months for their liberation.

In support of the operation, Dutch railroad workers had shut down the trains, cutting off transport of the V-1 and V-2 rockets that the Germans were launching at England from across the Channel. It was a sacrifice— more than 30,000 railroaders had to go into hiding—but it was also partial amends for their heretofore ignominious cooperation in transporting Jews, prisoners of war, and forced labor to the camps in the east. The larger sacrifice, though, was borne by the Dutch people at large. Without trains, the transportation of food slowed dangerously. Then the Germans retaliated by confiscating other means of transportation: the ubiquitous Dutch bicycles as well as the few remaining cars and trucks. Next, they embargoed all inland shipping of food, clothing, and medicine. Thus began what became known in the Netherlands as the Hunger Winter.

Cold and hunger, the evil twins that had decimated Leningrad during the first winter of the war, appeared together in the Netherlands for the final winter of the German occupation. It never stopped raining in November, and then temperatures plunged to the lowest levels Holland had seen in decades. The Germans, escalating their vindictiveness after the Normandy invasion, had cut off the gas and electricity. The coal mines in southern Netherlands were on the wrong side of the new front, so the only remaining fuel was wood. In spite of merciless German reprisals for looting, desperate citizens began to surreptitiously denude their parks and shaded avenues. They stripped the doors and floorboards from the abandoned homes of Jews. Under cover of night, they pulled up railroad ties and the wooden blocks on streetcar lines. Anything to stay warm.

Lidi got wind that the Americans had bombed an airfield outside of Utrecht, mowing down the surrounding trees. Together with their landlady, Marianne and Lidi took a pushcart and walked out to the derelict airfield. To their good fortune, no one else was there. They heaped the cart with splintered wood and branches and headed back home. It was a long walk with a heavy load, and they reached the outskirts of the dark city well after curfew. Pushing the creaking cart through silent streets, they cringed at each terrible rattle over the cobblestones. When the cart was stowed safely behind their garden gate, they stopped and listened. No footsteps followed.

At night curfews kept people inside, but even during the day the streets were deserted. Half the population was in hiding now, because every man between sixteen and sixty was being deported for slave labor in Germany. Those who weren't in hiding had little reason to venture out in the cold, since there were no jobs to go to, and nothing to buy in the stores.

Water was turned on for an hour each day, from six to seven o'clock in the morning. Marianne and Lidi rose in the frigid dark, filled a pot with water, and set it on their *majo*, the ubiquitous wartime stove, essentially a small empty can that required little fuel. They fed the stove a few sticks of wood, just enough to bring the water to a boil, and added a small ration of rice. Then they put the pot in a chest and covered it with a blanket. With luck, by nightfall, they would have cooked rice for their dinner.

AT THE END of the year, Lidi and Marianne bicycled from Utrecht to The Hague so Lidi could celebrate the New Year with her brother, who managed a large hotel. The hotel had been taken over by the Germans to house officers, but the brother lived in an apartment on the top floor.

Marianne and Lidi started the journey with two bicycles, but along the way one of them had to be abandoned on the roadside. In all likelihood, the bicycle collapsed because it had no tires. Rubber was a precious commodity, so the few Dutch whose bicycles hadn't yet been confiscated were riding on the rims or on wooden tires. It would have made for an uncomfortable 35-mile trip even with two bicycles, but Lidi wanted to be with family, so they took turns sitting on the back of the remaining bike for the remainder of the trip.

In The Hague, they spent a quiet evening upstairs in the hotel with the brother and his male lover, the four of them sharing a modest dinner and quiet conversation while the Germans downstairs celebrated riotously.

Marianne's old neighborhood, Scheveningen, had the dubious distinction of being the primary launching site for the V-2 rockets that had been terrorizing London since September 1944. The V stood for "Vengeance." Their predecessors, the V-1s, had been awful enough—unmanned rockets called "buzz bombs" or "doodlebugs" by the British because they signaled their approach with a terrible, loud buzzing. But the V-2 was larger, and because it was faster than the speed of sound there was no warning. The rocket impacted and tunneled thirty feet into the earth before it exploded, devastating everything within a quarter mile. The explosion, heard only by the survivors, was deafening.

The residents of The Hague were also terrorized by the V-2. The sight of these monsters rising up into the atmosphere on a cushion of flame was chilling, all the more so because the mechanisms were temperamental and frequently misfired, good for London but bad for the Dutch. When they heard a rocket launch, the locals reflexively began to count. After the count of thirty, they were safe.

At five in the morning, to ring in 1945, the Germans shot off a V-2 directed at London; it fell back to earth in The Hague, killing 38 people, destroying 76 houses, and shattering all the windows within a two-kilometer radius.

Lidi and Marianne were awakened by the blast but had to wait an hour until curfew ended before they could leave. They bid Lidi's brother goodbye and then crept downstairs through the silent hotel. The Germans in the hotel had either gone to the site of the explosion or were still sleeping it off. The two women went to the bicycle room to retrieve their bicycle, and then in a moment of daring they stole another one, a beauty with real rubber tires. They pedaled madly through the early morning streets until they were safely out of The Hague, and then kept up a good clip all the way back to Utrecht, scared they would be picked up with their stolen Nazi bicycle. Later, Lidi would sell it for food.

GERMANY LIFTED THE food embargo, in part because they feared a rebellion, in part because it was too demoralizing for German soldiers to have to watch people starve. This hadn't been a problem in 1941–42 during the siege of Leningrad—the Germans didn't witness the misery they inflicted—but now they were living among their victims. However, for a variety of reasons, lifting the embargo had no immediate effect. The Germans still took more than half the farmers' food to feed their own people. Distribution of the rest remained a problem because the railways were still not running, and the barge owners balked, fearing the Germans would confiscate their barges or the food or both. When the canals froze, the question of moving food by barge became moot.

By November 1944 the average Dutch person was getting only 900 calories a day; 600 to 1,000 calories is considered the minimum necessary to sustain life. The bitter joke was that the rations were just a little too much to die on but too little to keep you alive. In January, the daily ration fell to 460 calories and the joking ceased. The black market dried up. Cats and dogs disappeared from the streets. By the end of the war, the official ration stood at 400 calories, half the daily allotment for inmates at the Belsen concentration camp.

Even as people were starving in the cities, the farms had plenty. So people in Amsterdam, Utrecht, Rotterdam, and The Hague took with them whatever they had to barter and walked out to the country on so-called hunger trips. The farms closest in were quickly cleaned out or were inundated with household goods; signs posted on farm gates read "Gold or silver only." The "hunger trippers" ventured farther and farther out, sometimes walking more than eighty miles in search of food to bring back to their families.

Perhaps because they were attractive young women, Marianne and Lidi fared better than some. Lidi found work as a cashier in a restaurant patronized by Germans and collaborators, the only ones who could afford the black market prices on the menu. Marianne got a job in a military hospital on the outskirts of The Hague that had been taken over by the Red Cross. She got up at dawn to make the long walk to the hospital, and when she arrived she and another young woman went down into the dank basement and filled large metal canisters with the morning water before it was shut off for the day. They heaved the heavy canisters back up the steps into the hospital, taking turns carrying the can or pushing from behind. They helped the nurses distribute the patients' food and then spent a long day boiling sheets in a cauldron to sterilize them and scrubbing floors and walls. Taxing though the job was, Marianne was paid in food: two sandwiches, one of which she saved for Lidi. She also boiled milk for the patients and got a little additional nourishment by eating the skin that formed on the top. And then there was the other perk of the job: the hospital was kept warm for the patients.

Lying in bed at night, one might hear the shrieking sound of the V-2 rockets headed to England or the faraway thrum of the Allied planes headed to Germany, but the average citizen had few clues to the war's progress beyond the Germans' increasingly punitive reprisals and confiscations of property. Resistance fighters were no longer given trials but were executed in the town squares, their bodies left in the streets as a warning. If the Resistance members responsible for an action couldn't be discovered, hostages were taken and executed in their place. The eventual outcome of the war was no longer in doubt, but for many of the Dutch, hope faded that the Allies would come in time.

12 The Wild Goose

Furnished with false identity papers and large sums of cash in several currencies, Jan left Spain and made his way back to Paris and Brussels to meet his contacts there. From them he learned that his likeness had been posted in German headquarters and police stations across western Europe. He had a photograph made of himself to be sent out to his family and friends in the event of his death and then, like an actor taking on a new role, he changed his appearance. He dyed his hair dark and purchased a flashy wardrobe: striped silk shirts, suits made with smuggled British woolens, heavy silk ties, and a pair of pointed yellow patent leather shoes. Rather than trying to pass unnoticed by the Nazis, he would dress the part of the black marketeers and contractors who were traveling unchallenged around Europe. He wore a flower in his buttonhole, carried cigars to give away, and affected a cool and reckless demeanor to go with the new clothes, an alter ego that bore no relation to his ill and desperate private self. He was young, slender, and almost effeminate-looking, but backed by his posse of Gypsy toughs his appearance actually worked in his favor. People were afraid of him because he was such an anomaly.

He was charged with setting up an escape line to transport downed Allied airmen, Jews, and other endangered persons out of occupied Europe. Though stories sometimes circulated of people escaping by means of submarines off the coast or airlifts, in truth pretty much the only way out was over the mountains to Spain. Organizing escape lines to Spain was a logistical feat, dependant on the cooperation of many unconnected networks spread out over several regions. Local partisan cells along the way hid those escaping, but for safety's sake no cell knew where the escapees had stayed earlier, the next destination, or the contacts farther on. As a further precaution, the routes and hiding places had to be changed continually. It was exhausting work, and it took weeks to get out just a few people.

Eventually Jan and his cohorts came up with an audacious new plan: they would pose as recruiters for the Organisation Todt, the engineering arm of Nazi Germany that used compulsory labor—prisoners of war, mostly—to keep the war machine going. This would allow them to transport groups of half a dozen or even a dozen—and to do it on the long-distance German military trains. Because the men were supposed to be prisoners of war, there would be no need to hide or disguise them.

Jan knew some young Gypsy women who had passed themselves off as Germans and were now working inside the military administration; they assisted with the warrants to take the "recruits" into the south of France near Spain. Once at the foothills of the Pyrenees Mountains, the men would be handed off to professional smugglers who guided groups on foot over the treacherous mountains for a fee. On the far side, others waited to take the group to the safety of the Allies' consuls and embassies in neutral Spain.

The dangers of discovery increased exponentially with each run. Many escape lines before them had been infiltrated and exposed by German spies and collaborators. Also, it was inevitable that once delivered to freedom, some of those who'd been transported would tell their story and unwittingly endanger those still inside. However, for several months the plan worked. Since Jan spoke German fluently, he led these runs and became a familiar figure on the trains, making a total of some twenty trips back and forth between Paris or Brussels and Spain and escorting to safety more than two hundred people on what became known as the Visigoth Line.

Perhaps he looked exhausted; he was still feverish and giving himself daily injections of quinine to keep going. One day, another recruiter on the train—a *real* labor recruiter—suggested that Jan had been working too hard and should apply for the bonuses and vacation time that were surely coming to him. Jan replied that he didn't want bonuses or holidays: he was there only to serve the Fatherland. Whether out of generosity or to take advantage for himself, the coworker applied for Jan's benefits. And of course, the records turned up no one matching Jan's alias.

Upon Jan's return to Paris, the Dutch banker who'd been funding much of the expense of these trips contacted him and asked that they meet in the elegant Hôtel George V. He was waiting for Jan in the bar.

Your aunt is sick, the banker informed him. Furthermore, I am certain she won't recover.

The operation had been compromised.

The banker slid Jan an envelope stuffed with cash in various currencies. To take care of the hospital bills, he said.

The thing to do was to disband and disappear. Even at that moment, though, there were nineteen men hidden in Paris, waiting to be transported out of the country and to safety. Jan decided to take them.

Jan, in his guise as the "Wild Goose," with Roma in the Resistance, 1943. Courtesy of the Yoors Family Partnership.

They wouldn't be able to use the German military trains or any of their former accommodations. Nor could they make alternate arrangements with the usual care. Word went out that the nineteen men were to meet at an artist's studio in Montmartre under the guise of a party, and they would depart in the evening from there. Meanwhile, French identity and travel papers were quickly created for everyone: they would pose as workers from the region of the Pyrenees, going home on a ten-day leave from work on the coastal fortifications. In the past, Jan had preferred forging Swedish passports: since Germans were unlikely to know any Swedish, they couldn't question the escapees. This plan also meant traveling by the slower French civilian trains, which were checked more thoroughly by German police. But there was no choice in the matter.

Jan was dismayed when he met his fugitives—among them, a baby-faced politician, an escaping Jew, an officer in the Polish army, a French Legionnaire who was an escaped prisoner of war, and a tall Dutch secret agent. Even after they'd been costumed in old clothes and handed bundles and battered suitcases to carry, not one of them looked persuasively like a French peasant. They were given their instructions, which were, in essence, to attempt invisibility. Once on the train, they should sleep or pretend to sleep and let their "couriers" do any talking for them. Jan felt so certain of his impending death that he was momentarily tempted not to care about the fate of this hapless band.

They broke into smaller groups and found seats on the train. Fatigued, Jan slept until the first checkpoint, hardly waking to go through the motions before returning to sleep. The night wore on, the train's rhythm and forlorn whistle announcing their passage through the dark world. Another check, and then another, followed without any noticeable disturbance, so Jan assumed that somehow, inexplicably, the others were also passing undetected.

All the next day, the train continued to crawl south, often shunted onto sidings while the military express trains roared past. Passengers got off, others took their places, and the fugitives acquired a dazed and rumpled look, red-eyed and unshaven. At the appointed place in the south of France, they finally disembarked. No one was there to meet them. Jan opted to head for the next *point de repair*, Lourdes, by bus. There, they were warned away: the Germans were watching. All the locals seemed to be either staring at them or quickly averting their gaze.

At the next *point de repair*, a small village called Mauléon, again there was no one to meet them. The group was far too conspicuous to loiter at the station, so they set out walking. Night fell, and suddenly three women approached them and said, The men sent us. Jan didn't question what men these might be, but allowed the group to be split apart and taken to lodgings for the night.

The next morning, one of the women returned to the house where Jan had spent a fitful night, jerked in and out of sleep by the phantom motion of a train and its screeching whistle. The woman had a child with her and under the pretense of being a family, the three went into town so that Jan could hire a mountain guide.

In the past, Jan had hired smugglers to take his charges over the Pyrenees, a risky transaction since the smugglers were known to fleece travelers of their money and then turn them over to the Germans for a second payment. He had learned to convey an air of menace and to make persuasive the threat of retaliation if he were betrayed. This time, though, no amount of gold or intimidation could induce anyone to budge. As it happened, the Germans had arrested several smugglers just before Jan's party had arrived.

This explained why the whole town seemed on edge. It also went some way to clarify the unexpected hospitality they had later received. The Germans were known to punish entire towns where they uncovered fugitives, so the villagers were motivated to hide these conspicuous guests and then quickly see them gone. A farmer with a truck and a travel permit volunteered to take them over the border after nightfall. Jan considered that they might be walking into a trap, but he could see no alternative. The escape line was collapsing, and they had to get out quickly.

He rode beside the farmer, and the others hid in the bed of the truck, covered with a tarpaulin and sacks of potatoes. Rain spattered the windshield as they climbed slowly up the pass. Then, without notice, the farmer turned off the engine and opened his door. He listened. There was the faint whine of motorcycles some distance down the pass. The farmer leapt out, threw off the tarp, and frantically shooed the men out of his truck, pointing them toward the woods.

The Wild Goose

Panicked and stumbling, they ran up the muddy slope, ran until their lungs were heaving in the thin mountain air. Finally, they collapsed. Below, on the road, they heard the sounds of approaching traffic, a military vehicle, and then the excited barking of dogs. In their panic, they had left a messy trail. Luckily, in the dark and rain, the searchers missed the signs and drove on.

Jan led the nineteen men up the mountain, though he didn't know where he was leading them. The terrain was rough, and as they climbed, the rain turned to sleet. They shivered in their drenched clothes. Somehow he would have to find a guide.

Eventually, they came upon a clearing and a little mountain hut occupied by a Basque shepherd and his wife. The small, leathery old man greeted them with suspicion and an old carbine, but when Jan explained that they needed a guide to take them to Spain, the man set down his gun. It wouldn't be an easy trip, he said. Without a further word, the old man took his walking stick from the corner, threw a haversack over his shoulder and walked out the door, not even bidding his wife goodbye.

AT FIRST, the snow seemed fortunate: it would cover their trail and discourage the Germans from pursuing them. But as the group climbed single file hour after hour, perspiring and shivering, a cold wind bit into their skin and stung their eyes. It required all their effort to keep putting one foot in front of the other, picking their way over pebbled ground in their thin-soled city shoes. Worse, they were hungry.

Normally, travelers on the escape line would have been outfitted at their penultimate stop with spiked boots, heavy wool sweaters, and sheepskin coats. They would also have received provisions for the mountain crossing: two pounds of sugar cubes, a pound of smoked bacon, and a flask of brandy. However, there had been no time to arrange this and no way to carry such provisions from Paris without inviting suspicion. They had only the clothes they'd worn when they left the city. Jan had on his usual attire: a business suit, silk shirt, and patent leather shoes. One of the Poles, an old man, wore felt slippers.

Toward morning their guide took them to an abandoned goatherd's shelter hidden under the snow so that they might sleep for a while. They felt grateful to collapse onto the floor and to be out of the wind, even if there was no fire and no food. They took off their shoes and rubbed their sore feet, but their guide warned them to put the shoes back on again before their feet swelled. Exhausted, they slept like dead men until, hours later, the guide jabbed them in their sides with his walking stick. It was dark, time to move again. He produced three or four raw chestnuts for each man, and they nibbled their ration as they walked, revived by sleep and fresh air. The sky was clouded over and promised more snow, but the wind had let up.

At the end of that night's climb, they dug shelters out of the snow and huddled together in threes and fours. Though they were cold, it bothered them less than it had the day before. In fact, Jan experienced a peaceful, disembodied lethargy. Were it not for the clawing hunger, he might drift off . . .

He awoke to the guide kicking him in the ribs. This time, it was harder to shake off his lassitude and move again. As they set off for the third night of climbing, it began to snow. Soon, the sense of isolation and detachment Jan felt was made physical. He lost sight of the man behind him, and the man in front of him drifted in and out of sight. The Poles were the hardiest among them, and since the beginning they had made it their mission to move up and down the line like sheepdogs, keeping everyone together, bringing up the rear and then circling again to the front. The guide, meanwhile, seemed to have no concern for their miseries, no awareness of any individual's frailty. He just kept walking. When they finally stopped to rest, Jan looked around at the now unrecognizable men. Their faces were chapped and raw and their lips swollen like bloody sausages. Squinting against the snow, beards matted with ice, they had the appearance of strange Ice Age creatures come back to life.

They were trapped in a blizzard. Clutching one another, they found a rock overhang and dug down into the soft snow beneath it. Jan felt the cold slowly numbing his extremities, though his center burned with fever and he was unbearably thirsty. He noted these symptoms with blurry detachment and concluded that he was freezing to death. Though cocooned together with the others, he felt completely isolated, drifting peacefully into a white tunnel of oblivion. And then there was pain, repeated and sharp, in his side.

The guide was again kicking him in the ribs. This time he hated the man for interrupting his death, but he got up and the two of them kicked the others back to life. Under protest, the group began to move again. It was still daylight. They moved through a white landscape of deep, soft snowdrifts. It was peaceful. Jan thought in passing that the drifts resembled gigantic female nudes. When night fell and the temperature plummeted, a thin crust formed over the drifts that wouldn't support their weight. Step by galumphing step, they plunged forward, crashing through the ice, which cut into their legs.

As he had in prison, Jan began to hallucinate a world of riotous color. Then he was pulled back into the world by an inhuman sound. The guide had thrown himself down onto the snow, he was crawling forward and sobbing, and then crossing himself repeatedly. He pointed: there was a tall iron obelisk marking the border between France and Spain. Below lay the Pass of Roncesvalles, and beyond that Pamplona. Most of Jan's fellow travelers fell to their knees, and some kissed the earth. But Jan felt nothing. This was not yet liberation.

They found a small farmhouse and were welcomed inside like heroes, and treated to hot wine with cloves, boiled potatoes with lard, bread, and garlic. Jan gave the guide all the French money in his wallet, and after a show of gratitude, the man quietly slipped away.

When they were sufficiently revived, Jan tried to persuade the others that they, too, must push on: they were not yet home free, and until they had made contact with their respective home embassies or consulates they might still be arrested. Except for the four Dutchmen, though, the others declined to go back out into the cold.

Their numbers reduced to five, the travelers hiked down the pass into the village of Orba. Again, they were greeted as heroes. When they asked to use a telephone, they were told that the lines were down and the village was snowbound. They settled in at an inn and waited for communication to be restored. Eating and drinking with the hospitable locals, they freely spent the gold coins they'd brought for the journey, until the day when the last coin was gone. When Jan requested a loan to tide them over until communication with the outside world was restored, members of the Guardia Civil, the Spanish police, materialized with submachine guns and handcuffs. Their former drinking companions were nowhere to be seen, and the roads were now, miraculously, open. The five were arrested, taken to Pamplona and then on to Miranda de Ebro, the infamous Spanish concentration camp. The others in their party were already there.

POSTMARKED FROM SAN SEBASTIAN, Spain, November 18, 1943

Dearest Annabert,

I am here for a few days for a rest cure in this hotel that you see on this card. It is really nice! I hope that the war will be over soon because I would love to come to Holland to visit you

Woega

13 Annabert's War

All his letters were taken open by the Germans. He said, "Oh, I am now going to Spain, and there are such delicious oranges." Well, I don't know! It's nice to read it in a letter, but I didn't know what he was doing.

—ANNABERT YOORS

Sheltered and naive, Annabert experienced most of the war at a muted remove, as shortages, inconveniences, and the unvoiced anxiety of grown-ups. Just a young Dutch girl, and neither Jewish or Gypsy, she was kept ignorant of the horrors so many were enduring, but as she wrote later, [it] *vibrated in the atmosphere around me. This is worse because the truth concealed becomes monsters of imagination and fear.* On a few occasions, she saw things that troubled her. Once, coming out of school, she saw a soldier punishing one of her schoolmates, beating him for no apparent reason. Annabert ran over to the boy, and at the sight of his bloodied face, she began to cry uncontrollably. Even when a teacher came outside and tried to shush her, she could not be soothed.

A few weeks before the outbreak of war, her family had hurried home from Switzerland, where her father had been recuperating from tuberculosis. A little more than a year later, on July 12, 1941, the Nazis closed the Vrije School because it employed Jewish teachers. And that was that, as Annabert later recounted: she didn't see her friend Marianne anymore until after the war.

She transferred to another school, where she made new friends. On her summer holiday the following year, she went back to the camp where she and her family had briefly evacuated at the start of the war the previous year. There she made pottery in the mornings and went swimming in the afternoons. She also spent a week on a farm, where she got to ride an old wagon horse. In a letter to Jan that autumn, she innocently asked if he had ever sat on a horse—*I was really scared, but after that I loved it*—this to a young man who unbeknownst to her had spent his own summers before the war traveling with horse traders. In other letters, she chatted about playing Maria in the Christmas pageant, going skating, and taking dancing lessons.

In June 1942, after Jan was released from his first stay in prison, he wrote Annabert. *I hope you are not very angry with me but I am very, very busy with exams. As soon as I have finished (I hope that I got a good report card) then I'll go for a couple of weeks to rest in the middle of the woods. And after that I will start with moving. Moving, you say? Chikita, I am moving to Brussels. I don't mean that I will move totally out of Antwerp, not that, but I rented with a friend a big space in Brussels with a beautiful pavilion. And we are going to make it all livable, you know? . . . It is a pity that now we cannot send photos in the mail because I am very curious how you look without your braids, and I am also very changed in the last three years.*

Apparently, he sent another letter in the fall, wishing her a happy birthday. And then nothing.

Even before the war, the correspondence between the two had been circuitous. Jan was rarely where he claimed to be. When he was traveling, one of her letters might take weeks to reach him, going first to Antwerp, being forwarded and then finally picked up at whatever address or general delivery he'd given his parents. The war, of course, had complicated matters further: postal service slowed and was hampered by the censors. His parents were gone to England, and Jan dared not reveal his actual whereabouts. Still, in due time a reply had always arrived at Voorschoten Lane in The Hague, entreating her forgiveness for the delay.

Annabert's letter dated March 11, 1943—five weeks after Jan was arrested and imprisoned in Antwerp—conveyed a hint of worry. *Did you ever receive my previous letter that I sent in response to your birthday letter to me? I hope that you still visit the Troyentenhof, because I know no other address for you.* She then proceeded to tell him about her life in The Hague, the possibility that they might have to move soon, the Christmas play she had acted in, a bike ride. *There was a fierce storm yesterday coming from the East. You just were dragged along, but that was blissful. I went for a long bike ride, first with head wind, but afterward a wonderful back wind. I was simply flying, and with an arm full of catkins I arrived home.*

In her next letter, she dispensed with the chat and pleaded with him to please write her as soon as possible, that she and her family were very anxious.

At last, in July, a letter came.

Dearest Annabert, Jan began—this was no longer a time for Chikita and Woega—*I want to show that I am still alive, and that I still think about you. And that I am still as happy and healthy as before. I have heard that during the time of my long absence—more than six months—somebody I know was so sweet to write to you and to keep you posted. Were you not very shocked?*

Had Annabert actually received such a letter of explanation, one can imagine the shock it would have given her, who suspected nothing of his double life. However, no one had contacted her. And now Jan added nothing to enlighten her about his situation, no explanation or apology, only that he was happy and healthy and was going to the Ardennes to fatten up. *Write me then once in a while,* he asked, *because I feel very alone and miss my little sister very much. But then I study bravely through and I work hard to show the people that I love very much, to give them a beautiful surprise when the war is finished.* He quickly redirected his remarks back to her, asking after her family and if she was still acting in plays. After this letter, he disappeared off the radar again.

Annabert continued to write, but it must have felt like an exercise in futility because, except for three lines on the back of a postcard from Spain, there were no further replies. In December, after six months of one-way communication, she closed a letter to him with this: *Now something else, Jan: don't you think that we should stop writing? I don't hear from you at all, and I find it very difficult to write to somebody one doesn't know nor his thoughts and ideals. . . . If you write back, we will keep writing, but please be honest about it. I'd rather have you not writing, and keep the beautiful memory that I have of you. The letters get shorter and shorter. You are not angry with me that I write this to you? I wish you lots, lots, and lots of love. Annabert. P.S. Father is going to marry again. Do you know what that means? I don't know what to do about it.*

A few weeks later, a letter came in the mail, addressed to Annabert in an unfamiliar hand.

December 22, 1943

Dear Annabert:

Jan requests that I write in his place to wish you a happy Christmas and he wishes for a quick reunion.

    Jan, who is something like a young brother or a headstrong, adopted son, is not here anymore and cannot get your letters.

    And he has asked a very dear friend to ask me in case contact with you is lost. Many times in intimate moments he has spoken about you with a special expression in his eyes. Every letter from you means a great pleasure for him, but he didn't get any of your letters. He was a long time in prison, and at the end he was released because there was not enough evidence against him. Jan is a distinguished young man who looks very serious and gives the impression of being thirty years old. His friends all love him, even the ones who are thirty years older, and professors at the university talk to him as an equal (not of knowledge but of being an adult). Jan is not living an easy life since the war began. He could have lived the life of a spoiled prince, but he chose his freedom and lived away from his aunt and her circles. What I could offer him was a cozy, interesting bohemian life, but that was also too much for him. You have to know that Jan's social feelings are very strongly developed and he is constantly looking to help other people that are exiled. I will write you and send a friend with a photo and you can show to all your girlfriends that he is the most handsome movie star. (He looks like that in his photo but thank God, he is much, much better than a film star and much more serious.)

    Annabert, I know that Jan thinks of you with love constantly, and that he asks himself how you have developed your inner self. He is very serious when he is in contact with young girls, and he demands a lot of them.

    I have at the moment no address for Jan, but I will write you very soon on the condition that you write me first at this old address for Jan. I ask for forgiveness for this writing that doesn't hang together. I am a long time ill and I am not allowed to write letters.

    With many warm greetings from Betsie. I hope I am being a friend.

Was this the communication that Jan assumed had been sent months before? (*Somebody I know was so sweet to write to you . . .*) If so, the delay may have been due to the unspecified illness that prevented Betsie from writing letters: the Nazis. In the last year before Belgium was liberated, the Gestapo was tracking Betsie Hollants, and she had to leave Brussels and hide out in a house in the Ardennes belonging to a friend. It's probable but unverified that this friend was Jan Daelemans, and the house was the same one where Jan had stayed. When Betsie finally wrote Annabert, she was careful not to reveal anything that might compromise her work and Jan's. She elided his imprisonment in Antwerp and made no mention of the fact that he was now in a concentration camp in Spain. Her task here was to play Cupid.

And it was to this, rather than the news of Jan's imprisonment, that Annabert responded. *I'm so happy that you wrote all about Jan, although I was really a little bit shocked because I think Jan thinks I'm an ideal girl. Please will you say that I am absolutely not that. Omie always said, "Annabert, you are incurably messy."* She then added this cautious observation: *I believe that I don't know Jan at all. Of course that is logical because we haven't seen each other for ten years. We met when we were tiny little children, so we don't know each other.*

In these same last weeks of 1943, the German army commandeered the coastal neighborhood of Scheveningen—here they would stage the V-1 and V-2 rocket launches—and the van Wettum family was compelled to evacuate. Annabert's younger brother, Erik, went to Groningen to work on a farm, or so she believed, though in retrospect it seems more likely that he was sent into hiding there. Her father and grandmother moved to the Anthroposophical community in Zeist where Annabert had first met Jan. And Annabert was sent to Leiden, northwest of The Hague, in order that she might continue her schooling.

She was upset to be separated from her friends and family, and then was stunned to learn that her father was marrying her former teacher, Juffie. Apparently, Mr. van Wettum had had a long and warm friendship with his colleague, and when Juffie made the move with him to Zeist they decided to marry to preserve propriety.

He came to Leiden to break the news of his impending marriage to his daughter, and Annabert crumbled. When her mother had left all those years ago, Annabert had stopped eating and her father had hand-fed her twice a day like a baby bird. Now, the man she had worshipped ever since was allowing an outsider to displace her.

It was after curfew on a moonless night when she left their meeting and headed through the blacked-out streets toward the house where she was living. Distracted by her grief, she ran blindly into a lamppost and broke her nose. The next day, a doctor reset the bone without her receiving either anesthesia or the comfort of her father, who'd had to return to Zeist that morning. *Father, my father, who was everything for me*, she moaned in her diary, *I, a dear dumb little girl . . . I have lost the trust in my father.*

With no one left to confide in, she poured out her heart to the stranger who had written on behalf of Jan. *I find it so difficult to write to someone I don't know, but because of your sweet letter I have the feeling that you understand everything, and that I can tell you everything. At the moment, I'm in such a depressed mood that I could easily put my head on somebody's knee and cry. So much happened here, in this quiet time of the year, it is as if I live in a daze. Everything is very strange. I'm sure I will get adjusted again but it is very difficult to be pulled up, out of one's family where you feel absolutely happy and surrounded by love from your Oma and Father.*

The broken nose was the first in a string of physical ailments. When she broke her nose, she probably also gave herself a severe concussion, because for months afterward she was dizzy and unbalanced, and had such terrible migraines that she was frequently nauseous. Unnerved by her symptoms, her father insisted that she leave school and join the family in Zeist, where she bunked with Omie because her father could only find two rooms together for himself and Juffie. That year, she suffered from angina, a double ear infection, and an infection of the tongue, and then she contracted diphtheria from her brother when he visited, one of roughly a million cases of diphtheria that year in war-wracked Europe.

She tried to help her father in caring for and teaching the developmentally disabled children of Zonnehuis. *They are so sweet*, she wrote Jan, *and it can be so sad. You tell them a story and then you see their eyes empty. Where to? . . . I saw one child having an epileptic episode. There was nobody around and I had never heard of it. So incredibly scary that I could not sleep and dreamt of it. I really had trouble to get over it and get back to my work.*

In the end, she found their disabilities too emotionally distressing to bear, especially given her own delicate health. She collapsed. When the Hunger Winter came the following year, she was already weakened and thin.

THAT WINTER OF 1944-45, Annabert's grandmother, Omie, somehow procured a side of bacon—who knows what she had traded for such a treasure—and it hung in the bathroom. Every day, Annabert shaved off the tiniest little bit, just a taste, not enough to notice. But eventually, of course, many tiny little bits add up, and one day Omie discovered the desecration of her precious bacon. She railed at Annabert, called her a thief, and threatened to tell all her friends what a bad girl she was.

Everybody thinks only about food, Annabert wrote in her diary. Hungry as she was, though, Annabert thought deeply about many things besides food. She had again made friends with a small group of young people, among them a few she'd first met as children in the long ago summer of Pingola. They would sneak out after curfew to the van Bemmelman house, and spend their evenings reading aloud from Goethe, Schiller, and Wagner, revered texts of Anthroposophy. In heavy coats and boots, huddled around one tiny candle, they studied these German writers and philosophers, earnestly pondering Schiller's claim that a perfect civilization would be arrived at through aesthetics, deciphering the allegories in Wagner's operas, and taking parts and reading aloud from Goethe's masterpiece, *Faust*. They also spoke shyly about the difficulties in their own lives. And every night Annabert played music. It was her inspiration and her salve. She played the piano together with two brothers, a violinist and a cellist named Hans, on whom she had a little crush. They called it love, she later said, because she didn't know the difference between that and friendship.

Perhaps because Rudolf Steiner, the founder of Anthroposophy, had been German, and the heroes she knew of were all likewise German—Goethe's Parsifal and Wagner's Lohengrin—Annabert made distinctions. That they were being starved by Germany didn't mean that all Germans were evil. In fact, she was too naive to imagine real evil and much preferred to see the good in people, even the enemy. There was a mansion adjacent to Zonnehuis that had been commandeered to house German soldiers, just ordinary conscripts of the Wehrmacht, not SS, and many of them were boys away from home for the first time. Annabert later noted that they were kind to the disabled children of Zonnehuis and often gave them food during the Hunger Winter, without which the children might well have died.

Ironically, in Germany Hitler had long since begun killing off the mentally and physically disabled, part of his mission to create an Aryan super race. Germany wasn't alone in tinkering with such horrific ideas. The Anthroposophists' commitment to caring for and teaching developmentally disabled children stood in stark contrast to the eugenics movement, which had originated in the United States and become popular in the twenties and thirties. Proponents of eugenics theorized that social behaviors were largely genetic, and they advocated strengthening the human gene pool by applying the same practices used for centuries by breeders of animals: encouraging reproduction among superior individuals and discouraging it among those with undesirable traits. Many countries instigated programs of birth control and sterilization for those who were considered genetically inferior. Nazi Germany, however, took it to a whole new level, using eugenics as the rationale for exterminating not only Jews but also the disabled, homosexuals, and Gypsies.

In 1934 the German government began sterilizing those deemed feeble-minded. An estimated 300,000 to 400,000 suffered this fate. The advent of war allowed Hitler the cover needed to shift from sterilizations to so-called mercy killings because it could now be claimed that this population was using scarce medical resources and staff. Before public pressure from the churches led Hitler to halt the program in 1941, 70,273 mental patients were lethally injected or gassed in chambers that were later used to murder Jews. Even after the program was officially dismantled, the killings continued, expanding to include the mentally and physically disabled in Poland, Russia, and East Prussia. The dead totaled between 200,000 and 300,000 persons by the end of the war.

Annabert, of course, knew none of this. There were dark hints, but the monsters of her imagination were not nearly so gruesome as the actual atrocities.

One day, when she was sitting in a window seat that faced the street, she happened to see a man wearing white stripes shoveling snow from the pavement. An SS officer came up. Out! he yelled at the man, and pushed him to the ground. Annabert ran to her father and told him what had happened.

That is what they are doing, her father said. They are being very, very tough against Jewish people.

As THE WAR dragged on, the German net tightened around Holland. Some 300,000 "divers" were in hiding. This included some remaining Jews and stranded Allied soldiers, but the vast majority of them were Dutch men and boys. In daily raids, the Germans flushed them out to be shipped to the Eastern front as labor. Mr. van Wettum, Annabert's father, was picked up and taken to Amersfoort, the same transport camp near Zeist where Jan Yoors' father had spent the previous war. Annabert got papers from his doctor certifying that her father had tuberculosis and was thus exempt from service, and she bicycled to Utrecht to present these documents at German headquarters. She made several trips without food, returning home to a cold house because Omie was sick in bed and could not make a fire or cook. However, unlike Marianne, her efforts were rewarded: Annabert succeeded in getting her father released.

A curious line appeared in her account of this incident, written about a year later, that seems to suggest she rescued her father not so much for his sake as for her grandmother. *Omie's dear angry Gotthard. I really had to do that, I had to help his mother.* Gotthard was Annabert's code name for her father: it was the mountain pass that Goethe climbed to reach what he considered the most beautiful place in the world. In Goethe's iconography, the Gotthard symbolized a boundary to be crossed.

Annabert was about to cross the boundary of her father toward the real romance of her life.

Madrid, 4 February 1944

Dearest Annabert,

I write you finally once again a few small lines. I better tell you quickly that I am doing well and that I am still in Madrid. The last time I wrote you during Christmas from a very lovely little village in the mountains, where I went with a few good friends to play winter sports. Delightful!

Until now, I haven't received an answer to my letter. Please write me back directly, because I am waiting impatiently for some news of you. At Easter, I am going to spend a few weeks at my parents and my little sister. How much I would love to have you here with me! We have such lovely warm spring weather and all imaginable southern fruits. Here in Madrid, everything is lit very brightly at night. You would certainly enjoy it. There is a lovely museum you certainly have heard of, the Prado. Of course, I am there for hours. I will be happy when I am finally on leave and may come to you. Now it is very difficult. Will it come soon though? Let us hope so.

Please give my best regards to your father, your grandmother, and to your brother, Eric.

Stay strong, very cordially

Jan

14 The Ghosts

It was a spring day, and Marianne was standing on the roof of the hospital where she worked. She and the girl she worked with had spent the morning boiling sheets and were hanging them out to dry on the clotheslines. In the distance, they heard a thrumming, not the sound of a single plane but of a whole squadron, and then the horizon filled with Allied planes, B-52 bombers, at least fifty in formation, coming toward them one after another. They flew in very low, passed over the hospital, and then came back. Marianne and the girl grabbed a sheet off the line and began to wave it over their heads. One of the planes dropped out of formation and came so close that they could see the pilot. He was smiling and waving at them.

There was no radio, no news, so they knew nothing of the meaning of the planes until the next day when word came that the planes had dropped bundles of food. Everyone got a loaf of bread—white bread! people wept at the sight of it—and a bar of chocolate. Marianne stretched out her chocolate to make it last a whole week, each day marked with a square.

ON APRIL 30, 1945, Hitler committed suicide in his command bunker in Berlin. Five days later, Germany surrendered. Then on May 7—nearly five years to the day after Germany had invaded the Netherlands—the Forty-Ninth British Infantry Division rolled into the streets of Utrecht.

People streamed out of their houses to welcome the Allied troops. Those who'd been in hiding for months and even years blinked like moles in the unaccustomed sunshine. Old people, pale and thin, leaned on the arms of others. People wept and cheered. If they had flags, they waved them, and they showered their liberators with flowers. At night there were parties, called *hosse*, in the streets, with accordion music and dancing, and the Dutch people celebrated ecstatically. It was still considered risky to be out in the open—in Amsterdam on the first day, isolated German snipers had fired into a crowd, killing twenty-two people and injuring more than one hundred—but their jubilation couldn't be contained. Marianne went out every night that summer with her brother, Philip, who'd been in hiding, and she danced with the American soldiers.

There was also a shadow side to the celebrating. Marianne was standing on the corner of the main street one day when she saw a throng of people marching toward her. It was another parade. Resistance fighters had begun to round up collaborators—local officials and shopkeepers who had profited by working with the Nazis, even *moffenmeiden*, the women who'd had relations with the occupiers. They shaved the offenders' heads and painted them orange, and then paraded them through the streets to be humiliated, or worse. As the parade approached Marianne, bystanders jeered and some fell in with the mob. The Resistance fighters were indistinguishable from the rest of the crowd, except that they carried guns on their shoulders or used them to shove along their terror-stricken captives. One of the collaborators, a young man just a few years older than Marianne, caught her eye. His eyes pleaded silently, for rescue or perhaps only for compassion. It was only a split second. She turned around and walked away.

One afternoon in August, the doorbell rang. Lidi went to answer it. There stood the doctor's wife from down the street, all smiles and tears. Instantly, Lidi knew. Before the woman could say a word, Lidi ran past her, out into the street.

Henri Citroen was alive.

He'd been sent to Auschwitz-Birkenau on the same transport as Anne Frank and her family, on September 3, 1944. When he arrived, he was among the half who survived the initial selection for the gas chamber, and he was put to work in the laundry. It was warm there.

In mid-January 1945 the Nazis had stepped up the pace of the killings, but there wasn't enough time. They blew up the crematorium at Auschwitz to destroy evidence of the slaughter, and then they prepared to evacuate, rousting the inmates into the yard. Word got out: the Red Army was coming.

Nearly 60,000 prisoners were marched out of the Auschwitz camps, and some 15,000 died on the forced march that followed. Those prisoners deemed too ill to walk had been left behind for the SS to finish off.

But in the panic of the evacuation they were forgotten. Henri Citroen was among them.

When a Nazi with a machine gun came through the barracks and saw Henri lying on his bed, he told him to get out.

I can't anymore, Henri replied.

Instead of shooting him, the man just shrugged his shoulders and walked away.

Others who were not ill had hidden or pretended to be dead. Slowly, these inmates emerged and looked around. The camp was nearly empty, the Nazis gone. A few days later, prisoners standing near the gates saw what appeared from a distance to be ghosts approaching the camp. They moved ever so slowly, wavering like white apparitions, nearly invisible against the snow. When they drew close, it at last became apparent that they were not spirits after all but the Russians in their white winter camouflage uniforms and hoods.

Henri's circuitous journey home from Auschwitz took seven months. First, he was taken to Odessa, where he remained until the close of the war. He was then put on a ship to Le Havre, France, and from there he hitchhiked the 350 miles back to Utrecht, to find Lidi and his children.

THE CITROENS HAD nothing left; everything had been stolen by the Nazis. Henri took his two sons back to The Hague to look for a place to live. They went back to their old neighborhood, at the edge of the Haagse Bos, and walked the familiar streets. It was a warm summer evening, and the sun was still shining. All of a sudden, Philip bent over and picked up something off the ground.

That's Anneke! he cried. He held up a small crinkle-edged photograph. Their little sister, Anneke, dressed in a plaid jumper and with a large bow in her hair, gazed frankly out from the photograph, posed over her practice book, a pen clutched in her fingers, a confident little girl of six or seven.

Oh, look! Philip picked up another photograph from the lawn and another, and then pointed: incredibly, the family's old leather-bound family album was hanging in a bush.

As if this were not bizarre enough, the album was not found in Scheveningen, the seaside resort on the edge of The Hague where they had been residing when war broke out, but in the neighborhood where they had lived prior to that, very near where the photo of Anneke had been taken and where she had died.

If one discounts the paranormal, the more logical explanation remaining is that after Henri Citroen went into hiding, Germans must have moved into their house in Scheveningen. In December 1943, when Annabert and her family had had to evacuate, these same Germans would have needed to move inland as well. Coincidentally, it seems they moved to the Citroen family's previous neighborhood, taking the family's possessions with them. The furniture and linens and household goods disappeared forever, in all likelihood part of the vast quantities of loot shipped to Germany. Over the course of the occupation, the Nazis had systematically stripped Holland of anything and everything useful—from railroad cars and ships to church bells and blankets, from livestock, alarm clocks, and cigarette cases to Rembrandts and van Goghs. But apparently they had no use for the photographs of their victims.

This, however, doesn't explain the album surviving, its photos scattered in the street but as yet undamaged by the elements, or that, as though impelled by a gravitational pull, both photographs and living subjects had returned to their place of origin.

Here were photographs taken at the seaside: Anneke and Marianne holding hands, the pier of Scheveningen just visible behind them. An older photograph of the girls' mother, Ellie Citroen, sitting in a wicker beach chair, a chubby toddler in her lap, her eyes shaded by a cloche hat. And Henri Citroen, a young boy at the turn of the century, posed in the sand with his parents and three brothers, who in spite of the wicker chairs, the paint set and shovels, were all formally dressed and solemn as undertakers. Moving farther back in time, there were silver nitrate photographs. A wedding party long ago. The darkened image of an apartment house with barely visible figures on the front steps and balconies.

What must it have been, to happen upon those images of an irretrievable past, the faces of loved ones fluttering in the bushes like spirits from a world gone forever?

EUROPE HAD BEEN decimated to an extent that is impossible to convey. Hundreds of its cities were partially or entirely demolished, and many consisted of nothing but rubble and the occasional chimney or iron girder still upright. Cathedrals and castles that had stood for centuries were gone, repositories of culture and learning vanished. Britain had been pummeled by almost 50,000 tons of bombs, not only London but the small cities and towns as well. Coventry, a few miles from where Jan was stationed at the end of the war, had been bombed so relentlessly that its fate spawned a new German verb, *coventriren*, meaning "to obliterate."

In Scheveningen, the elegant resort pier had burned and then its charred skeleton had been dismantled lest it be used as a stage for an Allied landing. The Germans had destroyed the pool house and concert hall, too, and had salted the dunes with land mines. The neighborhood where Marianne had lived with the Kalkers was simply gone, bombed flat. Though the people now had peace and were grateful for it, they had almost nothing else; there would be more years to come of rationing and hardship, years to rebuild.

For Christmas 1945, Marianne wrote and illustrated an elaborate fantasy dinner menu made of foods remembered from another time. She named each of its many courses after some place or personage of the war—*Salade Allieres* for the Allies, ragout on toast points à la Stalin, the compote named for Truman, the potatoes for Queen Wilhelmina, a Churchillian pudding with pears and whipped cream—and the blood-red wines, vintage 1942, for Westerbork and Auschwitz. With imaginary cognac, they would toast their freedom.

They had learned to do without things. What was harder to live without were the people who were gone. Few had survived the war without having lost someone close to them.

Marianne got the terrible news about Dr. Kalker from her tutor, Leen, after she returned to The Hague. He had been in hiding, Leen said, and one day the doorbell rang. The people who lived there were not at home, but Dr. Kalker had gone to the window and peeked out. The Nazis saw the movement of the curtain. They arrested him and took him to the prison in Scheveningen called the Orange Hotel. There they interrogated him under torture until he was dead.

Jan Daelemans, who had harbored Jan in the Ardennes after he was released from prison, was dead too. Before Jan left for Spain, he had successfully persuaded his friend to join the Resistance. In his second week as a fighter, Daelemans was out on patrol with the group he had joined, and when they emerged from the woods onto a dirt road, Germans ambushed and shot the whole group. When Daelemans died, he left behind his bride of nine days, Roosje.

For some survivors, the numbers of those they had lost were unbearable. Of the roughly 300 or 350 people in Jan Yoors' organization, he later guessed that perhaps three had survived.

Pulika was dead. Kore. Nearly all Pulika's *kumpania* that Jan had drawn into the fight were dead. A half million Rom had been massacred in what their survivors termed the *Porajmos*, the "devouring."

The Jews. Family upon family, entire neighborhoods and villages. Six million souls.

The Allied soldiers. The Axis soldiers. The civilians on both sides lost to starvation, bombing, and disease. All the fathers and mothers and children.

And beyond Europe, in Africa and Russia, China and Indonesia. The terrible, fathomless numbers. Sixty million and more.

Horsemen of the Apocalypse; or, The Conqueror Shall Be Conquered, *tapestry, wool and cotton, 9 × 12 feet, 1958, Jan Yoors. Courtesy of the Yoors Family Partnership.*

WAR

PART TWO UTOPIA

15 Pingola Redux

Oh, isn't it beautiful to be young and liberated!
—ANNABERT YOORS

At the end of July 1945, the teachers of the Waldorf School in Zeist and the nurses and doctors at Zonnehuis organized a costume dance and carnival to celebrate the liberation. Annabert and Omie decided that Annabert would go dressed as the fairy of summer, an inspired choice since the privations of war had given her the delicate appearance of a nymph, with thin limbs and a large-eyed, pixieish expression. They made a wheat-colored skirt on which they embroidered cornflowers, poppies, and daisies, and they wove the same flowers into her hair.

The grounds near where Annabert and Jan had once built Pingola were lit with lanterns; violins and flutes played, and in the great meadow, princesses, clowns, knights in armor, and bears danced under the huge beech and oak trees.

Annabert was dancing with her boyfriend, Hans, when her father approached and interrupted them.

Someone wants to see you, he said.

Oh Father, I am dancing. Who is it?

He only answered, You will not regret it if you come with me.

She followed him reluctantly. Under the oak tree where Jan had carved his name a dozen years before stood a young man, arms crossed. He wore gray flannel trousers, and a light blue shirt with a beige tie. He stretched out his hand to her.

Chikita, he said.

Jan, she answered. She felt as though she had been struck by lightning, as if she were standing in light, with nothing else there—no music, no crowd of dancers—only Jan.

He took her arm and led her away from the festival, back to her grandmother's house where he had gone when he first arrived. He was stationed near Coventry, England, he said, and had crossed the Channel on an army ship to see her. He had five days' leave and so much to tell her, but just now he was very tired. Omie showed him the guest room.

In a daze, Annabert walked back to the dance. Hans was waiting there for her, and she would have to tell him. "I was a different person," she wrote later. "Woega had kept his promise. All these years he had been the dream of my girlhood."

Over the next four days, Jan told her about himself: about his travels with the Gypsies, his work in the Resistance, how he'd been captured and imprisoned in Antwerp and then again in Spain. He wanted there to be nothing between them, no more fictions. He wanted her to know everything.

During the time she thought Jan was working at the Prado Museum in Spain—so Betsie had written her—he'd really been holed up in the Miranda de Ebro concentration camp. Through the personal intercession of Foreign Secretary Anthony Eden, he was released after five weeks but then had been delayed in Spain waiting for a passport. Legitimate passports, it turned out, took a good deal longer to procure than the counterfeits he was accustomed to carrying.

Finally, papers in hand, he had sailed to England. He wanted to go see his parents in Surrey, but MI-6 detained him under guard at what was euphemistically called the London Reception Centre, housed in the grim Royal Victorian Patriotic School. Day after day, they interrogated him to verify his identity and make certain he wasn't a double agent. Frustrated, he slipped out the back one day, went round to the front entrance, and rang the bell. When asked who was there, he replied, "It is Jan Yoors. I just wanted you to know that I have escaped from Nazi prisons, and you cannot keep me here except if I agree to stay." When he was finally cleared, he had joined the volunteer Belgian Army. However, this too had proved frustrating, all humdrum drilling and no action, hardly better, it turned out, than being cooped up at Miranda.

Annabert listened to his stories, spellbound. Even had she not been predisposed to hero worship, Jan's stories were exhilarating. Then, too, she was in love.

"There was the moonlight-filled night," she later wrote, "when Jan closed me in his arms—at our feet a rippling canal like liquid silver, the scent of honeysuckle, and a windmill silhouetted against the sky—a kiss and life surging so intensely—Jan had to steady me—Love flooding us with delight. There was my small attic room and the sunset streaming golden over Jan's face, Jan telling me about his life, his youth—the gypsies, his artist father who created cathedral stain-glass windows—painting in glass and lead Christ's life—Saints and angels—His mother a poet who would play the piano and sing Botrello [*sic*] songs for her little son. Telling about the war—and I would let my fingers follow Jan's eyebrows, caress his high forehead, look in those mild blue eyes, and hold those small, strong creative hands—hear the strong beat of his heart."

Later, they would have her wedding ring engraved with a date: not the day of their marriage, but the last day of their reunion, when she committed to be his.

On August 15 of that year, Japan surrendered. Jan began a long letter to Annabert that night, and added pages each day describing the celebrations in the little English town of Leamington Spa, where he was stationed with the Belgian Army. *The V-Day is past and it is midnight, and again after a long walk I am in my room alone, but outside the people are screaming and howling.* He described for Annabert the beauty of the little village, decorated like a fairy tale with colored lights and flags, contrasted with the mobs who were behaving licentiously, getting drunk, and shooting off fireworks into the crowd.

Now I would like to kneel before you and put my tired head in your lap, and relieve myself in crying. Today I could do that. Why? No, Annabert, don't ask me why. It's just the way I feel and that's all . . .

On page after page, Jan scrawled his grief. *Far away the smoldering rubble of the totally destroyed cities are still burning. Hundreds of thousands of human beings lay crushed, doomed and senselessly destroyed . . . by people. That civilized people dare celebrate "victory" in such a* danse macabre *way.*

He felt intensely lonely, alienated even from his fellow soldiers. He worried, too, for the future. The atomic bomb would place the fate of the multitudes in the hands of even fewer than before. It was vital, then, that those leaders be men free of prejudice and race-hate, people sensitive enough to consider those who were smaller and weaker.

He caught himself and begged Annabert's understanding and indulgence. *Annabert, dear, you really must find me a sad, silly philosopher. Tomorrow, really, I will be myself again, full of hope and full of fire. I will be really honest towards myself and . . . towards you.* He was so grateful for her confidence in him, he continued, and so hopeful for what they might accomplish.

We have to place our ideals so high that we will have the rest of our long lives to reach them.

16 Christ on the Mountainside

When Jan and Annabert became officially engaged in September 1945, a friend of the family gave them a small gift of cash. In the wake of the war, there was almost nothing to buy; on the other hand, there was no point in saving the money because the old guilders were about to become worthless. The Dutch, along with much of western Europe, were embarking on drastic monetary reforms, in part to deprive war profiteers of their ill-gotten gains and to prevent people from buying off the black market. All money held in bank accounts or turned in for exchange would have to be accounted for. Jan and Annabert decided to celebrate their engagement with an overnight trip to Epe, a small town a couple hours east of The Hague; they'd use their guilders to buy a beautiful ceramic bowl from an artist there.

They shared a room at a little hotel. She slept chastely in his arms all night and woke up the next morning with her period. No one had ever explained to her why she bled every month; Omie had simply said, Oh, when you're forty-five it will stop. There was no hiding it now; her nightgown and the bedsheets were splotched with dark blood. And besides, Jan had said that from now on there would no secrets between them. Embarrassed, she confided her mysterious ailment to Jan. He took her in his arms again and with great sensitivity explained to her the anatomy of love, how babies were made and how they were born, all new information for this eighteen-year-old girl.

All that would wait until they were married, though. Jan believed that making love should follow a conscious decision to have a child, and that it was the man's duty to control himself during the period of engagement. For Gypsies, it was the measure of manhood to be in control of oneself in any situation. A Gypsy should be able to drink a bottle of vodka and still keep his tongue in his head. The same restraint was required with women: they considered it weakness to succumb to sexual temptation. As much as Jan and Annabert desired one another, they would wait until they were ready to marry and bring a child into the world.

Sensibly, they planned a long engagement. Jan had first to finish his service in the Belgian Army and then to find his place in a postwar world. He applied for admittance as a student to London University, claiming that all his transcripts beyond the sixth grade had been destroyed during the war. Apparently, his rare fluency in Romani and an endorsement from Sir Alfred Zimmern, the head of the Foreign Office Research Department, trumped a lack of credentials; the School of African and Oriental Studies admitted him, and at twenty-three years old, he began work on a degree in anthropology, studying under some of the leading social anthropologists of the time. He moved into a community center in the East End, Kingsley Hall, founded by a friend of his mother's, and was given the room that had been Mahatma Gandhi's when he stayed in England in 1931. However, because it had suffered bomb damage and was under repair—and probably also because he was lonely in London—he often spent weekends at his parents' home in Surrey. He built a studio in their back garden and immersed himself in sculpting and painting. His enthusiasms were scattered and half-formed, but he pursued each interest with his characteristic intensity. In a pocket notebook, he scribbled class notes alongside a drawing of a rooster or a fox, and he made lists of phonetically transcribed Romani words on one page and rough figure sketches for a sculpture or plans for a house on the next. He wrote articles for the Gypsy Lore Society. He also took courses in international law with the thought that he might someday end up working in the diplomatic world.

For all the horror and misery of the war, many of those who lived through it had taken inspiration from the cooperation among nations and the dissolution of not only national but also class and racial barriers. In order to defeat a common enemy, people had worked together without prejudice—Russians with Europeans, Rom with Gaje, workers and peasants with aristocrats. Now, that spirit was celebrated. From the ashes of war, new societies and organizations sprang up all over the world with the goal of peace and cooperation. Most notably, in April 1945, delegates from fifty nations met in San Francisco and drafted the charter for what would become the United Nations.

Jan's youthful longing for a utopian society, first sparked by his childhood reading of *Robinson Crusoe* and his father's tales of mythical heroes, reemerged in force now. He participated in an organization called Students in Exile, formed to redress the educational inequities created during the occupation, when only those students and professors who had agreed to collaborate with the Nazis had been allowed to remain in the universities. He wrote long letters to Annabert on the letterhead for another organization called the World Union. The mission of the World Union, proclaimed in blue across the top, was "to unite the peoples of the Earth under a World Government, to promote their welfare and secure the reign of law and order throughout the world. The World Union movement is open to all irrespective of party, race or creed, and does not seek to impose any new political doctrine."

Under this banner, Jan filled page upon page about his work, his thoughts toward his and Annabert's future, and the art projects that increasingly occupied his thoughts. He also admitted to her the dark moods and weariness that overtook him. These confessions, distressing to Annabert, would sometimes be followed by weeks of silence, and then he'd write again, saying that he was feeling much better again.

I don't want to acknowledge to myself or anyone else, but life here in the heart of London, the big city, and the university gets me down. I am ashamed of my shameful weakness, that I am so tired, so tired. Till now I have not been able to find peace. I feel pursued and the inexplicable restlessness of the war years comes up in me again as an unexplained fever. Physically, I feel so weak, broken. Who can understand me? Usually, I feel so strong with an indestructible power that not being used would shock me. I want to, I must find rest, hold on and persist until I am strong again. Where there is a will, there is a way.

One year, anyhow, I have to study. I want to, I want to show myself that I am strong, and also show others. But . . . does this studying make sense? The cold, hard knowledge of materialism, how you look at the world: without God, without art, without love, without life. Can a deeper knowledge of those miseries help me? Am I strong enough to be able to fight against it? Are these difficulties that are passing? Are they there to make me stronger or is this a sign that I should not go on in this way?

The war and imprisonment had taken a toll on his health. He continued to suffer the exhaustion and fevers that had plagued him since his release from prison in Antwerp. And as with so many returning veterans, his emotional equilibrium had been reset: he was like an engine perpetually running too high. For Jan, though, the problem was also older than the war. Even as a child he had struggled in school, not for lack of intelligence—he was brilliant and precocious—but because he had difficulty tolerating routine and remaining focused on what held little interest for him. Luckily, he had parents who were themselves iconoclasts and so could support their child's independent spirit, even to the point of allowing him to leave home and travel with the Rom. He had always been restless, and never quite sure where he belonged in the world. As the Gypsies had said, he was a wild goose, a *vadni ratsa*.

When Annabert expressed the wish to become a nurse or doctor, he confessed to her that after the war, he couldn't bear to spend more of his life surrounded by suffering and death. We have to build a new world, he told her, one that would be an affirmation of the joy of life, the beauty of the soul, and man's need for beauty. Perhaps, he reflected to Annabert, his salvation lay in his art, in becoming a sculptor.

THE SUMMER AFTER they were engaged, and with the permission of her father, Jan took Annabert on a five-week pilgrimage to show her the landmarks of his war. In Antwerp, they went to the house where he'd been born. He also took her to the gates of the prison where the Nazis had held him for six months. In Brussels, he introduced her to Betsie Hollants. They walked down the twisting, cobbled streets of the Marolles, the old quarter that was home to the poor. Jan stopped and whistled: up and down the street, windows flew open. Putzi! people cried. These, Jan explained, were the Sinti Gypsies who had helped him after he got out of prison.

Jan and Annabert took a night train to Paris and stayed in the convent across from the Santé Prison where he had first met Monsieur Henri and where, later, they hid people before smuggling them out of France. Jan was given his old room. The writer and philosopher Marie-Madeleine Davy, a Resistance fighter with whom Jan had worked, invited them to dinner. In her diary, Annabert expressed shock to meet a theologian so worldly that she wore a sheer dress and lipstick. The young couple also visited the anthropology museum Musee de l'Homme, Notre Dame Cathedral, and the eternal flame to the war heroes. Jan took her to the flea markets at Porte de Clignancourt, and he introduced her to the Kalderash Gypsies with whom he had stayed just before the outbreak of war. They returned to him a suitcase stuffed with his letters and documents, his photographs and negatives; at no small risk to themselves, they had held all his papers in safekeeping throughout the war. In Montmartre, too, there were Gypsies: an old woman approached Jan on the street, and the two chatted eagerly in Romani, with him translating bits and phrases to Annabert. The old woman brought them to a café, sat them at a table, and left. She returned shortly, her apron heavy with food: hard-boiled eggs, bread, and tomatoes collected from who knows where. She broke an egg, gave half to Annabert, and blessed the wife-to-be of Putzi.

After Paris, they traveled to the Belgian Ardennes, and Jan sought out Roosje, the young widow of Jan Daelemans. Her sweetheart-shaped face, once so open and cheerful, was just as openly sad now as she recounted to Jan and Annabert the circumstances of her husband's death. The three of them hiked up into the mountains, and Roosje pointed out the rocks alongside the trail under which she and her young husband had hidden messages and letters to each other. They hiked up farther, through a meadow of wildflowers, and came upon a stone quarry.

Do you remember this place? Roosje asked Jan.

Of course he did. He and his friend had dreamed of building a theater and cultural center here.

It was also here, Roosje reminded him, that you suggested Jan go with you to Spain.

Jan nodded. It haunted him, his sense of responsibility for Jan's death.

But Roosje saw it differently. If I had let him go, she continued, I might still have a husband.

The three went on to Orchimon to visit the spot where her husband had fallen. A small wooden cross with the sign of the Maquis marked the spot, and fresh flowers were heaped there.

I feel Jan so close around me, Roosje said. Jan's father is so bitter and angry and doesn't want to remember him. Now my life is so empty, every day the same. The days go by so slowly.

Near the little village of Samson, Jan and Annabert hiked up a mountain overlooking the Maas River. Below, the Battle of the Bulge had been waged the previous year, and the valley was a picture of desolation, strewn with the skeletons of burned trees and ruined houses. Here and there, against the rocks, stood charred wooden crosses indicating where guerrilla fighters had been executed. The carcasses of airplanes, too—broken wings and fuselages, twisted and blackened monuments to war—littered the mountainside.

The air was tangy with the smells of wild thyme and marjoram, and the setting sun poured gold and fire from behind black clouds. Watching the sun sink over the valley, Jan had an epiphany. He would dedicate his life to art. Exhilarated, he described his vision to Annabert. He'd make a monumental statue of Christ on the cross as a memorial to his friends who were killed in the war, and to all who had suffered and lost their lives. And he'd place it here, on this mountain.

It will not be a meek Christ, he explained, a lamb offered for the sins of others. It will be a young man in the strength of his life, rebellious and trying to free himself, pushing himself away from the heavy wood— from his fate, his suffering brought upon him by his fellow men.

And then, with cinematic drama, thunder cracked across the sky and the clouds burst open like ripe fruit. In the drenching rain, they made their careful way down over the slippery rocks.

Jan took her hand to steady her. She looked like a little drowned mouse, he joked. But then, he probably looked no better.

No, she said, you always look like a god, even when you are soaking wet.

In spite of the graveyard setting, they were laughing and holding hands, in love and giddy with their visions of art.

JAN WAS STILL in school, they had no money or home of their own, and both were still physically debilitated from the war. But in the end they couldn't wait another year to begin their life together. They married on November 27, 1946, at the City Hall in The Hague, and then moved to

England to live with his parents in the village of Purley, just south of London. Eugeen Yoors designed the wedding announcement, depicting the stained glass window he intended to execute for the newlyweds once they moved into their own home. On it, a childlike couple dressed in white faced each other, their hands pressed palm to palm like Romeo and Juliet, their faces upturned. Above them a white-haired Heavenly Father spread his arms wide, unfurling a rainbow, the symbol of His faithfulness toward His children.

Jan's dreams were Annabert's dreams. She believed that her husband was destined for great things, and it's a measure of this lifelong faith that she saved for posterity the flyers, cards, and catalogs for every exhibit of Jan's work, every newspaper and magazine clipping, and every letter they would ever receive. Well, nearly every letter. Among the congratulations and gifts that arrived at the house in Purley in the months following their wedding, a letter came addressed to Annabert. It was from a Gypsy girl in France. She accused Annabert of stealing Jan from her and put a curse on the bride and the marriage. Jan provided some explanation for the girl's claim, but the curse itself he dismissed as superstitious nonsense.

They swept the Gypsy girl's letter under the carpet, literally lifting the edge of a rug and tucking it out of sight. It was a gesture they would repeat in future with other unwelcome correspondence. Gypsy curses had no place in the fairy tale they envisioned for their life together.

17 The Other Girl

The Citroens came back to The Hague to reclaim their old life, but it was gone. When he went into hiding, Henri Citroen had left a brother in charge of his business; now that he had returned unexpectedly from Auschwitz, the brother was reluctant to relinquish control. Family relations frayed and snapped. In his own home, too, Henri's children couldn't be tamed back into submission. Every night they disappeared. He battled fiercely with his two sons, and even his daughter defied him. On her father's first night home from the concentration camp, Marianne had gone out with her boyfriend rather than stay home and listen to her father's stories. Now, she went out every evening and came home late.

One day, the family went to a warehouse where, as reparation, Jews were being given furniture, clothing, and housewares donated by Americans. Picking over tables piled high with clothing, Marianne searched for a sweater to replace the one she had long since outgrown, something that wouldn't look so childish and shabby. During the war, there had been no new clothes to purchase and she'd had to make do, letting things out as she grew, piecing together two skirts to make a larger, motley one, clomping around in wooden shoes. Now, with the war over and the boys come out of hiding, Marianne wanted to be pretty, to be noticed.

Newly blossomed into womanhood, Marianne *was* pretty. Her hair had darkened to a glossy caramel, and her body was strong and lush. Beyond her physical attributes, she also radiated a nascent sexuality that invited notice. It caused older women to distrust her and to keep a closer eye on their husbands and sons. At the same time, she was naive to a degree that would be hard to credit today. Like Annabert, she'd had no mother to instruct her. When she was living with Leen, she had once shyly asked her tutor how babies were made, but Leen was so embarrassed that Marianne quickly let her off the hook. Is it by kissing? she asked, to which Leen had said yes and changed the subject.

Marianne had her first little romance at the age of seventeen, while she was still living on the farm with Lidi's parents. It was innocent: a farmer boy rode his bicycle to her after work, and they would stand at the gate and hold hands and talk. Then in Utrecht, there was a student named Hans, but his mother nipped their romance in the bud, saying that her son was too busy studying for medical school to have time for a girl.

After Hans came Harry, who was hiding upstairs in the house where she and Lidi rented rooms. The housekeeper reported to Marianne that this boy was in love with her, a notion that thrilled her. She went upstairs to the attic, and one night she decided to stay. Only then did it come out that he was pining for another girl who had died from tuberculosis. Out of loyalty to the dead girl, he refrained from touching Marianne.

A short time later, after moving back to The Hague, she confessed her misadventure to Lidi, who was horrified. If you slept with a man but didn't consummate it with intercourse, she told Marianne, it could go to his brain and make him crazy. Marianne wrote to Harry in Utrecht and said that it was urgent he come visit her. When he arrived, she explained to him in all earnestness that his sanity depended upon his having relations with her. He complied. Afterward, he asked shyly if she was thinking about her dead mother while they did it, a bizarre question presumably prompted by thoughts of his dead sweetheart. She lied and said yes.

Some weeks later, mistakenly believing she was pregnant—perhaps her period was late, perhaps she simply assumed that this was the inevitable outcome—she went with her brother to Utrecht to see him. But Harry put her off and made it clear he had no interest in seeing her.

Next came the requisite bad boy, a rich and spoiled young man who rode a motorcycle. When Marianne was away for a weekend, he cheated on her with a friend of hers, and that was the end of that.

Though the boys might change, the pattern remained: Marianne was always the substitute, the other girl.

Sometime in that first year, she bumped into her childhood friend, Annabert, who had also returned to The Hague with her family. The world had changed since they'd last seen one another, and each of them had changed with it. Shy little Annabert, frail and thin as kindling, was engaged to a Belgian war hero, the handsome blond boy whose photograph Marianne had seen on her dresser when they were young.

There was nothing momentous in Marianne's first meeting with Jan, nothing to foreshadow what would come. She came home one afternoon and found the young couple in the parlor visiting with her father and stepmother. Before anyone noticed her, she ducked upstairs and changed clothes so that she could show off her new riding boots. Then she snuck back downstairs and outside so that she could make an entrance.

The three young people sat in the parlor and talked, and Marianne thought that her friend's fiancé seemed like a nice fellow, good-looking and courteous. They were so deep in conversation that when it was time to go, Marianne walked with them back to Annabert's house. Jan suggested that she should stay and have dinner with them, but Annabert had to retract the invitation because Omie hadn't prepared enough food for an unexpected guest.

Marianne met another young man when she went to the beach with Philip and a group of his friends. The young man asked if he could take her out, and she said yes. He was Jewish and had lost all his family except for one sister somewhere in the south of Holland and an uncle in Rotterdam. He was in the Dutch Liberation Army. This, she thought, might please her father, and so she brought him back to the house one evening and introduced him to her parents before they went out to the movies. Afterwards, they went back to his room.

This was the first one that felt serious, and it lasted several months. What ended it wasn't the revelation that there was someone else, an older woman who lived in the boarding house where he stayed when he was off-duty. Marianne was by now more or less resigned to the fact of other women, past or present. No, what ended it was that her period was late, and when she went to him with the news, he received it in silence.

She suggested an abortion, and noted his relief. He went to his uncle in Rotterdam for help in finding a midwife. When he returned, he repeated a joke his uncle had told that made light of her trouble. Crushed and angry, she stormed out of his room and never saw him after that.

Desperate, she confided to her friend Annabert that she was pregnant and was going to get an abortion. Annabert tried to talk her out of it: she and Jan were opposed to abortion. But there was no way that Marianne would carry a child without a father. It was unthinkable. She withdrew a large sum from her bank account, and Lidi made arrangements for someone to come to the house while her father was away. The midwife performed the procedure, and then told her to get up and walk—walk and walk and walk—advice intended, presumably, to pass the fetus. She and Lidi walked around The Hague for hours, but there was nothing, no blood and no pain.

The next day, their family doctor came to the house. He examined Marianne and pronounced her fine. As her father was letting the doctor out, he gave Marianne a terrible look of reproach, but he never acknowledged that he knew what had transpired.

In fact, Marianne had probably never been pregnant in the first place, but this was something that she would realize only upon telling the secret some sixty-five years later.

As PART OF her latest efforts at schooling, she was earning educational credits by taking care of children in one of the state's Orange Houses, community centers where malnourished children were helped to recover. Surrounded by a circle of little skeletons, Marianne read the children books and sang to them. One day, holding an infant in her arms, she called out for the nurse to come and help. The child's muscles were so weak that its intestines had slipped out of its body.

Marianne decided she had to get out, get away from her family, away from her failed affairs, away from the postwar bleakness of The Hague. Somehow she came up with the idea of going to England and working as a nanny, a plan her father disapproved of. Why should she work? And why as a nursemaid? However, she was adamant, and so Henri Citroen used his connections to find a position for her in a house in Leatherhead, Surrey, that paid one pound, fifteen shillings a week.

At the end of November 1946 Marianne sailed for England.

18 The Apocalypse Tapestry

In the spring following their wedding, Jan and Annabert went to see a show at the Victoria and Albert Museum, *Masterpieces of French Tapestry*. Two hundred tapestries illustrated the august history of the art form. Pride of place in the exhibit was rightfully given to the oldest surviving French tapestry and without doubt the most stunning: the Apocalypse Tapestry. At 130 meters—more than the length of a football field and the largest tapestry ever woven—its six sections depict Saint John the Divine's vision of the final battle between good and evil that culminates in the triumphant return of Christ. Though the message was intended ultimately to uplift, the images of death and destruction, of devils and hydra-headed beasts are ghastly, a mood reinforced by the slightly larger-than-life scale of the figures, the sheer size of the piece, and the semidarkness in which old tapestries are displayed. Visitors to the London exhibit in 1947 would certainly have projected the tapestry's chilling allegories onto their own recent experiences of war, just as the original creators in the late fourteenth century had woven in references to the conflict of their time, the Hundred Years' War.

The history of tapestry following the medieval period was one of long decline. Beginning with the painter Raphael, whose designs employed shadow and perspective and increased tonal variety, tapestries increasingly imitated paintings. Examples of the Baroque and Rococo included classically themed works by Boucher and Perrott, tapestries so detailed that it took up to a year to weave a single square foot. As feats of craftsmanship, they are extraordinary, but as art they appear vaguely lifeless, like something that might result from an incredibly meticulous paint-by-numbers set. The thousands of man-hours required to execute such intricate designs meant that eventually they were priced out of reach for all but a very few, and the number of weavers declined almost to extinction. By the turn of the twentieth century, the once-great workshops of Gobelin and Aubusson were reduced to turning out reproductions of old paintings and third-rate kitsch for tourists.

What prompted the Victoria and Albert's ambitious exhibition, though, was a renaissance of the medium. In the twenties the owner of a French design firm, Marie Cuttoli, had commissioned the Aubusson workshops to weave designs by some of the foremost modern artists: Picasso, Braque, Miró, and Rouault. Modern art translated well into wool, recapturing the purity and primitive strength of early tapestry. In the years before World War II, a handful of artists began to create designs specifically for tapestry, most notably Jean Lurcat. Inspired by the Apocalypse Tapestry, he championed a return to simpler designs, limited palettes, and a stouter weave. The war put this fledgling revival on hold, but in the year of the exhibition, Lurcat formalized the movement with the creation of a society, the Association des Peintures Cartonniers de Tapisserie, and several examples of their work hung in the London show.

The show also featured working demonstrations by an Aubusson master weaver. Watching him at work charged Jan's imagination. As a child, he had amused himself with a small loom he found in his parents' home. It was a simple skill, as easy to learn as knitting, and recently he had taught Annabert to weave, thinking they might earn some extra money making shawls. Of course, weaving a tapestry is a considerably grander undertaking—as mastering a soufflé is to scrambling a few eggs—and it's a measure of Jan's self-confidence and Annabert's faith in him that they weren't dissuaded for a moment by their relative ignorance of the craft. On the contrary, Jan was so excited that he went home and started designing on the spot. He had found a medium to match his ambitions and temperament.

As an artist, Jan had been molded by his father. Some of his fondest childhood memories were of the times he accompanied Eugeen Yoors to a church or cathedral on business. The grand scale of stained glass windows and their play of intense color and light against the backdrop of gray stone inspired him, and the heroic and spiritual subject matter conformed to his inherited belief in the elevated purpose of art. He appreciated, too, the physicality and artisanship involved in constructing a stained glass window. However, as much as he admired his father and wished to emulate him, Jan could never be comfortable working in his shadow. Because he had monumental intentions, sculpture had initially seemed to be the answer. However, in the postwar austerity, the cost of granite and marble was prohibitive, and bronze out of the question, so he had largely been restricted to modeling in clay and making plaster casts. At the end of his life he would return to sculpture, but tapestry proved a more accommodating medium, allowing him to honor his artistic legacy and at the same time make his own mark. He could design "windows" to be woven in wool.

19 Betwixt and Between

Don't forget, we came out of the war. *Neer geslagen*—what is the word in English? After a storm the woods are ripped out, the trees are flying, everything is gone, and you have no more roots. Everything is chaos. And after that chaos you have to try to find a meaning in life again. The war was behind us, and it was a new focus.

—MARIANNE YOORS

Jan's moods and energy swung violently. One day he might be working at his art, full of enthusiasm and grandiose plans; the next he was too depressed to get on the London train to attend classes. Or he'd head out for a walk and not return for hours, sometimes even days. He slept little and was always on edge, with the hypervigilance of the hunted. When he didn't like something he had made, he tore it up. He made a model for the crucifix he had first envisioned in the Ardennes with Annabert, but then destroyed it in a fit of rage. His inability to control his emotions shamed him. *Where is Putzi?*—he wrote in his diary—*who saw his friends go to war, never to return . . . without others ever suspecting his deep inner struggles. Putzi who was proud to control himself, to be master over his feeling in the presence of others. . . . Now when I am tired and think about the loving people around me, I ask myself if that strong self-control and strength of will was not also megalomania (too strong a word—haughtiness? Pride?).*

He tried to explain himself to his starry-eyed bride, to tell her what he had seen and suffered in the war, but his stories distressed her to the point of illness. One evening, they went to the movies. A Russian newsreel preceding the main feature showed graphic footage of Nazi

137

atrocities. Sitting in the dark theater, Annabert flinched at the black-and-white images flickering on the screen: corpses stacked like cordwood or heaped in ditches, survivors like walking skeletons. She got up and ran from the theater, nauseated and in tears.

Jan had imagined a union of perfect symbiosis, a partner with whom he could share all of his secrets, someone who would understand all facets of him. But he recognized now that he risked despoiling the very thing that had attracted him to Annabert: her purity. By now she was also carrying his child, a second innocent that needed his protection. He made a decision to shelter her as best he could from the darkness in the world, including the darkness he carried inside himself.

JAN NEEDED A model but couldn't afford to hire one. Annabert was too thin for an artist's model, and now she was pregnant as well. Between the two of them, they thought of Marianne. Duly, Annabert sent a letter to the Citroens' address in The Hague, inviting Marianne to come over for a holiday. The Citroens in turn forwarded the letter back across the Channel to Marianne in England. Unbeknown to the three young people, they were living in neighboring London suburbs less than twelve miles apart.

Marianne was excited to learn that her friend was so close. She had been lonely in a strange country, and isolated by a new language. Her first job hadn't worked out—her employers had fired the Irish maid for a mistake that had been Marianne's, and so Marianne had quit in solidarity with the girl. She was now employed as a housekeeper by a mother and daughter who lived in the same village of Leatherhead. Both were quite nice, but they were employers rather than friends. On her first day off, she took the train to Purley and spent a happy day with Annabert and her new husband.

On Marianne's next visit, Annabert broached the subject of modeling. Jan wouldn't ask her himself, as that might appear improper. Even so, Marianne was shocked. Her bourgeois upbringing had schooled her in the belief that artists and bohemians were people of low character. And artists' models were loose women, no better than prostitutes. Is that what the two of them thought of her? She was deeply offended.

No, Marianne told Annabert, she could never do something like that.

Why not? Annabert asked. You are exposing yourself already.

Marianne was indignant.

I can see everything, Annabert insisted quietly, and she gestured at Marianne's beautiful organdy blouse. You are showing your whole body. So what's wrong with modeling for Jan?

Whatever Jan wanted, Annabert wanted for him, and so she coaxed and cajoled her friend around to the idea of modeling. Reluctantly, Marianne agreed to at least give it a try.

At first, she kept a bedsheet wrapped around her torso like a Greek goddess. Even so, it felt awkward being nearly naked in front of a man and permitting him to study her body. He sketched her back and shoulders, and in this pose she didn't have to face him, but only heard his voice behind her and the scratch of charcoal on paper. As he sketched, he told her stories about the Gypsies and about the war, and gradually she began to feel at ease.

Lower the sheet a bit, he encouraged, so I can get the line of your lower back. Yes, that's better.

And they returned to conversation. He wanted to know her stories, too, and he listened with such empathy. It was the first time in her life she'd felt *heard*. Eventually, she let the sheet slip to the floor. He made no remark, just kept talking and sketching.

When he was done working for the day, she would dress and the three of them would go for a walk or prepare dinner together. Jan's mother, Magda, was out of the country much of the time, but Eugeen Yoors would join them for dinner, and the conversation flew around the table, the talk about art and religion so lively and impassioned, especially compared with the buttoned-down silences at Marianne's own family's table. It was wonderfully invigorating, and when evening came it was with reluctance that she got back on the return train.

> *Jan and Annabert Yoors*
> *are happy to let you know that*
> *their first son Johannes was born*
> *on the 2nd of September, 1947*
> *at*
> *88 Haydn Avenue, Purley*
> *Surrey, England*

Marianne's work visa was set to expire in November. As she was considering asking her present employer to sponsor her, a better solution presented itself: Jan and Annabert offered to take her in as an au pair for their newborn son, nicknamed Janneke. First though, she returned to Holland for her twenty-first birthday. She spent a month or so with her family while she waited for her new permit to come through. If her father had been dubious about her working as a nanny, he was even more leery of her taking up residence with artists, but Marianne wasn't asking his permission.

She returned to England, wrapped like a film star in the new fur coat she had gotten for her birthday, and moved into the house in Purley. As it happened, she arrived on Annabert and Jan's first wedding anniversary. In the immediate, immersive way particular to young people, she was swept into their life, caught up in their passionate idealism and the romance of their plans. Jan didn't approve of smoking, so she quit on the spot, leaving her carton of rationed Camels on the doorstep for the milkman. Because Jan and Annabert were both religious, she began to study the Bible. And she made herself indispensable, helping Jan with his various projects.

It was Marianne who found a ramshackle forge a short distance from the house, and arranged with the old blacksmith to rent it for Jan's use as a studio. She paid the rent up front, so that Jan wouldn't feel beholden to her. In the mornings, Jan would sketch her there, or they'd prepare the clay for his sculptures. Then in the afternoons, they walked over to Jan's land. The Cadburys, heirs to the chocolate fortune and devout Quakers, had been giving Eugeen and Magda Yoors a small monthly stipend to support Magda's peace and reconciliation work. Now they had also donated a small plot of land in the same neighborhood so that Jan and his bride could build a home. First, though, the lot needed to be cleared of the hawthorn that had grown over it in fairy-tale proportions. By the end of each day, Marianne and Jan were physically exhausted and covered in scratches.

Meanwhile, Annabert spent long hours alone with the baby. Sometimes when loneliness got the better of her, she'd bundle up little Janneke and go find her husband and her friend. She couldn't help with the physical labor—she was frail and undernourished from her wartime illnesses, and pregnancy had weakened her further—but she'd find an excuse to interrupt, bringing them food or something cold to drink. She'd admire all the work they'd done and she'd ask Jan to show her again where the front room would be, and which direction the nursery would face, and what would be the view from there. Sometimes when Jan and Marianne went back to work, she'd stay on and watch them, rocking the baby in her arms.

When Annabert's grandmother came to England to see her grand-daughter and new great-grandchild, she was dismayed to find Marianne unexpectedly in the mix. One day while Jan was away at school, Omie unpacked elegant gowns she had brought for Annabert. As a girl, Omie had worn these same evening dresses when she served as hostess for her widowed father, the governor of Dutch Borneo. Now that Annabert was married, she would be entertaining and would want something nice to wear. If not now, well, she could save them for later. Meanwhile, Omie said, it would be fun for the two girls to try them on. She selected one dress for each girl to model. Annabert's was demure, but the dress she handed to Marianne was black lace with a pink satin slip underneath. Here, Omie said, this suits you.

Marianne understood the tacit suggestion.

With her granddaughter, Omie was more direct. Marianne is going to take Jan away from you, she warned.

Omie's observations were accurate, but her conclusion was faulty: though she had begun to fall in love with Jan, Marianne had no intention of stealing her friend's husband. And while Jan badly wanted to make love with Marianne, he wasn't about to leave or deceive his new bride. What he *did* have in mind would never even have occurred to Omie: he wanted to keep them both. Jan was working out a way to fold his physi-cal desires into a larger vision of utopia and a morally defensible choice.

In his anthropology studies at the university, he had learned that polygamy was actually not an uncommon practice in the world; in fact, the number of societies that allowed it far outnumbered those that insisted on monogamy. There was even biblical precedent in the Old Testament. Look at King Solomon, he said to Annabert. Look at Abra-ham. It made a kind of sense, and even more so now, given the shortage of young men at the end of the war. Why should a young woman be left unprotected and unloved simply because the war had unbalanced the ratio of the sexes? And why, after all the barbarism and inhumanity he had seen practiced by so-called civilized societies, should he conform to their narrow and hypocritical ideas of propriety? On the contrary, as an artist he was obliged to travel to the far edges of human experience, seeking out the higher truths. He had already experienced one end of the spectrum in prison, when he was being tortured. Now, he needed to find out if there was an ecstasy equal to that pain, perhaps even surpassing it.

MARIANNE AWOKE AND found Jan standing at her bedside, holding a candle. Annabert had sent him, he whispered. He brushed a bit of hair from her face and then lifted her chin as he sometimes did when he was posing her. He and Annabert knew how lonely she had been. His wife had sent him downstairs to comfort her. Did she want comfort?

She nodded dumbly.

Jan eased himself down onto the edge of the narrow bed and snuffed out the flame. In the blackness she reached out for him, but her arm knocked the candlestick as he was setting it on the night table, and it hit the floor with a deafening clatter. He pressed a finger to her lips. She strained to hear sounds of stirring upstairs, but her heart was drumming in her ears.

Annabert's grandmother might investigate, Jan whispered hoarsely, and that would not do.

His weight lifted from the mattress, and he was gone again as suddenly as he had come.

It was a temporary setback.

After that first visit, Marianne lay awake every night waiting, tense with anticipation, hoping he would sneak back downstairs to her, hoping he would not. The household would say their goodnights and go to bed, and after an hour or so, he would sometimes appear. They would have sex, and when he was finished he would leave her bed.

Annabert is so good, he'd apologize. I have to go quickly back to Annabert.

During the day, she continued to model for him. She would disrobe, and as he sketched her they would talk as they always had, about his travels with the Gypsies and his work as a saboteur, about her time with the Kalkers and then with Lidi. They talked of everything except what happened at night between them. Nor was anything said of it between Annabert and Marianne. The two childhood friends lived side by side in quiet torment and confusion. It was intolerable.

One night, Marianne lay weeping in the dark when she felt a presence behind her. She turned. It wasn't Jan but Annabert, her childlike body shrouded in a long white nightgown.

You stop that, Annabert scolded. You keep us all awake.

Marianne's anguish finally drove her to conclude that, though she had nowhere to go, neither could she remain where she was. In the middle of the night, she snuck out of the house with only the clothes she was wearing. She doesn't remember how far she got, but she must have been less than stealthy in her departure, for Jan quickly caught up to her.

Where do you think you are going? he asked.

To London, she answered. She would become a prostitute, she figured, the only option she imagined was left to her.

He calmed her down and brought her back to the house.

In his 1909 book *Les Rites de passage*, the noted French ethnographer and folklorist Arnold van Gennep coined the term "liminal" to describe the disorienting middle period when one is neither here nor there in the social order, for instance, no longer a child but not yet an adult. Victor Turner, who later developed and advanced van Gennep's theories on liminality, described the period as being "betwixt and between," "a gap between ordered worlds where almost anything could happen."

As a student of anthropology, Jan would have been familiar with van Gennep's work, but would he have recognized how well it described his own present circumstances?

In a strange coincidence, Victor Turner was a fellow student with Jan at London University. Jan and Turner shared the same teachers and mentors, and studied the same theories of social and cultural anthropology. Not only that, but during the last years of the war Turner had lived in a Gypsy caravan near Rugby, England, a few short miles from where Jan was stationed at Leamington Spa. Turner was also a pacifist and conscientious objector and so may well have been acquainted with Jan's mother, Magda. In short, it seems almost certain that Jan and Victor Turner knew one another.

Turner's lifelong work focused on liminality, and he expanded the definition from rites of passage to include any disruptive periods of transition in societies, such as the whole of Europe was experiencing in those early postwar years. In these threshold periods, Turner posited, a society takes stock and reevaluates its social, emotional, and spiritual structures. Taboos weaken, and individuals can step outside of their normal roles and choose alternative social arrangements and values. In other words, when a society is in transition, anything goes.

Raised by parents with a bohemian bent, Jan was destined from birth to cut his own path. The same could hardly be said of Annabert and Marianne, though. That the two friends found themselves in love with the same man was exquisitely painful and confusing. Perhaps the only thing more bewildering was Jan's apparent intention that they should simply share him.

Such a thing would have been impossible had not the repeated shocks of divorce and death upset the order of their childhoods and made them vulnerable. The terrors and privations of war further loosened the bonds of their Dutch bourgeois upbringing. Even so, it took all of Jan's considerable patience and charisma to persuade them to take this next step.

20 A New Family

Marianne came to live with us when Janneke was only a
few weeks old—and with her came a time of great jealousy,
insecurity and fear that stems from insecurity for me. All
my values I so much had dreamed about had to change.
I was not anymore the only Mrs. Yoors—Jan's one wife.
In our society, in all of Europe, it was seen as a great shame
when a husband had another love. It was and still is illegal.
We had to break with convention. We had no money. I was
very young and knew nothing of marriage, except that I
was now married to Jan for better or for worse to care, to
go through life together.

—ANNABERT YOORS

Annabert had just turned twenty-one and had no mother or older female
relative to guide her through the mysteries of motherhood. Magda
Yoors, having been invited by Gandhi, was away in India, and Marianne
knew only a little more about taking care of an infant than Annabert did.
In the wake of war, the medical community was too overwhelmed to pay
much mind to a frightened new mother. When Annabert followed the
English midwife's advice to nurse only every four hours and never at
night, her milk stopped coming in, and she struggled to feed her baby.
The welfare doctor who came to the house to give Janneke his smallpox
injection said Janneke was too thin, and after that they had to go every
week to the welfare center in Purley. Annabert was horrified: the place
stank of illness and filth, and the overwhelmed doctors had no supplies or
medicine to treat their sick patients, not even a bandage.

On a February night in 1948 when the baby was six months old, Marianne was looking after him while Jan and Annabert took a walk. Though the doctor said it was nothing to worry about, Janneke had had a little cough for weeks, and now Marianne couldn't persuade him to eat. Very suddenly, he turned feverish. When Jan and Annabert came home, and Jan picked up the baby, he went limp in Jan's arms and a strange moaning sound passed out of his chest. In a panic, Marianne ran down the hill to the house of a doctor who lived on the road to Croydon. The doctor, in turn, took the baby to the hospital. Janneke was diagnosed with pneumonia and put in an oxygen tent. Jan, Annabert, and Marianne were sent home: there was nothing left but to wait and see if he would pull through. The hospital would call if there was any change. All through the next day, Annabert prayed. She went out walking by herself and gathered wood anemones for her baby's homecoming.

The next morning, when the baby seemed improved, a nurse took him out of the tent. He was dead within the hour.

Many years later, on what would have been her child's twenty-fourth birthday, Annabert wrote of that terrible day: *Kneeling next to that little baby whose face had an expression of surprise I could cry out, "Why?" A question to answer for the rest of my life.*

IN PLACE OF the family she had dreamt of—mother, father, and child—Annabert found herself part of a different sort of threesome, one that included her childhood friend as her husband's lover. She had made some sort of rugged peace with this arrangement and did her best to conceal her jealousy and grief. But then she went a remarkable step further: she accepted Jan's vision of the three of them as a family. This acceptance was predicated on her belief that Jan was an exceptional person to whom the ordinary rules didn't apply. He was a war hero and an artist and, in Annabert's eyes, a young god who was going to do remarkable things in the world. She called him her Lohengrin, the knight in shining armor from the Wagnerian opera of the same name. In the opera, Lohengrin rescues Elsa and then asks for her hand in marriage, but on the condition that she mustn't ask his identity. Annabert made a similar pact. Her husband's various identities—as Woega, as Putzi and Vanya—remained mysterious to her, but she was resolved to support him unquestioningly and to be a helpmate in all his endeavors. Nothing made her prouder than when he called her his cornerstone.

In August 1948, seven months after Janneke's death, Jan went to Belgium to help Betsie and Roosje design a chapel to be dedicated to the memory of Jan Daelemans. He sent letters back to England addressed communally to Annabert and Marianne, and they answered separately.

Oh my angel, it is so sweet that you write to both of us, Annabert penned. *Marianneke is beaming. It is so good between us. We have a good time together, but we only see each other once in a while . . . and we do a lot of weaving, as little spiders. The whole day and the evening till it is dark, we are weaving.*

They were hard at work on Jan's tapestry designs in preparation for his first exhibit, at the Archer Gallery in London. *Another long day has passed,* Marianne reported, *a day with a lot of sunshine, a sky so blue as the background of the small Maria. The weaving is getting along nicely, tomorrow evening finished.* Marianne was weaving an image of the Virgin Mary, one of a pair, while Annabert executed their first large tapestry.

Nadara, *tapestry, wool and cotton, 6 × 8 feet, 1948, Jan Yoors. Courtesy of Matthew A. Voorsanger.*

Worked today, Annabert wrote, *like all the days, so hard and much. Again tied from behind and stretched on, drew on a new chalk, and wove a whole part still. Oh dearest, what colors, what a gorgeous deep red, with the black of the shield, against it vermillion and deep blue. The gold yellow of the leg, light crème and brown of the horse, wonderfully beautiful—I enjoy the colors so much.* Like the two Mary tapestries, the subject matter of this tapestry—a knight on a rearing horse—paid homage to medieval tapestry, but it was updated to honor those who had fought in the recent war. Written in Sanskrit across the knight's shield was a Romani word, *Nadara*, meaning "Do not fear."

DO NOT FEAR. Easier said than done. For the rest of his life, Jan would carry beneath his skin the psychological scars and habits formed by war. He stayed on the shore when others went swimming because his experience of torture had left him with a paralyzing fear of being underwater. Whenever he entered a room, he made a mental note of where the windows were located and if possible sat near them, always facing the door. He avoided carrying more than he could throw out of a window if he had to escape. He also balked at giving out personal information, and as a consequence never finished filling out the paperwork that would have qualified him for veteran's benefits. He reflexively distrusted the police and authority figures in general, an attitude instilled by the Gypsies and reinforced during the war by his dealings with the Nazis and their collaborators.

And so, one day in the early weeks of 1949, Jan intercepted Marianne on the road as she was coming home. He grabbed her arm and turned her around. Walking swiftly and speaking in a voice tense with fear, he told her that British officials had been at the house inquiring about her. She had never seen him like this, and his panic was contagious. He took her directly to the station and put her on a train back to Holland.

In all likelihood, the officials had simply wanted to follow up on Marianne's visa, which had expired. She might have remedied the infraction by simply going to the consul and requesting an extension. However, when Jan and Marianne recovered their wits, they discovered that now, in order for her to reenter the country, she would need a new sponsor because Jan and Annabert could no longer claim the need for a nanny. Anxious letters flew back and forth across the Channel, the three of them trying to figure out how they might reunite, and also reassuring each other that this was in fact what they desired.

Who knows what first piqued her father and stepmother's suspicions, but something prompted them to investigate. In Marianne's room, they found and read the letters that had been coming to the house with nearly every post. Jan hadn't implicated himself by writing to Marianne directly, and Annabert had disguised some of the matter in a private code. Still, Henri and Lidi Citroen could put two and two together: these were love letters.

They didn't confront Marianne with the evidence, and when Marianne saw that her letters had been disturbed, she too held her tongue. Still, the unspoken tension in the house was palpable and came out in veiled comments and criticisms.

But this is the same old egoism, she explained in a letter to England. *Children, we are so happy. Here they see me only happy and enthusiastic when I am busy for you and talking about you. They cannot understand it, and I get sarcastic remarks. . . .*

Would it not be possible for me to get a job in England taking care of little babies in the neighborhood near London? I can then earn some money. I bicycle here from one side to the other side to save pounds. If I hear of something, I go straightaway there to earn two or three pounds. Then I feel myself closer with you and hope that it doesn't take so long, so I don't have to stay here too long, because the mood is very tense. . . . We have conversation and conversation and all this goes around to the same thing: they are so afraid I will not marry. What can I say about that?

Jan eventually enlisted a friend who applied to sponsor Marianne as his housekeeper. When she got the news, Marianne responded with exuberance, writing that she would come just as soon as she could get her passport renewed. She joked that Jan should wear an orange ribbon on his lapel when he came to the airport to meet her, so that she would know him after their long, three-month separation. On April 7, 1949, Marianne cabled that she'd be arriving at Northolt Airport that evening at 5:20.

When she arrived in England, though, she was pulled aside at customs and taken into an office to be interrogated. Why was it that she was going to work for this man? What use did a bachelor have for a housekeeper? And what was her relationship to Jan and Annabert Yoors?

Either it didn't occur to Marianne to lie or she didn't know how. Next thing she knew, the immigration officials had confiscated Annabert's letters from her suitcase and had brought in a Dutch speaker to translate them. Marianne sat, humiliated, as the man read them aloud. Then he stopped.

What is this word? the translator asked.

Marianne felt herself blush to the roots of her hair.

Because Jan considered the English and Dutch words for sexual parts too coarse, the three of them used Romani words instead. Annabert had written that Jan, as a creator, had many little stars in his *kar* with which to populate the world. Marianne was forced to explain to the officials in the room that *kar* was a word for penis. And that *mish* meant vagina.

She was denied entry to England and sent back to Holland on the same plane. Later that night, sitting in a compartment on the train from Amsterdam to The Hague, she tore the sheaf of letters to shreds.

21 A Threefold Cord

Marianne became convinced that her father had tipped off the authorities and orchestrated her forced return. His opposition, though, only strengthened her commitment to Jan and Annabert, and her resolve to get back to her life with them. She left the house late one night, after her parents had gone to bed, and started walking. It was only when she reached the beach at Scheveningen that she realized she had been walking due east, heading in the direction of Jan and Annabert as if she were a homing pigeon. Looking out at the black water, she imagined the two of them waiting for her on the other side of the Channel, in London. This water was all that stood between them—nothing and everything—and if she really were a pigeon she could lift her wings and cross it. She was miserable, but in the darkly romantic way of a twenty-two-year-old girl. When she had cried herself out, she got up and walked the several miles back to her parents' house, seeing no one either coming or going. When she arrived, the house was lit up brightly. Lidi answered the door. Marianne's father stood behind Lidi in the living room. They had been frantic with worry. Marianne didn't care. Jan and Annabert were all that mattered to her now.

She drained her bank account to help them with the expense of mounting their upcoming exhibition and to buy them extravagant gifts. On an impulse, she purchased several large cans of butter on the black market and mailed them to England. She also insisted that Lidi take her to the most luxurious men's store in The Hague to buy Jan a sweater. What with postwar privations, the store's shelves were nearly bare and there was only one sweater, red. Marianne bought it, along with a pair of shoes, yellow socks, a shaving brush, and eau de cologne.

Jan and Annabert reciprocated with tokens of their love. On their dead baby's feast day, they made a present to Marianne of the birth announcement that Jan had illustrated and Janneke's baptismal cross. One can imagine how doubly galling it must have been for Henri Citroen, a Holocaust survivor, to see this cross hanging at his daughter's throat. He never discussed or even acknowledged his daughter's relationship with Jan but, through Lidi, Marianne understood how deeply opposed they were. She enlisted the support of the upstairs neighbor, the distinguished elderly widow of a judge. Mrs. Landsberger had a daughter in Paris who was mistress to a married man but, unlike Marianne, was kept in a separate apartment and visited at his convenience. Mrs. Landsberger tried to persuade Lidi and Henri that, all things considered, they should be grateful for Marianne's more open and equitable arrangement. However, it was too much to expect a bourgeois Dutch couple to see bigamy as a legitimate alternative.

Jan and Annabert Yoors in London studio, 1947. Courtesy of the Yoors Family Partnership.

UTOPIA

In a letter to Annabert and Jan, Marianne wrote, *This morning I talked to Lidi and she said, "A man cannot have two wives. Never shall a wife accept another wife." I did not say anything. What would she say if I let her read Annabert's letters. They will never understand if I say I knock against the wall of convention.* Showing Lidi Annabert's letters was out of the question. Once bitten, Marianne was careful as long as she remained under her father's roof to burn her letters after she had read them. On one occasion, though, Jan broke pattern and wrote to Marianne directly, and this letter was too precious to destroy.

May 6, 1949

My dearest sweet Marianneke,

Don't think it too difficult to be away because then you get constantly dear, sweet names. The days here are full and very busy—full of tension, full of hope, full of strength, and full of work. Also full of longing for a letter from Marianne! . . .

Yesterday I made a portrait of Mrs. Allan, the wife of Elkan Allan, our new friends. It really went fine. Tomorrow I have to finish it. At about nine o'clock, Elkan and Michael Howard, Secretary General of the Consulate, came. We discussed the exhibition, and everything is coming along wonderfully. Friday they will come again. Everything has to be organized now with the contract. Then I can ask them to help you come over again. With this exhibition it will all help. Then everything will be all right again. They are so incredibly enthusiastic especially Michael Howard, over the Apocalypse, the torso, and the statue "To Go Forward." The chances with those people are great. Maybe they will buy a house here and we will be the owners.

Dear Zoeteke [a Flemish endearment] *soon you will be really here! And then . . . everyday we make plans, big plans, oh such great plans! And do you know that my plans always come out right. It will be a little bit longer than we thought, because in my optimism I always hope for a little more, but it will always come out. Really! Really! Really! So, a little bit more patience, prepare yourself because it will burst. . . . If the exhibition goes through and this is quite sure, we have maybe two months! So*

1) we have to finish weaving the Apocalypse. Annabert finished the border, and then we will put on a new warp.

2) approximately ten large drawings.

3) one large male torso as opposite the female torso.

4) 25–50 small designs, framed, plus charcoal drawings.

5) 10–15 portraits (cast, but that will done by other people).

6) all those plans must be organized, plans from how to exhibit, painting, etc. lighting, where to hang everything, press releases, and messages.

It will really be a hurricane! But oh what a life, so intense, wonderful and rich. Also I would like to sculpt small groups like the "Pieta," "man, wife, and children," etc. in small format.

We will have of course all the money we need and will be able to concentrate totally on our work. No money worries will stand in our way. No upstairs neighbors, downstairs, on the side, only our own studio. No more P-muzen [complaining] *only hard work, intense life without borders and only happiness! . . .*

Oh Marianneke, I'm so bursting full that I can hardly write from impatience! So full, my head, that it hurts—this all has to be constrained for some short while! But when we sign the contract and you are here, oh then! Tell us quickly what you're doing, thinking, feeling, what is going on inside you—if with us you feel hope, longing, if you are building with us in your thoughts, making plans. "Do you live in the future?" How much do you think about that, "for us (3)" (all we do is for "us"—3) how much you dare to long, how you're growing, how pure you're getting, how you prepare yourself, how much you think about little pattotertegs [literally "baby potatoes," a Flemish endearment for children].

Do you still remember how much we belong together?!!! Will you still remember how wonderful and strong it is with the three of us together? Do you still remember how it feels to be crushed in my arms? Can you still remember how intense and strong love is and how much greater and stronger it will be when you become my bride, wife and mother!!!

If you can answer with a jubilant, thundering, courageous "Yes," come then to my arms and sleep satisfied, peaceful, and pure, to make yourself strong for a new morning and all the mornings that are coming to us. With all, all good wishes, thoughts, and longing from Annabert, and with all my intense thoughts and fervent longing, my dear little wife, from me!

Me

(your husband!)

Marianne replied with affectionate indignation. *Oh silly ones, what are you thinking? Shall Marianne blow out the holy flame? First was the flame so small but now it burns strong and clear. Everybody sees it. Many try to extinguish it, but the angels are protecting the flame with their powerful wings. I was never so convinced and conscious of my task. Do you think that anyone can stop me now? Not a hundred! Because I'm not alone. We are three and together we are one. Who can fight against a threefold cord?*

In their letters, they began to reconfigure Marianne's formerly undefined role to that of a second wife, and they recast their relationship in biblical terms. The reference to a threefold cord came from the book of Ecclesiastes: *Two are better than one; because they have a good reward for their labour. For if they fall, the one will lift up his fellow: but woe to him that is alone when he falleth; for he hath not another to help him up. Again, if two lie together, then they have heat: but how can one be warm alone? And if one prevails against him, two shall withstand him; and a threefold cord is not quickly broken.* The passage is more commonly cited in support of traditional marriage, but they caught hold of that last line and claimed it for their purposes. Marianne was also cast as Hagar, the handmaiden whom Sarah gave to her husband Abraham. Less flatteringly, she was at other times Mary Magdalene to Annabert's Virgin Mary. Jan, they compared variously to Peter, John the Baptist, and Jesus.

WHEN THE GESTAPO sentenced him to death, Jan had sworn that if he got a second chance he would do only the things he cared for. He did not, as it turned out, care for being a student any more now than he had as a child, and he stopped attending classes entirely in favor of his art, this in spite of the fact that his immigration status depended on his remaining in school. In the beginning of 1949, the university had sent him a friendly note offering an appointment to discuss his trouble with the Home Office. Through charm or evasion, he somehow managed to forestall the inevitable for several more months until after his show opened, but eventually his visa was revoked. He and Annabert were forced to leave England.

Annabert went back to the Yoors' family home in Antwerp. Jan continued directly on to The Hague to collect Marianne, and arrived unannounced at the Citroens in the late morning. Marianne was beside herself with joy. Slipping away into the next room, Lidi put in a call to her husband at the office. Forewarned, Henri declined to come home for lunch that day as was his habit. Instead, Lidi, Marianne, and Jan ate in the dining room and afterwards Lidi and Jan talked downstairs while Marianne packed a suitcase. It was all very polite, very civil. Then they were gone.

Henri Citroen made one last desperate attempt to retrieve his daughter. He wrote Marianne a letter promising that if she would come home, he would not persecute Jan. She thought, well, she could at least go home and talk with them, and she booked a ticket. She arrived at the house, entered the living room, and all of a sudden there were two plainclothes detectives behind her.

They arrested her and held her overnight in jail, but as there was nothing they could charge her with, she was released. From the jail, she went to her brother Phillip's house, called Jan, and asked him what she should do.

Take a train and come back, he said.

As it turns out, he, too, had been arrested and brought before a Belgian magistrate. Annabert had testified on his behalf, saying that she approved of his relationship with Marianne.

I wish more women were like you, the judge had answered. I would have less trouble.

Though her status wasn't recognized by the outside world, Marianne came back to Jan as a full-fledged wife. With this came the privilege of his staying in her bed through the night. As Sarah had with Hagar, it was Annabert who voiced this new arrangement. Jan would sleep one night with Marianne and the next with her. The three would share everything equally. For a visible sign, Eugeen Yoors provided Marianne with his own mother's wedding ring.

In practice, though, the three were back under Jan's parents' roof and surrounded by the strict bourgeois mores of Catholic Antwerp. There was no way for them to remain in Belgium, which was too cramped, with too many nosy neighbors and too many painful memories. They needed a new plan, a place where they might live the life they envisioned. When Betsie Hollants wrote Jan from San Francisco where she was posted as a reporter, he took to heart her suggestion that he come over to America. Betsie had an apartment in New York where he was welcome to stay, and she helped arrange for him to get a press card with the Catholic Belgian Press Agency so that he could travel as a journalist. On the strength of this, he left Annabert and Marianne with his father in the house in Antwerp and set sail for America.

22 The New World

After a long, boring trip between knowing and not knowing . . . the arrival was magnificent. We sailed from three
o'clock up the Hudson till six o'clock we were at the pier,
but in the light mist slowly grew the silhouette of Manhattan on one side and the Statue of Liberty on the other side.
Manhattan, an enormous group of buildings reaching up
to the heavens in the most strange forms and colors, in the
shape of pagodas and cupolas and then small houses and
then again very high, so high that you are afraid they will
fall over, in white, red, gray, and tan colors. Miniature,
small brownstones and still giant when you see those tiny
little yellow taxis going back and forth between the red and
green lights, advertising flickering before your eyes and
over you. Anyway, we still saw this all from a distance but
it made an enormous impression.

—ANNABERT YOORS

Jan went to New York in April 1950, thinking it would be a six-week
visit. A year later, on his twenty-ninth birthday, Annabert and Marianne
joined him. Jan and a friend met them at the pier and, after they'd cleared
customs, drove them to the sparsely furnished two-room apartment in
Greenwich Village that Jan had taken over from Betsie. At the door was
a shopping bag full of mismatched china, a housewarming present from
a young artist's model named Phyl whom Jan had been sketching.

The two young women, dazed and happy, freshened up before going
out to dinner and then took a whirlwind tour of the city: to Rockefeller
Center, with its skyscrapers lit up and its plaza displaying the flags of

all nations, with its golden statue of Atlas holding up the world; then on through Central Park, which Annabert pronounced the most beautiful park she'd ever seen; and over the George Washington Bridge, twinkling in the darkness like an arc of stars spanning the Hudson. For Annabert, the only damper on this fairy-tale evening was that Jan chose to finish it with Marianne in his bed. She hid her hurt and waited her turn.

In the first few weeks, Jan took them sightseeing all over the city, from Harlem to Coney Island. Annabert wrote to friends back in Antwerp about the strange charms of New York. *In the city you see everywhere the White Castle, a small cafeteria built in the shape of a castle's white tower.* In Chinatown, Annabert reported, *you can buy dried octopus and all different kinds of strange animals, black and transparent seaweed and fishes and all delicious things for the Chinese.* They walked over to the Lower East Side where on market days, vendors spread their wares on the stoops: Spanish olives, avocados, large loaves of black bread, paprika, red pimentos, enormous watermelons, and vegetables they'd never seen before. *For ten cents you can buy an Italian pizza—that is a pancake with tomatoes and anchovies.* As it happened, they had only a nickel, so they bought a knish instead and shared it between the three of them.

Even the sticky summer heat was a delightful novelty, *a happy warmth* Annabert termed it, that occasioned the natives to don clothing made of a special summer fabric called seersucker, and to open the fire hydrants and make rainbow fountains in the streets. Every apartment there had a refrigerator, as well as an unfamiliar device for which Annabert could find no Flemish translation: the electric fan. *Special air coolers*, she called them, *an instrument that you can put in front of the window and that cools the air when it comes into the room. And those ventilators are in all the shops and offices and in the trains and subways, and if you leave it on for a couple of hours it will cool off the air.*

One day, returning from a ride on the Staten Island Ferry and passing through the turnstiles, they were approached by a group of Gypsies who knew Jan. Because Marianne and Annabert were with him, Jan talked for only a few minutes. He didn't introduce them; nevertheless, within twenty-four hours the word had gone out in the Gypsy community: Putzi had been seen with two bareheaded girls who wore their hair in pigtails. In Gypsy culture this sent a mixed message, for when a girl married she showed her new standing as a woman by braiding her hair and covering her head with a scarf. The phone in the Yoors' apartment began to ring with calls from Gypsies who were making roundabout inquiries concerning the marital status of these girls. Were they available? Somehow Jan deflected their curiosity, but after that, though he continued to visit the Rom with some regularity, he generally went by himself.

The Gypsies weren't the only ones who took notice. In addition to their long braids, Annabert and Marianne observed the Gypsy codes of modesty, covering their legs in long skirts and dark stockings. Even in Greenwich Village, home to bohemians and misfits of every stripe, it was a look that set them apart from others. Neighbors assumed that the two young women must be Amish or Mennonite sisters. When Jan needed to, he encouraged this misperception, introducing Annabert as his wife and Marianne as his sister-in-law. But explanations were rarely required. After all, this was the Village, where people were free to dress however they wished, to be whoever they chose, and to sleep with whomever they pleased, no questions asked. As John Reed had put it, in his 1912 poem "The Day in Bohemia":

> There's pleasure or near it for young men of spirit,
> At Forty-Two Washington Square!
>
> But nobody questions your morals,
> And nobody asks for the rent—
> There's no one to pry if we're tight, you and I,
> Or demand how our evenings are spent.

One of the charms that had lured the first bohemians to Greenwich Village was the cheap lodgings. But it wasn't quite true that nobody asked for the rent, at least not in 1951. On a Saturday morning a few weeks after Marianne and Annabert arrived, the landlord appeared at the door and angrily demanded several months' of back payment. Jan went off with the man and was gone for a couple of anxious hours. When he returned, he told the two women that the landlord had agreed to forgive the debt. Still, they would have to move.

They lived briefly in a tiny, squalid tenement and then illegally sublet another artist's studio, sneaking in and out for a few months, before they found a place to call home. 96 Fifth Avenue was a commercial building filled with other artists, all of them living there unlawfully and sharing a single communal bathroom. In their fifth-floor loft, Jan built a high platform on top of which they hid a mattress out of view. The platform concealed a bathtub underneath. The elevator stopped running at seven, and on Friday nights the building's furnace was shut off for the weekend, so that in winter the skylight would sometimes ice over, a cold wind would blow through the studio, and they'd work wrapped in blankets, freezing, freezing, freezing until Monday morning came. But the ceilings were high and the space huge, with more than enough room for the large-scale tapestries Jan envisioned. And the light in the loft was beautiful. At sunset, they could look out over the tar roofs, chimneys, and water towers of Greenwich Village and see the old buildings painted gold by the last light.

In the "Help Wanted" section of the *Villager*, Annabert and Marianne found babysitting and housekeeping jobs. Annabert went to work for a nice Italian couple and Marianne babysat for the children of the writer James Agee and his wife, Mia. At thirty-five and forty cents an hour, the two women were able to bring home about $125 a month. After paying the rent, they had roughly $35 left for the electric and phone bills, groceries, art supplies, and anything else that might be needed.

Annabert was terribly underweight, still suffering the ill effects of wartime starvation. They could hardly afford a doctor, but by a remarkable coincidence a woman whom Jan's mother had helped save from the Nazis lived just across the street. She was a doctor, an Austrian Jew who'd stayed with her family in the Yoors' Antwerp house for an entire year before finally getting papers to emigrate to America. Annabert was a bit frightened of her—perhaps it was her stern manner and Germanic accent—but the doctor was willing to treat Annabert for free. She prescribed a pint of cream a day to help Annabert put on weight. Even cream represented a formidable expense for the Yoors—other than Annabert's cream, their diet consisted mostly of bread, salad, and potatoes fried on a little hot plate—but they managed. Sometimes they'd walk over to a little fruit and vegetable stall run by Italians on the corner of Greenwich Avenue and Sixth. At the end of the day, Ma and Pop Balducci put out the fruit that was about to spoil, and Annabert and Marianne could buy a basket for a nickel. Phyllis Stevens, or Phyl, the model whom Jan had befriended, sometimes invited them to her cold water flat for meals and gave them five dollars here and there from her own earnings. When Jan sold a drawing, they ate a little better; when he didn't, they ate more potatoes.

And when Jan started experiencing his own troubling symptoms—unquenchable thirsts and a constant need to urinate—he found another doctor. He met the man at a cocktail party, they struck up a friendship, and for nearly twenty years after that the doctor treated Jan free of charge. What seemed like a bargain at the time would eventually have dire consequences, but that was many years off in the future.

One evening during the holidays, the elevator man came to the door to wish them a merry Christmas. Francesco had often snuck them up on the elevator after hours, and they loved listening to him sing his Spanish songs while he mopped the hall. They were sorry, Jan apologized, but they couldn't give him a tip. They had no money. An hour later, Francesco knocked again at the door. He was carrying trays of appetizers left over from a Christmas party in the building, so that the four of them might have their own party.

In true Gypsy fashion, poverty didn't prevent them from entertaining and throwing big parties. One night a group of the Rom came to the studio, and one of them, Mishka, played the guitar and sang while the others danced. The next morning, there was a full bottle of scotch that hadn't been opened at the party. Marianne and Phyl went out and tried to sell it. That's how broke they were. They went round to the liquor stores, but of course the stores couldn't buy it. Finally they found a willing customer on the street.

Another time, they made soup from garbage scraps. They had nothing to eat, but the night before they had had potatoes, so Marianne began to go through the garbage and pick out the peels. Annabert scrubbed them clean and threw them in the pot.

Oh look, Marianne said, and held up the end of an onion. It's our lucky day.

The two began to giggle. When Jan came into the kitchen, wanting to know what was so funny, they were breathless with laughter.

This was what the Rom understood, that having nothing was a gift, the only freedom anyone ever had. As Jan explained, "The moment you can't up and leave the moment you want to—because you have engage-ments, you have a house, plants to water, you have cats to feed, you have dogs to walk—you are a slave to your possessions. Possessions should be there to please you. So the less you have, the freer you are."

23 Faux Boho

The Village's reputation as the Left Bank of America first found expression in the years leading up to World War I. Writers, intellectuals, and freethinkers—among them Djuna Barnes, Eugene O'Neill, Theodore Dreiser, Edna St. Vincent Millay, Upton Sinclair, Emma Goldman, and Margaret Sanger—flocked to the Village, first because it was affordable and then because everything new, radical, and racy seemed to be emanating from there. When the Yoors arrived in 1950 and '51, they were part of the second wave. Alongside the refugees from Europe, artists and square pegs were fleeing the stifling conformity of their hometowns in Indiana or Connecticut or Oregon. As the writer Dan Wakefield recalled, "Our generation in the fifties needed the Village and all it stood for as much as the artists, writers, and rebels of preceding generations—maybe even more."

Following two decades of Depression and world war, America had turned resolutely middle class and amnesiac. Rosie the Riveter had been sent home from the factories and retooled as a cheerful suburban housewife vacuuming in high heels and pearls. In 1950, Disney's *Cinderella* was Hollywood's top-grossing movie, and John Wayne its number one star. Anxieties about the Korean War and the Cold War with the Soviet Union, pushed underground, bubbled back up as a toxic, formless fear of the Other. The most visible face in politics during those years, Senator Joe McCarthy, made his name by conducting a national witch hunt for communists, and the charge of "un-American" was being leveled like a gun at anyone or anything perceived to be different. In the fifties, if you were, as writer John Cheever put it, "a man with a beard, a garlic breath, and a book," the Village was the only place where you were welcome. It was a one-and-a-half square mile protectorate for those who didn't conform to the enforced normalcy of Eisenhower America.

This new generation of Villagers appropriated the identifying marks and behaviors of their forebears. They dressed the part of bohemians in berets, turtlenecks, and sandals. They put their mattresses on the floor and ate cheap spaghetti dinners in restaurants with drippy candles stuck in empty Chianti bottles. They hung out in bars until the wee hours. Poverty was a badge of honor, and sexual license a form of social protest. But something was lost in the translation. "What I couldn't see back in the fifties," Wakefield mused, "but now seems clear is that a major shift had taken place in the order of the world since World War II, and that out of it a new kind of shattered experience had been born—a rootless, drug-stoked, existential, kaleidoscopic assault on the soul by modern technology and its weapons." Unlike the original bohemians, who had earnestly championed trade unions, family planning, and socialism, this generation no longer hoped to change the fallen world. Instead, they channeled their alienation into art for art's sake. Perhaps the most famous symbol of their alienation was Holden Caulfield, the disaffected protagonist of *The Catcher in the Rye* who saw the world as a bunch of phonies. Equally telling was J. D. Salinger's dismay at his novel's huge popularity. After all, how great could it be if the general public appreciated it?

Salinger's attitude toward fame and the Establishment was echoed by the visual artists and musicians in the Village. The artists now commonly referred to as Abstract Expressionists or the New York School—the painters Jackson Pollock, Willem de Kooning, Franz Kline, Mark Rothko, and others—were too individual, too anarchic to be a school in any traditional sense of the word, but what they did hold in common, in addition to a rejection of representation, was utter disdain for bourgeois tastes. If they didn't agree on what Abstract Expressionism *was*, one of Robert Motherwell's many philosophic declarations cataloged what it *wasn't*: "I allow no nostalgia, no sentimentalism, no propaganda, no selling out to the vulgar, no autobiography, no violation of the nature of the canvas as a flat surface, no clichés, no illusionism, no description, no seduction, no charm, no relaxation, no mere taste, no obviousness, no coldness."

Jan, who had never fully belonged to any group, didn't embrace Abstract Expressionism either. Though his tapestries would later migrate to the abstract, in the fifties his art was both representational and autobiographical, drawing on themes of the war and the Gypsies. His personal manner, too, was more formal and European than his fellow Village artists. Whereas Jackson Pollock wore jeans on all occasions and was a famously belligerent drunk, Jan dressed like a banker, had an abhorrence of drunkenness, and charmed whomever he met, men and women alike, with his elegant manners and Continental accent. Still, the Yoors exemplified the zeitgeist of the Village. Given that Jan had inherited his bohemian bona fides from his birth family on the one side and had acquired them on the other side from his Roma family, one might even be tempted to claim that he was the most authentic of the lot, the last of the true bohemians. However, the very notion of authenticity is slippery when the first Villagers were themselves creatures of self-invention.

Shortly after the Yoors moved to 96 Fifth Avenue, a socialite acquaintance insisted on introducing Jan to a fellow Gypsy, the Village legend Romany Marie. Between 1914 and 1949, Romany Marie had owned a succession of cafés in the Village where she hosted a veritable who's who of painters, musicians, poets, and writers. She had generously encouraged those who were up and coming or down on their luck, showing their work on the walls of her restaurant, feeding them even when they couldn't afford to pay, and rolling out mattresses after closing time for anyone who needed a place to sleep. Purportedly, she kept the playwright Eugene O'Neill alive during 1916 and '17 when he was in the depths of alcoholism and fed the architect Buckminster Fuller throughout the Depression. Harry Kemp, the so-called "Tramp Poet," was ensconced for years at the Poets' Table in the back of her café and would happily declaim for tourists who came to get a glimpse of "real" bohemia.

The elderly Romany Marie—dressed flamboyantly in full skirts, colorful peasant blouses, bright lipstick, and bangles—looked like every illustration of the archetypal Gypsy woman. In actuality, she was born Marie Marchand, a Jew from Moldavia who had assumed the persona of a Gypsy when she arrived in America.

Amusingly, when these two pseudo-Gypsies met, Romany Marie greeted Jan in her native Romanian and Jan answered her in Romani, the language of Gypsies and not remotely similar to Romanian. Marie finessed the potentially awkward moment by reaching out to him like a long-lost friend and declaring, "Yes, he is a Gypsy!" They all became great friends, and in an ironic twist a journalist later established Jan's Gypsy credentials by citing this friendship.

A few years later, when Marie was down on her luck and needed help with the rent in order to stay in her apartment, Jan, Jackson Pollock, the journalist Alma Reed, and a few others tried to organize a benefit to be held on her behalf at the restaurant Toots Shor. In spite of all Marie had done to help others, they were only able to raise about $60 in start-up money, and the plan never got off the ground. Instead, Marie had to move. Jan walked the streets and helped her find a new place to live.

In May 1951, Jan gave a lecture at the Village Art Center: "My Life with the Gypsies & Their Influence on My Art." Afterwards, the audience was cordially invited to visit the studio. Perhaps it was this event that caught the attention of the *New Yorker* magazine. A few months later, a staff writer set up an interview for a possible "Talk of the Town" story about the tapestries. This was a perfect chance for Jan to get his work in the public eye. The two sat in the dark and woody elegance of the Yale Club's Tap Room and began to talk.

Tell me about yourself, the reporter asked. How did you come to do tapestries?

Jan was a marvelous storyteller, and out came tales about the war, his life with Pulika and the Lowara tribe, and the inside scoop on the habits and attitudes of the Gypsies. If he remembered to mention their influence on his art, it wasn't evident in the article that later went into print. That Jan Yoors happened to design tapestries was mentioned only in passing.

Jan liked to quote an old Rom saying—*yekka buliasa nashti beshes pe done grastende*—with one rear end, you cannot sit on two horses. Yet that was exactly what he was trying to do: be both an artist and a Gypsy. He'd made the choice to come back to the Gaje world and follow in his father's footsteps as an artist, and yet when he was given the chance to promote himself as such, he preferred to talk about the Gypsies. Perhaps his connection to them was how Jan thought to set himself apart in an overcrowded field of aspiring talents; certainly, it was an irresistible angle for journalists. The *New York Times* headline for a showing of his work in 1956 was fairly typical of those that would follow him for the rest of his career: "Tapestries Made by Gypsy Prince."

He was ambitious, unquestionably, but opportunism is too cynical an explanation. For Jan, the gravitational pull back toward that life was a potent blend of nostalgia, grief, and survivor's guilt. As Annabert wrote many years later, "in our young hands and minds was the hope of all those who died, an inheritance so immense we could only do very little, but we did and we are doing our best."

There was also in Jan the inherent duality which had first found expression in his double life with the Rom and later as an undercover operative. He really was a wild goose, belonging neither here nor there, never fitting in.

24 Rubie

The first break came to them in 1951 through Jan's best friend in America, the man who'd squired Marianne and Annabert around town on their first night in America. Jean-Claude Landau worked as an engineer for the Atlantic Chemical Corporation in New Jersey, a company that specialized in the formulation of synthetic dyes. One evening he took Jan to meet his boss, Rubin Rabinowitz. Sixty years later, Mr. Rabinowitz remembered the introduction well.

One day he called up and said, "Rubie, I'd like to come over with a friend who was very helpful to my uncle"—I think his uncle Herman—"from concentration camp days."

So he came with Jan, and we sat around the living room there. We were going to have dinner. We had drinks. And I said, "Jan, what do you do?"

"I'm an artist."

"And what kind of art do you do?"

"I do painting. I do sculpture. What I'd really like to do one day is a tapestry." Who thought up tapestries, you know? It was an unusual thing. And I said, "You know, Jan, if you look at our dining room here"—which had a beautiful cover of Italian burl walnut—"there's a whole fifteen-foot wall above the buffet that's totally empty." But it was beautiful to look at because it had the gnarled wood. It was gorgeous.

And I said, "I would like to have a tapestry." And my wife, Phyllis, looked at it and said, "Yeah, that would be a good idea."

So he said, "Well, let me do a cartoon."

I didn't know what a cartoon was. I thought it was going to be about this big. Lo and behold, he comes back with brown wrapping paper that covers the entire wall. And there was a magnificent drawing—I think he probably used acrylic paints—of a fisherman with nets and everything else.

This was the chance for Jan to execute something on the scale of his dreams. Ever since he saw the *Apocalypse* at the London tapestry show, he'd wanted to make a tapestry that would overpower the viewer with its size. Because this tapestry would be narrow and long—six by fifteen feet—he designed a river scene, a line of bare-chested native fishermen pulling in nets full of fishes. It was reminiscent of Gauguin, a primitive cacophony of reds, violet, and warm browns.

The drawing was a gorgeous thing, Rubie admits, and he can't recall what exactly they objected to, maybe that it was *too* powerful, too busy. After a couple of months, he finally took Jan to lunch and broke the news that he didn't want this design. Rabinowitz asked him to design something else for him. Jan said he couldn't.

I never saw a man as sad as that in my life. Rubie shakes his head.

And here is where the versions of the story part briefly, depending on who is doing the telling. In Annabert and Marianne's version, Jan was furious—*this* was the design he had created and that he wanted to execute—but they were hard up for money. Rubie says that Jan returned some time later with a second design; Marianne says that he only relented when Rubie came back and asked him again.

The new design he called *The River Crossing*. Perhaps it was an inside joke or a bit of residual stubbornness, because without the title a viewer might not notice at first the blue border that undulates along the bottom. Again, he used a palette of brilliant colors and another bare-chested native, this time a warrior astride a black stallion. The warrior clutched a screaming scarlet rooster by the foot. In his wake followed another horse carrying a beautiful woman playing a lute. Behind her trailed orchids like colorful starbursts and the suggestion of yet more horses.

The design was headily romantic and perfectly suited to a client whose business was creating color. The Rabinowitzes immediately fell in love with it.

So I said, "Jan, let's go."

"Well," he said, "there's a problem."

I said, "What's the problem?"

"We have no loom. Tapestries were never woven in America, so there is no loom."

So I said, "Well, we'll build one for you. Just tell me what you need."

And he told me the size lumber he needed, which would hold a ten-story building. It's about eight inch squared wood. I said fine. Their studio was on Thirteenth and Fifth Avenue. Jean-Claude, my brother, and Jan, and whoever else, I have no idea, schlepped all those wooden things up to the—what floor, fifth floor?—and they built the frame. They drilled, they put this thing together. The thing had to maintain enormous tension. So the loom is built.

And then Jan said, "But Rubie, I need thread. I have to have linen thread."

Well, it happened that somebody living near me in Clifton was the linen thread company. I said, "Just tell me the kind of linen thread you need, we'll get it." We got the linen thread for him. So now he was able to make a warp.

He said, "Now we have another problem."

"What is that problem?"

He said, "The problem is simply that the only wool I would like to use is Iranian wool. That's carpet yarn, and the carpet yarns are all in very, very dull colors. Madder red and dark colors.

I said, "Jan, no problem. We'll get the wool, and we'll dye every color you want."

And every one of these colors and every piece of yarn was dyed in the laboratories of my company. And at times Annabert came down and Jan came down and Marianne came down and did the dying in the laboratories. They moved the dye around and we selected the dyes. The black is Palatine Black. The scarlet is Brilliant Scarlet 3R. These are colors that are very brilliant and are not used in carpets, but this is what Jan wanted. This is the way he drew the cartoon, and this is what we were going to give him. And when Jan didn't

The River Crossing, *tapestry, wool and cotton, 6 × 15 feet, 1952, Jan Yoors.
Courtesy of Jonathan D. Rabinowitz and Joshua W. Rabinowitz.*

like the shade, we dyed it again. And when he didn't like that, we dyed it again. He was fussy. . . . So we finally had it all complete, and Annabert and Marianne went to work on it.

The weaving of the tapestry took six months. The women would come home from their respective jobs and prepare dinner. Afterwards, the three of them would weave, accompanied by classical music on the radio, until eleven or midnight. They were up again at seven the next morning, but for all the hardships and long hours, this is what they had longed for: to be independent and free to make their art.

The only missing piece was children. Ever since Marianne and Annabert were young girls playing together with their dolls, they had dreamed of having babies. However, after the devastating loss of little Janneke, a death they attributed to postwar destitution, Jan was determined not to bring another child into the world until they could afford to adequately care for it. Their circumstances were still precarious, but they would work very hard, weaving like patient little spiders, and someday Jan's genius would be recognized, they felt sure. Every stitch put them closer to that dream.

25 A Lesson in Weaving

The teamwork demanded by the making of tapestries as
we practice it is one of the purest forms of romance and
personal fulfillment.

—JAN YOORS

When the Yoors built their first loom, theirs became the only tapestry
studio of its kind in America. No one else was doing this. Their pre-
decessor, Herter Looms, had closed its doors in 1934, but it had been
a commercial producer of luxury textiles, an offshoot of the famous
Herter Brothers who furnished and decorated the turn-of-the-century
mansions of industrial tycoons. Herter tapestries typically favored the
Gothic Revival; even when the subject matter was purportedly American, they mimicked tapestries several centuries older.

The Yoors wove their tapestries using older methods, but Jan's
designs were unmistakably modern. They exploded traditional notions
of framing by bleeding off the edges, calling to mind the cropped imag-
ery in photographs. In contrast to the painstaking detail and delicate
shadings prevalent in tapestry design since the seventeenth century, Jan
employed large color fields and used a limited palette of bright jewel
tones that reverberated against each other. As Nobuko Kajitani, former textile conservator at the Metropolitan Museum of Art, once said,
"[Jan] is the only person who can use two contrasting colors to make an
area three-dimensional. That's his magic." Often he also mimicked his
father's stained glass by separating those colors with a heavy black line
echoing the demarcation of lead and further intensifying the colors. The
bold effect showed the influence not only of his father but also of Matisse
and Rouault, his father's contemporaries.

The designs were then woven with heavy-gauge wool and fewer knots per inch, lending them visible texture and heft. The renowned *New York Times* art critic Robert Hughes said of Jan's work, "There's this sense that the thing is conceived entirely in terms of its medium. He is an absolute master of weaving; he designs in terms of the weave and the knot. And this gives his work—despite its simplicity and its extreme straightness and boldness of design—a really sumptuous quality, which you don't get very much in twentieth-century tapestry."

Hughes' praise gets at an important truth about the organic nature of the Yoors' tapestries. The European tradition of tapestry weaving, based on a master-apprentice system, isolated designers from weavers. Often tapestries were simply copied from paintings, but even when an artist created a cartoon, the preparatory drawing for a tapestry, he would then send it off to a workshop to be enlarged and translated by artisans into wool or silk. If it was a successful design, these cartoons might be used repeatedly for years, with duplicate tapestries coming off the line like Model Ts.

By contrast, Jan not only designed the tapestry but also was closely involved in every step of its creation. Though he wasn't temperamentally suited to the repetitive nature of weaving and eventually left this mostly to Annabert and Marianne, he knew the craft as well as they did. All three were self-taught and had arrived at their mastery together. For their part, the two women were much more than mere technicians. Jan discussed his designs with them and asked their opinions, and though they didn't make the ultimate decisions about color and line—Jan's full-scale color cartoons were affixed to the loom directly behind the warp threads—the sumptuous quality that Hughes described is the visible expression of their intimacy and shared vision.

When the weaving was completed, the Yoors usually destroyed the cartoon, guaranteeing that each tapestry was a unique work of art rather than one of an edition.

Amidst the deprivations and scarcities of postwar England, the Yoors had woven their first tapestries of whatever materials they could lay their hands on: ordinary knitting wool and cotton threads that were sometimes not even colorfast. They later destroyed most of these tapestries because they deemed their early workmanship too crude and the materials inferior. In America, though, Jan could be exacting, and he was. It was his good fortune to have as his first client the owner of a synthetic dye company, someone who could appreciate and indulge Jan's obsession to match wools to the colors in his head.

Later, Jan befriended Harry and Karnig Paternaya. The two brothers had fled Turkey in 1915, sole survivors in their village of the Armenian genocide, walking first to Palestine and later making their way to New York. Using their knowledge of the rug trade, they started a business importing and dying the finest-quality Persian yarns. To this day, Paternayan yarns are coveted worldwide for their superior durability and luster. Not surprisingly, the Paternaya brothers found a common bond with the charismatic young hero of the Resistance, and they became yet another link in the network of immigrants and survivors who supported Jan. When money was tight, they extended Jan credit, often carrying the debt for years at a time and thus enabling the Yoors to keep working. (Many were enlisted to help in the Yoors' cause. Later, when Jan took up photography, he found a former Hungarian freedom fighter, the

Marianne and Annabert in 96 Fifth Avenue studio. Courtesy of the Yoors Family Partnership.

A Lesson in Weaving

owner of Motal Custom Darkroom, who developed and printed his photographs on credit.)

Jan would bring in a bit of fabric to the Paternayas, a yellow silk scarf, let's say, and while one of the brothers dyed yarn to match it, Jan and the other brother would talk politics. When the dying was done, Jan would check the color. He knew exactly what he wanted. It had to match a particular yellow he had seen in his prison window, and he wasn't satisfied until it did. Eventually, the brothers had created a whole palette of Jan's colors customized for his use alone.

ACCORDING TO MARIANNE, there is nothing especially difficult about weaving.

"Do you know how to darn a hole in a sock?" she asks. "You stretch like that and then you go up and down, like basket weaving. And then you beat it down, so that you don't see the white side. So the technique is very easy, but you have to learn the tension because if you put the thread in too tight, it shrinks; if you do it too loose, it starts to bubble, and you have to see that the lines are straight."

However, if the necessary basic skills can be acquired fairly quickly, the practice requires extraordinary patience. When Penelope, the faithful wife of Odysseus, wished to stall her overeager suitors, she told them that before she could remarry she needed first to weave a burial shroud for her dead husband. Each night, she would undo part of what she'd woven during the day. It's a measure of just how glacial the process of weaving is that she could maintain this charade for twenty years.

The loom Penelope used was probably not much different in design from the one the Yoors constructed: a vertical, or high-warp, loom. There are two types of tapestry loom, the vertical and the horizontal (low-warp), with the vertical being the older of the two. This was the style most often used to weave the great medieval tapestries. However, by the time the Yoors built their eight-by-eighteen-foot loom, it was likely the only one of its size apart from the famous Gobelin looms in Paris. The two styles of loom produce the same stitch, but the horizontal loom displaced the vertical for this simple reason: on the horizontal loom, the weaver moves the treadle with her feet, so it's faster. Speed comes at a price, though. The weaver faces the backside of the tapestry and can only see the front by looking down through the warp threads at a small mirror that reflects a reverse image. This and the increased speed are thought to increase the likelihood of errors, and for this reason, the high-warp tapestry is considered the gold standard.

It generally took the two women a full eight-hour day to weave a square foot. The fact that the tapestry designs were simple didn't necessarily make the work go faster. As Marianne likes to say, "Simplicity in life is much more difficult." With busier designs a mistake isn't so visible, but in the Yoors' tapestries every stitch shows. "After the tapestry is unrolled six months later, you cannot say, 'Oh, oops, that line is not straight,' and then you cannot take it out. You have to be absolutely concentrated on what you are doing. You cannot have your mind wandering away."

Their first commission, *The River Crossing*, was 90 square feet, which translates to something in the neighborhood of 720 hours of weaving, not including the many hours needed to prepare the loom—first measuring, cutting, and stretching warp threads onto the rollers; then making the string heddles and attaching these to the warp threads; and winding the yarn onto bobbins.

The process of weaving is repetitive: the colored weft yarn is threaded horizontally between two alternating sets of the vertical cotton warp threads that are separated by a shuttle. Traditionally, weavers use a special comb or beater to pack the weft thread down tightly against the previous row, but Marianne and Annabert used the tip of a screwdriver because that was the only tool they'd had available when they first started. The rows of warp threads are then switched, and the process repeats. Over and over and over again. With the large color fields in Jan's design, they might weave nothing but blue for days before black or orange began to emerge at the edge.

Yet, what might seem tedious to some, they found soothing. They would sit next to each other, weaving, and their backs and arms became strong because they were always sitting. As they worked, they sometimes reminisced about their girlhoods in The Hague. They sang Dutch songs, songs that over time Jan learned, too. Or they'd listen to classical music on the radio. Their Siamese cats lounged in squares of sun, and the rapid beating down of the thread made a soft, thudding percussion, the constant beating heart of the studio.

Months later, when the weaving was completed, they cut the tapestry off the loom. For tapestry makers, this *tombé de métier*, fall from the loom, is a solemn rite recognizing that, like a tree, a tapestry takes a long time to grow but only a brief moment to fell. It was always exciting because while they were weaving, only the section they were working on had been visible, with the rest wound over the roller. Now, for the first time they would see their months of work in its entirety. They spread it out on the floor of the studio and admired it, before sitting down to do the final work of knotting and hemming the edges.

26 The Patrons

Given the amount of time it took to weave a single tapestry and the fact that the women could weave only on nights and weekends, the Yoors struggled to build up a body of work to show. In October 1953, when the Hugo Gallery staged the first solo show of Jan's work in New York, the entire exhibit amounted to six tapestries and a handful of charcoal drawings of torsos. The Yoors had brought four of the tapestries with them from England, including *Knight of Nadara* and *Descent from the Cross*. The fifth tapestry, *The River Crossing*, they borrowed back from Rabinowitz to display in the show. As for the sixth, a piece called *The Sun* commissioned by Jan's friend Leonardo Casanova, it was completed only just in time. Marianne and Annabert wove round the clock for two and a half solid days until, on the afternoon of the opening, they finally cut it off the loom. Jan hurried uptown to hang it before the first guests arrived. Marianne and Annabert would meet him there; they had to stop at a department store on their way uptown to buy two pairs of nylon stockings. Knee socks would not do for an opening at the Hugo.

In the forties, the Hugo Gallery had championed Surrealists, such as Salvador Dali, and the abstract painter Arshile Gorky, and had cemented the international reputation of René Magritte. Only the previous year, in 1952, it had debuted the work of another up-and-coming young artist, Andy Warhol, who'd done a series of drawings inspired by the stories of Truman Capote, with whom Warhol was obsessed. Up till then Warhol had been working as a highly successful commercial artist, but he hadn't been able to cross the divide over to the fine arts. However, possibly because the founders themselves stood outside the ranks of the art world, the Hugo Gallery was willing to take chances. In any case, they could afford to promote what might not sell. Elizabeth Arden, head of a cosmetics empire and one of the wealthiest women in the world, was a backer, as was an Italian prince, Maria dei Principi Ruspoli, and a baron, Robert Rothschild. Rothschild also happened to be a Belgian diplomat and, given that Jan frequently socialized with the French and Belgian diplomatic corps, Rothschild was probably the connection that opened the Hugo's doors to him.

MARIANNE'S DAY JOB was keeping house and taking care of the three children of James and Mia Fritsch Agee. Mia was an editor at *Fortune* magazine, where James Agee had worked as a journalist at the beginning of his career. Agee's masterpiece, *Let Us Now Praise Famous Men*, had been ignored at the time of its publication in 1941, and his literary reputation would come only after his death, but throughout the forties he had wielded considerable power as the film critic for *Time* and then *The Nation*. By the time Marianne came to work at the house on King Street, though, he'd quit these positions and was freelancing out of the house, writing magazine articles and working on screenplays. His alcoholism had caught up with him, and Marianne found him an unkempt and difficult employer. He kept the hours of a drinker, staying out late and often not appearing downstairs until the afternoon. Once, when Mia was out of town and Marianne was looking after the children, he called and asked her if she could stay the night. She declined—she wanted to get home to her own family and their weaving—but six o'clock came and went and still he didn't return. As the night wore on, the children, in a wild mood, tore open pillows and blanketed the house in drifts of feathers. When Agee finally returned in the early hours of the next morning, Marianne demanded to be paid on the spot and refused to clean up the feathers.

She disliked the job and the pay was paltry, but they needed every cent. The Hugo show had been prestigious, but it hadn't resulted in sales or commissions. Instead, they'd continued to weave on spec, going into hock to the Paternaya brothers for hundreds of dollars' worth of yarn. It had taken them an entire year to weave two tapestries. In May 1955 they were about to finish the second one, *The Fishermen*, the design Jan had originally conceived for Rubie Rabinowitz.

On Friday the 13th, Jan spent the evening at the East Hamptons farmhouse of Jackson Pollock and his wife, Lee Krasner. Over dinner and rounds of martinis served in large water glasses, Pollock gave Jan some career advice: when this new tapestry was completed, he should throw a big party to celebrate, do a lot of advertising around it, and invite lots of important people. When Jan returned home at 3:30 the next morning, he woke Annabert to discuss the idea with her.

The following Monday afternoon, Marianne was at work when the Agees' doorbell rang. Agee had left the house just moments earlier to go to a doctor appointment, so Marianne answered the door. The police stood on the other side. Mistaking her for Mrs. Agee, they told her that her husband had died of a heart attack in a taxi. For a confused moment, Marianne thought they were talking about Jan.

James Agee was forty-six years old. Grief-stricken, Mia took her husband's body to be buried on the Agees' family farm upstate and then stayed on there with her children after the funeral.

The week after Agee's death, Annabert finally wove Jan's name and the date, 1955, into the left-hand corner of *The Fishermen*, and they cut it off the loom. Following Pollock's advice, Jan invited architects and interior designers, collectors, gallerists, and curators to a cocktail party at the studio. The Yoors dipped into the rent money to buy alcohol, glassware, and pâté de foie gras. So long as Mia Agee and her children remained in the country, Marianne's wages would go missing from the cookie jar, but they were too excited to fuss about household accounts just now. They would worry about the rent later. Rubie Rabinowitz sent over bottles of whiskey and sherry, and Jan spent the day before the party installing hanging spotlights to show off *The Fishermen* while Marianne and Annabert swept out the studio and fashioned fancy hors d'oeuvres.

On the evening of June 3, 1955, forty-five guests showed up for cocktails. In attendance was Consuelo Cloos, whom the Yoors had nicknamed the White Consuelo to distinguish her from another Consuelo of their acquaintance and because she powdered herself to a deathly pale elegance. Always dramatic, tonight she was dressed in a floor-length gown that emphasized her wraithlike thinness and made her seem to float as she moved about the studio. Cloos was a poet and a much admired Abstract Expressionist painter, one of the few artists beside himself approved by Salvador Dali, who called her work magnificent. Though a Boston gallery had offered her up to $1,200 apiece for her paintings (more than $10,000 in today's dollars), she refused to sell any of her "children."

Pollock and Krasner came, too—after all, the party had been their idea—along with Roloff Beny, a young abstract painter and printmaker whose work had already been widely exhibited and included in shows at the Metropolitan and the Museum of Modern Art. He'd recently taken up photography, at first simply to record images from which to paint, but he would go on to cement a considerable reputation with books of photo essays documenting his travels around the world.

Many others in their circle also came to support Jan and to make it a party. But there were prospects in the crowd, too, and after the last of the guests left, the Yoors, Romany Marie, and Consuelo Cloos adjourned to the restaurant El Charro to eat tamales and review the evening. Rubie and Phyllis Rabinowitz had bought a painting, and an architect and his wife planned to return for a watercolor portrait. Annabert had spent a long time talking to the wife of the director of the Cincinnati Museum, who seemed very enthusiastic about Jan's work. But the coup had been the arrival of a fellow Villager, the so-called den mother of modern art, Dorothy Miller. As the first curator at the Museum of Modern Art, Miller worked alongside its director, Albert Barr, and was one of the most influential people in American modern art. While Barr tended to stay uptown with the white glove set, Miller had spent years hanging out at Romany Marie's café around the corner from her apartment, finding the talent where it lived and bringing it uptown. Through her intercession, the world would come to know the work of Frank Stella, Robert Rauschenberg, Louise Nevelson, and Jasper Johns. Apparently, Miller had been impressed by what she saw that evening, because she invited Jan and Romany Marie to come to her Eighth Street apartment the following week and to bring some work to show her husband, Holger Cahill, who had headed the WPA's National Art Project during the Depression.

The Yoors were giddy with possibilities. So much was riding on the success of the evening.

An artist might spend a few dollars for brushes and paints and then complete a painting in a week. Sketches cost only pennies for charcoal and paper and were a daily exercise for Jan. By contrast, an uncommissioned tapestry represented a high-stakes gamble. It was probably no mystery why the Yoors were among the very few practitioners and were unique in opting to work on such a large scale: weaving monumentally sized tapestries hadn't made any kind of economic sense since the days of feudal princes and peasants. Nowadays, it was hard to come by artisans like Marianne and Annabert, who were willing to work for nothing or next to it. On the other side of the equation, there were precious few patrons left who had both the wherewithal and the independent judgment to shell out large sums for something that couldn't readily be quantified.

The Yoors were also working against public expectations that art might be expensive but crafts should be a bargain, and that textiles should be purchased by the yard. A machine-made tapestry might be had for a few dollars, while the prices listed in the Hugo show topped out at $2,000. To put this sum in perspective, the average annual salary in 1953 was just over $4,000. Given that a large tapestry represented the labor of two artisans for half a year, $2,000 *was* a bargain, but a bargain few could afford.

As Jan saw it, postwar Europe was awash in luxury but without comforts. America, by contrast, had a great deal of comfort but no luxury. Still, he was betting that there were Americans out there who could be persuaded to appreciate—and pay for—grandeur; he just had to find them, and before the rent came due again. Nights, while the women stayed home and wove, Jan went out into the world, making the acquaintance of anyone who might be of help, cultivating important friendships, and following the string of connections. It required the same brash self-confidence he had deployed while working as an undercover operative, and the charm he had used to persuade two women to share a husband and devote themselves wholly to furthering his artistic ambitions.

At the end of the summer, Mia Agee returned to New York and asked Marianne to come back to work. Marianne said no. Annabert was quitting her housekeeping job, too. They'd gotten another commission for a tapestry, and they were making the leap to start weaving full-time.

Unfortunately, the commission came with disquieting concessions. A New York interior designer had hired them to weave a portrait from a photograph. Jan carried memories of his father's bitter struggles with committees and officials over commissions for church windows, and had never before allowed anyone to dictate a design to him. He bridled at even small compromises of his vision. Earlier that summer, in the wake of their cocktail party, an architect and his wife had returned to the studio carrying fabric swatches to see if the watercolor portrait they had liked would go with the couch. Once they determined that it did, they then asked Jan to go back in and paint over a naked breast. He complied— they needed the money for rent—but it put him in a foul mood.

This, though, was worse. The client, and the subject of this tapestry, was to be General Rafael Trujillo, the dictator of the Dominican Repub- lic. Given Jan's hatred of fascists, it's doubtful he was aware of just how racist and brutal a man his subject was, but even if he was completely in the dark, taking this commission still represented a compromise of his utopian ideals. For the Yoors, it was bad enough that they were hired hands, executing what they knew to be bad art.

The photograph they were to work from showed Trujillo in military uniform, astride his horse and perched on an ornate saddle that Marianne and Annabert were compelled to copy in all its embossed and glittery detail. At intervals, unnamed men in overcoats and dark glasses showed up at the studio and stood behind them as they wove, silently observing the unfolding design.

Mr. Yoors, they said, could you make General Trujillo's face just a little bit lighter?

Jan explained that his figures were always woven in this same rich, warm brown, regardless of the skin tone of the model. The men shook their heads adamantly. The General was not dark-skinned.

Jan agreed to redo the face. The women unwove the tapestry back down to the General's upright braided collar and rewove the face, using a lighter shade of wool.

When the men came back, they looked at the tapestry. Generally, they were very pleased, but there was just one problem: the General's skin was still too dark.

Jan smiled congenially and said, Of course. Only his years as an undercover operative allowed him to conceal his displeasure.

I had only a black-and-white photograph to work from, he demurred. Please excuse me for a moment.

He turned and strode to the other end of the studio and returned shortly with a basket. I am only the artist. You know your General better than I. Perhaps it would be best if you chose the color.

He set down the basket, full of yarn samples in various skin tones. The two men chose the lightest shade of yarn in the basket, a color matching

Jan's own pale complexion. Again, the woman pulled out their work and rewove it. The general now looked as bleached as a Swede. The men came back and pronounced it good.

Jan had been treading on the violent prejudices of a man who, in 1937, had "whitened" the Dominican Republic by committing large-scale genocide against the Haitians in his country. Although his own grandmother was Haitian, Rafael Trujillo whitened his skin twice a day in order to disguise his heritage.

In the end, Marianne heard that after the tapestry arrived at the presidential palace in the Dominican Republic, someone had lightened Trujillo's face even further, dabbing white paint directly onto the wool. She also thought she heard that the tapestry was destroyed after Trujillo was assassinated in 1961, but perhaps this last was only wishful thinking.

DEVOTING THEMSELVES FULL-TIME to art, the following year, 1956, the Yoors had two exhibits of tapestries, at a midtown design center called Thaibok Fabrics and then, in February, their first museum show, at the Montclair Art Museum in New Jersey. In a letter to his parents, Jan was exuberant.

Our big exhibition opened on February 15th and we are all very satisfied. The opening was a big success and the reaction from the public was a thousand times better than our greatest hopes . . . The room is immense, very well located and we are showing seven very big tapestries and I really think that we are beginning to pierce through. I am waiting for a visit from Maria Gevaert Salas who will arrive from Miami one of these days and about whom you will sooner or later get the full report. This is probably my first exhibition for which I am <u>completely</u> satisfied. All that we are missing is . . . a sale. We have many offers for other exhibitions here in N.Y. The people that go are all decorators and architect types, very put together. It's really a milieu that could launch us forward. Also we are preparing for our exhibition in Mexico. I am running around a lot, meeting lots of people, all interesting, and have less desire to simply make myself get back to work. . . . For the first time I know that I have a foot in the door and that without fault I <u>will succeed!</u> in this extraordinary and limitless foreign country.

A little less than a year later Annabert described coming home at the end of an evening and getting a phone call from a Mr. Parker from

Venezuela who had bought a small tapestry at the Thaibok showing. He explained that he'd been saving money since then to buy *The Cockfight*, another small tapestry he'd seen. He arrived at the studio half an hour later. Marianne asked $600 for the tapestry, and in the space of fifteen minutes, Parker had taken the tapestry and left a check. *It is unbelievable*, Annabert wrote in her diary. *We had six dollars left for the rest of this month. Paternayan, the wool company, was pressing us to pay the old bill of wool—312 dollars. And Jan's suit is completely worn out. I had to patch the knees of his trousers. Now Jan can have a new suit. This one was made the autumn of 1953 after our exhibition at the Hugo Gallery. Since it is Jan's only suit, he has been wearing it day in, day out. . . . We walked through the Village to our Italian Pizza restaurant in MacDougal Street, the Masquerada. Nowhere else can we get such delicious pizzas, made by an old Italian man who was a barber before he opened this restaurant. He makes his pizzas with love like an artist. Afterwards we bought three pastries to celebrate this great event of selling* The Cockfight. *I wove* The Cockfight *just before the exhibition in the Hugo Gallery in 1952 and 1953 in the small studio on a primitive frame. One has to now be able to reap. We meet people and years later they come back and buy. We work and over the years these finished tapestries go away to the place where they belong.*

27 *The Family of Man*

What amazes me about [Jan] was the fishlike ease with
which he could slip through all the layers and become
part of almost any situation into which he had strayed. He
knows the city and understands it in a way in which almost
nobody that I've ever met does—consequently, he's full
of surprises.

—ROBERT HUGHES, *NEW YORK TIMES* ART CRITIC

In 1955, *The Family of Man* opened at the Museum of Modern Art
and changed the world of photography. The renowned photographer
Edward Steichen conceived the show in different terms from the more
traditional exhibits he'd previously mounted at MoMA. This was to be a
celebration of humanity's common experience and a visual plea for peace
and brotherly love, in the spirit of the fledgling United Nations. As such,
he invited submissions from all photographers, professional and amateur
alike, and in his statement he explained: *We are seeking photographs covering the gamut of human relations, particularly the hard-to-find photographs
of the everydayness in the relationships of man to himself, to his family, to the
community, and to the world we live in.*

Over two million photographs flooded into the offices of the
museum, and from these Steichen culled down to just over five hundred.
He included famous names—Henri Cartier-Bresson, Alfred Eisen-
staedt, Dorothea Lange, Robert Doisneau, and Ansel Adams were all
represented—but gave equal room to unknowns. His selections favored
photojournalism over art and were grouped thematically, without regard
for the status of the photographer or the integrity of the photograph as
an object. Some photos were blown up to the size of murals, others were

hung on wires from the ceiling, and still others were wrapped around poles, cut into silhouettes, or collaged.

It's fantastic, Annabert wrote in her diary on February 22. *A very large photo lit up by the moon, almost an abstract of light and dark, and next to it a photo of an enormous round stomach and breast, the beginning of life. . . . You have children who are playing, mothers and children, death, hate, loneliness. And the question, "Will we have war with the atomic bomb?" It's very beautifully designed, but also there is a lot of very unimportant photographs and sometimes very ugly. It could have been so much more beautiful, but we see it from the art point of view.*

In our image-saturated present, when the lives of ordinary people are omnipresent on Instagram or Facebook, it may be hard to imagine the full impact that a show like this had. For many, it was like seeing the world for the first time. Although photography purists and aesthetes had reservations, the public responded to the show's ecstatic, theatrical displays and its inspirational message with awe. Every day, lines of people stretched around a city block waiting for the doors to open; by the end of its fifteen-week run, 270,000 viewers had seen the show, the most for any photography exhibit in history. Subsequently, the show toured six U.S. cities, breaking attendance records wherever it went, and then traveled on to thirty-seven countries. By 1961, at the end of its world tour, estimates put the number of people who'd seen the show at nine million, and the accompanying catalog—a dollar for the paperback or ten dollars for a deluxe hardbound edition—had sold over a million copies.

In the thirties, Jan had taken casual photographs of the Gypsies using a Brownie camera. In some ways, they are ordinary family photos: mothers, fathers, sisters, and cousins posed in front of their caravans or their horses just as another family might pose on Grandma's front porch or in front of a shiny DeSoto. Two boys clown for the photographer, demonstrating a knockout punch. A young woman stands holding a pitcher, a long dirt road unwinding behind her. She looks at the camera with a disarming lack of self-consciousness. Part of what makes the photos affecting is the realization that these people, usually hidden behind layers of myth and prejudice, are familiar. We know them. They are us. Three girls in their finery, their long skirts swirling, dance gleefully across the frame. In another photo, a small boy stands in front of the camera and spreads his arms wide, as though defying the viewer to notice the others behind him. There, in the background, tall and pale among all these dark-eyed Gypsies, is a young man with a serious demeanor, Jan, the adopted son.

Jan went back to see the *Family of Man* again right before it closed in May. In her diary entry for that day, Annabert wrote, *Jan is in his thinking, quiet period.* "*Isn't it strange to be an artist and do nothing else the whole day but paint?*" *That was one of Jan's sayings today. Jan said that I should not be upset that he was not full of plans and enthusiasm because to have a period of thinking is also very good.*

19 FEBRUARY 1957

Jan finished his "Blue Fire"—or "beginning of the end." A very unusual work for Jan, and a kind of reaction against his very tender and sensitive work he made from [the model] *Ernestine. Jan wanted to make something very strong and powerful, so we measured a big piece of paper—11 x 9 feet—and hung it against the wall. Jan had flames in mind but it had to be an "all over" pattern and powerful. It is indeed very powerful and striking. The forms are abstract—pure abstract forms, which make a strong pattern in black and blue. It is the opposite of the women figures in "The Women by Moonlight." It is crushingly powerful, but it is Jan's work. . . . In Jan's work you can see clearly the two sides of Jan's personality (better said two of the more obvious sides of Jan's personality). The very sensitive, tender, and respectful side of Jan— and the other side, an unexpected powerful and more primitive side.*

Jan's "period of thinking" culminated in a tidal shift in his work: he began designing huge abstracts of sinuous organic shapes, some of them drawn from leaves and other matter he had first photographed in extreme close-up. In their size and use of color—often one or two intense jewel colors throbbing against a black background—the tapestries retained a vestigial influence of his father's stained glass windows, but he was moving away from biblical themes and figurative storytelling, and coming into his own as an artist. They also kept getting larger. "For me," he would later explain, "tapestry is an epic format. It must stay monumental. A small tapestry, for me, is a table mat."

Private homes didn't generally have interior walls large enough to accommodate the scale that he was working in, but public and corporate spaces were another story. Trends in commercial architecture were advancing the Bauhaus aesthetic of unornamented concrete, glass, and stone, and the advent of air conditioning allowed these new buildings to have vast, windowless walls. Jan's tapestries brought humanizing warmth and color to these modern cathedrals of the fifties.

IN 1959 THEY had to move their studio. Like so many old buildings and commercial spaces in the Village in those years, 96 Fifth Avenue was being demolished to make way for a high rise.

On Forty-Seventh Street near the United Nations, they saw a "For Rent" sign on a three-story commercial building next to a vacant corner lot. There had been a fire. The owner had repaired the roof, but the building was empty. Inside, on the top floor, was a cavernous open space with a wall of windows on each end, a twenty-by-thirty-foot mezzanine, and skylights high above. To the west, it overlooked a little garden with trees and flowers; to the east, past the huge empty lot, it faced the United Nations Park, the East River, and Queens on the far side. The lease-holder told the Yoors they could have the loft for six months, until he could move back in. As it turned out, they would stay there for eight years.

The place was filthy. They scrubbed it out, painted, hammered, sewed, and hung lights. Jan built stairs up to the mezzanine, what they called the hayloft, and they painted its floor yellow. Up here Jan would work, sketching from a model or painting, and the family would eat and entertain friends. On the main floor, spare private quarters—a little refrigerator and electric burner to cook on, a closet and a mattress—could be concealed behind dramatic floor-to-ceiling draperies. The public would see only a vast open space with Chinese red floors, filled with light and dominated by the enormous looms and the bright tapestries hanging on whitewashed brick walls.

When they were finished, the space was breathtaking. People began coming to see the studio, every week someone new. The photographer Tony Vaccaro did a shoot for *Look* magazine, posing fashion models in front of the tapestries. Dizzy Gillespie played a benefit performance in the studio for the civil rights organization CORE (Congress of Racial Equality), raising money for their campaigns to end segregation. (Two years later, at the start of the 1964 Freedom Summer, the Yoors would again open their studio for a benefit in support of desegregation, this time in conjunction with the NAACP.) A few weeks after the CORE benefit, the Yoors hosted a reception for the Mexican poet and diplomat Octavio Paz. They frequently threw cocktail parties, and a stream of visitors passed through, including the photographers Cartier-Bresson and Edward Steichen (curator of *The Family of Man*), and the modernist architects Philip Johnson and Abraham Geller. Among the regulars were James Johnson Sweeney, director of the Guggenheim; Monroe Wheeler from the Museum of Modern Art; James Rorimer, director at the Metropolitan Museum of Art; and Thomas Messer and Susan Swann from the Guggenheim. Japanese, Greek, French, and Indian diplomats from the UN crossed First Avenue to mix with the arty crowd. And then there were the people whom Jan invited simply because they interested him. At one party, the model Phyl found herself talking to a Mohawk Indian who was one of the daredevil ironworkers making their livings on girders up in the sky, erecting the skeletons of new skyscrapers.

Dizzy Gillespie at Yoors studio, photo by Jan Yoors, 1962. Courtesy of the Yoors Family Partnership.

"Jan had parties like that," Rubie Rabinowitz recalled. "He had people from all over the world. Everyone was crazy about Jan. He was a wonderful, wonderful guy. I don't think anybody ever really knew Jan as he knew himself. The rest of us were just onlookers to this very wonderful guy, pleasant guy, affable mostly. You didn't know what was going to come out of his heart."

Some few of the visitors to the studio crossed an invisible line into the private life of the Yoors and became family friends. Often these were the models who posed for Jan.

When one of these young women, a very beautiful Filipino, got married, the Yoors hosted the wedding reception at their studio. This is how they met the next model, Cynthia Mead; her husband was a friend of the groom. By coincidence, just a few days later, they saw her again at the Brooklyn Museum of Art. As they all stood around talking, Marianne drew her aside.

You know, Jan would very much like to have you be a model for him. Are you at all interested? Have you ever done that?

Cynthia replied that she hadn't.

Well, think about it, Marianne encouraged her. It would be for tapestries or drawings, just two days a week for a couple of hours.

Cynthia's husband thought it was a great idea, but Cynthia herself wasn't sure she could do it. The first day, she wore a long dress that buttoned all the way up.

She had very long, straight hair and high cheekbones, a look that Jan told her he liked. You could be Polish, he said. Or Czech, American Indian, South American, you could be anything.

She was flattered. He told her his stories about the Gypsies and his adventures in the war. At twenty-two, she had never met anyone like him, and she was intrigued to be the object of such a man's attention. She began coming to the studio two mornings a week to model. Jan hung big sheets in the hayloft for privacy, and here he would draw her. Downstairs, Marianne and Annabert went about their business, weaving or doing whatever they were doing, and after a few hours they'd carry up bowls of soup and bread and cheese, and the four would sit on pillows around the low table and eat lunch.

NEW YORK CITY in the fifties and sixties was a patchwork of neighborhoods defined by ethnicity—Chinatown and Little Italy, the Irish West Village, Harlem and El Barrio, Spanish Harlem, the Jewish neighborhoods of Brooklyn—and Jan had friends in all of these places. It was one of his talents to cross borders, to slip through the barricades of race and language and class. He conversed easily in a number of languages and had learned at a young age how to assimilate into whatever community he entered. When he was in the company of the Rom, for instance, his manner mutated almost imperceptibly to match theirs; he walked and spoke with a bit more swagger. More importantly, though, Jan was a genuinely cosmopolitan person, comfortable wherever he went and wholly without prejudice.

He went out at least four or five nights a week, cultivating connections with architects, designers, and influential people in the art world or going to visit friends. Sometimes he mixed business and pleasure, and took a potential client or a visitor from the UN along with him to visit his Gypsy friends. Occasionally, he'd ask one or both of his wives to accompany him to a gallery opening, or the three of them might go out with members of the French delegation for a Chinese banquet. However, even had they spoken French or Romani, Marianne and Annabert lacked Jan's ease with strangers. They much preferred their private outings, exploring the city with Jan as they had done since they first moved to America. In their long, flowered dresses and sneakers, and Jan at his most casual in blue chambray shirtsleeves, the three would walk down to Little Italy during the Feast of San Gennaro or to Chinatown for the New Year parade. They took picnics up to the Cloisters at the northern tip of Manhattan or out to the Botanical Gardens in Brooklyn. They took the train up to Harlem to hear Daddy Grace preach or to meet Malcolm X. They visited the museums. And often they simply walked the streets, taking advantage of one of the great pleasures afforded by the city.

These were Annabert's happiest times, strolling arm in arm with her husband in the evening, or sitting on a bus, just the two of them, holding hands, and hearing him whisper to her, *Je bent mijn liefste*. You are my dearest.

Marianne also treasured their walks, though for her they evoked mixed emotions. When the three of them were out walking, it was Jan and Annabert who went arm in arm. She was always on the side, the sister. And somehow she always found herself a little out of step; perhaps her gait was longer, but she could never find the rhythm of their walking. Now, if she were alone with Jan in Chinatown or midtown or the lower East Side, it was a different story: they would walk arm in arm. But the moment they came into their own neighborhood, Jan would let go of her arm. She tried not to notice, not to let it bother her, but it did.

IN 1961 HENRI STORCK and Luc de Heusch, Belgian documentary film-makers, approached Jan. They wanted to make a film on the Rom and proposed that Jan be their go-between. Initially, they suggested, the three of them should make a short research trip to Europe to make contact with the tribes and scout locations. It was a flawed plan: you couldn't go meet Gypsies and then expect to return later with a film crew and find them still in the same place. The only way to successfully film the Rom would be catch as catch can, and Jan thought he'd convinced them of this. When the men showed up at the airport with their wives, their girlfriends, and their copious luggage in tow, he was angry but decided to make the best of the situation and look on it as an expense-paid road trip. For his birthday, a few of his friends had chipped in and bought him a Pentax camera so that he could document the trip, and so for two and a half months Jan traveled through the Balkans, Turkey, and Greece, following the *vurma*, the signs the Gypsies left along the side of the road, making new acquaintances and photographing them. Wherever they went, Jan was fêted and revered for his heroism during the war; the Rom shared with him and his companions their meals and their stories.

"This is the pleasure of getting together with other Gypsies," Jan explained, "and Gypsies you haven't met before: there's always stories to be told. That's the main reason why Gypsies travel. Because if you remain neighbors over ten years' period, what can you still talk about?"

The film was never made, but Jan had caught the bug. Back in New York, he began taking his camera with him wherever they went walking, and he would photograph street scenes: black-and-white images of shoeshine boys and sidewalk merchants. The ice cream man in his billed cap, bow tie, and spiffy white uniform. A hot dog vendor lost in thought, a cigarette dangling from his lips. The doughy woman on the Lower

East Side selling pretzels out of a basket, five cents each. Often, Marianne or Annabert served as a decoy: he'd pose them in front and just to the side of whomever he really wanted to photograph so that he could capture the subject unaware. Kids sprawling on a brownstone stoop or squatting on the sidewalk, engrossed in their play. People walking under an awning advertising "The Originator of Kosher Chinese Foods." A little girl, her hair in foam rollers, reaching out with both hands through a barred window to catch a sparrow on the sill. This was the New York that tourists—and even most natives—rarely saw, though it was hidden in plain sight.

Jan loved the spontaneity of photography, so different from the slow and formal process of tapestry. It also spoke to his democratic impulses. Because tapestries took so long to make, only the rich could afford them. But photography was a medium for the masses. Kathy Komaroff Goodman, a New York art dealer who knew Jan during this period, feels this was the medium in which his talents soared. "There is a notable humanity in them. A love for people. A gorgeous use of black and white. They are also emotional photos."

In the following year, 1962, another French filmmaker, Pierre-Dominique Gaisseau, visited the city. Gaisseau had just won an Oscar for *La Ciel et la boue*, or *The Sky Above, the Mud Below*, a film documenting a seven-month expedition into the wilds of New Guinea and the explorers' contact with tribes of headhunters, cannibals, and pygmies. He had a background in ethnography, as did Jan, and they also shared the bond of having served in the Resistance during the war. Not surprisingly, the two men intrigued one another, and they began excitedly to plot a new film: it would be an expedition into the little-known cultures of New York. They'd film it the way Jan had hoped to do the Gypsy documentary, inconspicuously and on the fly, each of them strapping a 45-pound camera on his shoulder, and carrying a portable tape recorder for sound. It would be like working as operatives in the Underground again.

28 Only One New York

Only one city with so many delights and dangers. Only one city where the evil and the exotic rub shoulders from dawn to dark. Only one entertainment like this in all the world!

Eight million people . . . Eight million passions . . . Eight million personal stories . . . all rolled up into the most remarkable motion picture ever made! Filmed where it happened . . . as it happened . . . in the Wonder City of the World!

—ORIGINAL MOVIE POSTER FOR *ONLY ONE NEW YORK*

That fall, Jan flew to Paris to negotiate and sign contracts for the film. He was to be paid the lordly sum of $1,000 a month for seven months. To celebrate, he bought Marianne and Annabert a brand-new oven range to replace the little hot plate they'd been cooking on for ten years. Even more wonderful, he determined that they could start planning for children. Commissions for tapestries were coming at shorter intervals, and Jan had been selected to represent the United States at the International Biennial of Contemporary Tapestries in Lausanne, Switzerland. On the strength of these improved prospects, and with the knowledge that the two women had just turned thirty-six, he decided—and it was always Jan who decided—that it was time to feather the nest. Finally, their utopia was materializing.

A few months later, Marianne was cooking a roast in their new oven, and the smell of the cooking meat induced waves of nausea in Annabert. It had been so long, but Annabert remembered the symptoms.

IN JANUARY 1963 Pierre Gaisseau came back to the city, along with a sound man, Jean Hamon, and they began getting permissions and filming. The master calligrapher Jeanyee Wong and her husband Wei, friends from Jan's first days in New York, introduced them around Chinatown. Then the three men headed out to Coney Island to find the Rom. When they got there the amusement park was deserted and clad in ice, and the Gypsies had moved on, but they shot some film of the deserted park anyway. Jan arranged to film at a Romanian restaurant owned by an architect acquaintance. They visited churches in Harlem, and met a group of African Americans who were attempting to recover their lost heritage by practicing voodoo startlingly similar to what Pierre had witnessed in Nigeria: drumming, dancing, and spinning to achieve an ecstatic transport, a state helped along when necessary by pressure on the eyelids. In a strange version of life imitating art, it came out in conversation that their source for information on these rituals was actually a book that Pierre Gaisseau himself had written about an expedition in Africa.

Morocco, a practitioner and master teacher of Middle Eastern dance, met Jan when the group was scouting locations and ended up being featured in the film.

There was an all-night beauty parlor called Larry Matthews, and this was when there were still dancers at the Roxy and when Radio City Music Hall was the hot spot and Lou Walters' Latin Quarter was going strong. This beauty parlor catered to the dancers and performers who worked later hours, and they were open all night, and they were also part and parcel of the same people that owned the Roundtable [the club where Morocco was dancing]. *So they sent another dancer and myself over there to get some pictures taken because Jean-Pierre Gaisseau and Jan were filming a segment for the movie* Only One New York, *and they wanted to get the club's name in there. And I'm not letting them touch my hair; Emra's getting hers teased up even higher cuz she's like five foot two, and I'm sitting on the counter watching them do that cuz I ain't letting them near my hair.*

And Jan asked me, What's your name? Where are you from? Are you really Moroccan?

And I said, Shit no, I'm Roma.

And it was like, Oh really.

Yeah, really.

So he says something to me in Romnes, and I say something smartass back to him, and he realizes I wasn't kidding.

And he says to me, Listen, we're going to be filming at a restaurant called *Harout's. It was right near Washington Square Park and the NYU building* *but they didn't have that big complex then. He said they were going to be* *filming there Friday. I should come down in costume, and I could get into the* *film, dancing. So I did and they did, and the rest is history.*

JAN ARRANGED AN introduction to the famous Chabad-Lubavitch rabbi Menachem Mendel Schneerson, thought by his followers to be the Messiah. The rabbi invited Gaisseau and Yoors to his home for dinner, and the three had a long, lively conversation in French about their wartime experiences—Schneerson had fled the Nazis in Berlin for Paris in the early thirties and lived in France for seven years until he finally escaped Europe in 1941. As with many others, the rabbi and Jan founded a friendship on this shared history and would remain in contact for the rest of Jan's life. Nevertheless, though Jan talked for hours that night until he was literally hoarse, Rebbe Schneerson declined to approve filming their ritual baths.

Jan turned next to the leader of the Bobov Hasidic sect. A fantastic man with an impressive beard and an embroidered brown silk caftan, the Grand Rebbe Shlomo Halberstam welcomed them into his office. Again, talk turned to the war. The rabbi had lost his whole family in Auschwitz but for one son. Jan told his stories about the Rom, and as they talked, the two men kept saying, There's something familiar about you, something I know, and I don't know what it is. How do I know you, I must know you . . .

Suddenly, Rebbe Halberstam pulled open a drawer and scattered a bunch of photographs across the desk. They were false papers showing a young beardless man. The rabbi, too, had been a secret agent helping to get Jews out. Somewhere in Europe, he and Jan had crossed paths.

In theory, Hasidim were not allowed to be photographed—this was considered to be creating graven images—so it's a measure of Jan's powers of persuasion that he convinced several congregations to allow him to film their religious ceremonies. He promised they would be very respectful, nearly invisible—only two handheld cameras, and no crew, no lights. They were given permission to film a ritual bath of purification, the reading of the Torah, and finally, a noisy Shabbat dinner in the

Jan on location of Only One New York, *1963. Courtesy of the Yoors Family Partnership.*

synagogue. After dinner, the men got up to dance, and Pierre and Jan worked a spiral around the edge of the crowd. With only the available light inside the synagogue, it was difficult work to find focus and a depth of field, and to keep the heavy cameras steady while the stream of men flowed around them. "I admit I wouldn't want to do it for money," Jan said. "I only do it for love."

ONLY ONE NEW YORK is a wonderfully odd and historically important film. It opens with an image of a changing city—a wrecking ball demolishing an old building—then the camera pans up the facades of soaring glass skyscrapers. To the tinny swing of an early sixties score with clarinet and organ, a narrator pontificates in voice-over. "How beautiful these shining towers are. They rival the ancient splendor of the pyramids. Never has there been a city in the world like this, not Babylon with all its hanging gardens, not even the vanished mythical Atlantis. Architecture expresses an attitude, it reveals the psychology of the builder, and it occurs to me that people who expect a bomb to fall don't build their walls of glass. A city of glass is like a declaration of peace."

UTOPIA

Then the filmmakers turn their lens on the inhabitants of this brave new city. They visit Chinatown, going backstage for the rehearsal of an opera and peeking into a community center classroom to watch children practicing calligraphy. "How much longer," the narrator wonders, "will these colorful remnants of an older culture be able to survive? How sad it will be if they vanish." The film records the rites and ceremonies of an array of subcultures within the city, from parishioners celebrating Easter at a Russian Orthodox Church to Playboy bunnies playing touch football with customers in Central Park. A Gypsy wedding features accordion music; a Ukrainian wedding culminates in a traditional sword dance. Beautiful women model the season's new fashions in a Fifth Avenue salon, and uptown in the Abyssinian Baptist Church. Japanese Buddhists stroll down Riverside Drive in full costume, celebrating the Festival of Flowers. Bands march up Fifth Avenue in the Saint Patrick's Day Parade. Italians celebrating the festival of St. Anthony of Padua carry a float on their shoulders bearing a twenty-four-piece orchestra and a twenty-foot tower. Greek dancers limber up on the sidewalk in preparation for a parade celebrating their independence day. Dance and song are shown to be universal human activities, and their cultural permutations seemingly endless. South American dancers do the cha-cha and the mambo in a Times Square dance hall. In Harlem, the parishioners of the United House of Prayer for All People of the Church on the Rock of the Apostolic Faith dance and sing gospel music. In Sunnyside, Queens, the Knickerbocker Orchestra thumps out a polka while men in lederhosen dance. At the end of the festivities, the audience rises to its feet and sings the national anthem of Germany, sometimes called by its refrain, "Deutschland, Deutschland über alles." In Brooklyn a line of Hasidic men, their hands on each other's shoulders, "dance and sing in the synagogue," the narrator informs the viewer, "as they danced and sang around the ark of David. It is also a matter of record that the Hasidim sang on their way to the Nazi crematories."

This was Jan's version of *The Family of Man*, an astonishing collage of all that he loved about his adopted city. Also like Steichen's show, it juxtaposed its uplifting message with the shadow anxiety of the Cold War era. The film ends in the lobby of a skyscraper where an exhibit displays huge models of the atom, "this terrifying new energy." The narrator waxes eloquent on the promises of the future and concludes, "Already these New Yorkers have achieved something entirely new and very important. With all their differences, they have learned to live together. Which I think is what all the peoples of the world will have to do if they want to survive."

29 Baby Book

Jan called Annabert *Kik*, from *Kikker*, the Dutch word for frog. It was an affectionate reference to her skinny limbs, but also to her buoyant spirit. Though she was now thirty-seven and prematurely gray-headed, she still had the tireless energy of a girl, the same bright look and childlike delights. And like the fabled frog in the pail of milk, she never gave up hope. As a girl, she had lived in expectation for eleven years before she was reunited with Jan. This time, her faith had been tested for fifteen years, but with the birth of her daughter Lyuba (named after the matriarch of Jan's Gypsy family), Annabert realized her long-deferred dream to be a mother again.

She converted her diary, formerly a record of their artistic and professional lives, into a baby book wherein she described her little worries—many fewer this time, thanks to Dr. Spock and her great joys. Nursing, she wrote, was indescribably fulfilling—"the warm little head leaning against my arm, the lovely, sweet blue eyes looking so serious and so full of love and trust." Sometimes in these pages she addressed herself directly to her daughter, as when she confided that "Mammie and Pappie want to have a little brother or sister for our treasure, and if possible more than one."

Annabert was pregnant again within six months of the birth but miscarried in the first trimester, a setback she could now afford to view philosophically because it was only temporary. The original plan—that Annabert would have the first baby and then it would be Marianne's turn—had been abandoned; it would have meant discarding Marianne's cover as Jan's sister-in-law and announcing to the world their polygamy. From the war, Jan carried deep fears of authority and imprisonment, and he wasn't ready to risk that kind of attention again. So, even as Annabert had once adjusted to sharing her husband with her friend, Marianne had to content herself with mothering her friend's child.

Marianne loves our baby almost (almost!) more than I do, Annabert wrote in her diary. *And how Lyuba loves her. Marianne shows her everything when she walks with her—a doll in a shop window, pigeons on a lamppost, etc. Lyuba loves it. How lucky our baby is to have two mammies!* Calling herself Mammy and Marianne Mammyjan, Annabert recounted a trip to Central Park, the two mommies with their baby. It was spring and Lyuba had learned to make kisses; when Marianne bought her a little bottle of milk, she showed off her new trick to the delight of mothers and child. They fed bread to a "Mammie duck with three little ones," Annabert happily reported, and even saw a "Mammie rat and her baby." New motherhood painted Annabert's world in pastel colors.

Today our baby took her first steps alone. Marianne held her by her middle. She walked so proudly like that—very conscious that it was not like other times. Then Marianne took her hands away and held them protectingly around her but without touching her—step, step, step—how her little face shone with joy and pride.

Babies change a marriage, even when that marriage is polygamous. Finally, the Yoors felt, they were truly a family. A baby gave them a sense of permanence and stability. They took Lyuba everywhere with them, to movies and openings, even to a formal dinner where, much to the consternation of the hostess, Annabert insisted on keeping Lyuba in a basket next to her chair rather than relinquishing her to the nanny upstairs. For many parents, a baby narrows the parameters of their world, at least temporarily, but for Annabert and Marianne, the opposite occurred: their formerly cloistered existence expanded, and their lives began to revolve less exclusively around Jan. In the morning, while Jan was drawing a model, the two women would take Lyuba across First Avenue to the United Nations Park, where they met other parents with their children. They were also befriended by Rose, the secretary downstairs who fussed over Lyuba and, to Jan's annoyance, got into the habit of dropping in; and by Mary, the Italian woman next door whose family lived over the luncheonette, and who brought them care packages of meat from the butcher and cake and ice cream.

A measure, perhaps, of this shift is that Annabert made no mention in her 1964 diary of the release of *Only One New York*. The film, produced by Joseph Levine and Embassy Films, previewed on August 13 to an enthusiastic crowd at the Gallery of Modern Art in Columbus Circle. It then ran as a double feature with *The Outrage*, a remake of Kurosawa's *Rashomon*, and opened nationwide in October.

Perhaps Annabert's oversight was simply a reflection of how busy she was. Not only did she have the demands of a toddler, but she and Marianne were rushing to finish a very large tapestry—seventeen by nine feet—commissioned to celebrate the new merger of the Belgian and German photographic film companies, Gevaert and Agfa. They had been given only six weeks to complete the tapestry by October 13, a feat they'd never before undertaken. While Lyuba slept in a cradle next to the loom or crawled around on a finished tapestry in pursuit of one or another of the Siamese cats, the two women pushed themselves to weave for hours and hours on end until they met their deadline. Add to this that Annabert was pregnant again—she would give birth the following April to a boy, Vanya—and it's probably more surprising that she wrote anything at all. The entries became more and more sporadic, and with two young children filling her days she wouldn't start a new diary again for seven years.

It may also be that the opening of *Only One New York* received no mention in Annabert's diary because in the end Jan was disillusioned. The credits and reviews listed him as Gaisseau's assistant. This reflected Pierre and Jan's relative status in the public eye, but entirely misrepresented Jan's contribution as a collaborator. It was only through Jan's connections that they had gotten access to most of the communities they filmed, and ultimately the film was his vision of the city, his New York. He never said a word against Gaisseau, but he certainly hadn't expected such treatment.

Also, the film hadn't done well at the box office, perhaps not surprising given the subject matter. It had received sensational reviews from the *New York Times* and from Judith Crist at the *New York Herald Tribune* but ended its national run after the first week. The rest of the country in 1964 was buying tickets for *Goldfinger*, *Mary Poppins*, and *My Fair Lady*; they felt ambivalent about New York, and for precisely the reason that the film extolled the city. At best, ethnicity was something to be overcome and erased in the "melting pot"; at worst, it was an uncomfortable front-page problem that summer, with young New Yorkers riding on buses into the South to register black voters. Most Americans were nowhere near ready to celebrate the diversity that Jan found so inspiring.

At the end of his life, he looked back on the project and described it as "a heartbreak because of the realities of commercial life so easy to overlook for the visionary." Then, catching himself, he added, "The heartbreak (what a big word in hindsight) was well worth the adventure."

EARLY IN THE filming of *Only One New York*, Jan had made the acquaintance of Michael Korda, a young editor at the publishing house Simon & Schuster, who would go on to run the company for decades and become renowned in the publishing world for bringing out big books like *The Rise and Fall of the Third Reich*, *The Story of Civilization*, and the memoirs of Nixon and Reagan. Korda was a fellow European, the scion of an illustrious Hungarian filmmaking family. (His father, Vincent, and two uncles, Zoltan and Sir Alexander, were responsible for such films as *The Thief of Bagdad*, *Jungle Book*, and *The Third Man*.) Korda had spent a privileged youth in England and France, and during the Cold War had served on a top-secret intelligence operation with the RAF. This was another basis of his friendship with Jan: they had a mutual and unspoken understanding of what it meant to be an operative.

Out of this friendship initially came a contract for a companion book to *Only One New York*, consisting of still photographs that Jan had shot. The book was published in January 1965, to coincide with the New York World's Fair, and they threw a book party and art show at Art Lugoff's legendary Village Gate.

More important, though, Korda was captivated by Jan's stories of his life with the Rom and thought they'd make a fine book. Jan had actually begun writing about the Gypsies many years earlier, first a few articles for an academic journal called *Gypsy Lore*, and later with the idea that he might publish a book with Sheed & Ward, the Catholic publisher that gave him his first commissions in New York as an illustrator. With Korda's encouragement, Jan dug out these old pages and began to compose in earnest.

His early drafts were scholarly in tone, a monograph intended to correct the morass of misinformation and prejudice surrounding the Rom. Because the Rom had no interest in setting down their own story, all accounts and histories had been written by Gaje, and in Jan's view even the most well-meaning of these were rife with inaccuracies. "I think close to five thousand books have been written on the subject," he said, "and I doubt there is a single one I would dare to recommend offhand." Korda persuaded him that rather than adding another anthropological treatise to the heap, he should set down on paper the tales he'd been entertaining listeners with for years about his time with the Gypsies. It was this first-person account that would captivate readers.

Jan was a gifted storyteller but not a natural writer. His talents had been shaped by his years with the Rom, for whom storytelling ranked among the most respected of skills, but who distrusted written communication. As Jan explained, "They like to speak face-to-face; they say a letter can be written by anybody. How can you tell it's true?" The war reinforced this reticence in Jan, when it was dangerous to put anything potentially damning on paper. Add to this the difficulty of writing in a language not one's own, and then throw in the daily hurdles that even the most practiced writers encounter, and it's no wonder that Jan found the process of writing painful. The first line of the finished book begins,

"I want to evoke a mood." He yearned to re-create the effect on listeners of sitting around a campfire and listening enthralled for hours at a time. As he had with his visual art, he wanted to make something artful, something passionate and beautiful. He wanted to tell the true story, to correct the record without betraying the family he had lost, the people he loved. He wanted with all his heart to honor them, and yet he had never cultivated a daily routine—routine was anathema to the Gypsies, and something that Jan also found distasteful. In the afternoons, while the women wove, he'd sometimes repair to the little blue desk under the stairs and wrestle with his memories until he couldn't remain in his chair any longer. Then he'd grab his camera and ask Marianne to go with him on a walk. In the evenings, Annabert typed out his handwritten pages. The book grew slowly, but it grew.

30 Tiger and Chipmunk

In January 1964 Andy Warhol moved into his first Factory, a block west from the Yoors, but the two studios might as well have been on different planets. Called the Silver Factory because it was decorated entirely in silver spray paint, tinfoil, and broken mirror, 231 East Forty-Seventh Street became the epicenter of the early sixties avant-garde scene. Warhol called it a factory because he wanted to produce art the same way manufacturers made their products, en masse. To that end, he hosted amphetamine-fueled, nonstop happenings where a mix of druggies, drag queens, bored socialites, and hipsters were put to work silk-screening Warhol's self-portraits or making three-dimensional Brillo boxes. They also performed in his unscripted experimental films, from the aptly named *Sleep* (five hours and twenty minutes of a man sleeping) to *Kiss*, *Blow Job*, *Nude Restaurant*, *Taylor Mead's Ass*, and *Vinyl*, his spectacularly bad adaptation of Anthony Burgess's novel *A Clockwork Orange*. A number of his Factory superstars got their fifteen minutes of fame as a result: Ultra Violet, Nico, Ondine, and perhaps most memorably the gamine Edie Sedgwick. Everything they made, Warhol put his name on and sold for huge sums, which he then funneled back to keep the party going. The musicians Lou Reed, Mick Jagger, Bob Dylan, and Jim Morrison hung out there; Allan Ginsberg, Salvador Dali, and Truman Capote showed up now and again. In the sixties, the Factory parties were the hippest place to be seen and were a highly coveted invitation.

Marianne and Annabert didn't even know the Silver Factory existed, much less that Jan visited there occasionally, but this is probably how the Yoors initially met and fell in with Tiger Morse. The straw-haired fashion designer with the foot-long cigarette holder and wildly oversized sunglasses was a Warhol girl who'd starred in two of his films, one of which bore her name.

Tiger came to the Yoors' studio and was blown away. A short time later, she reciprocated by inviting Jan to visit her home off of Central Park. Marianne went with him. Tiger came to the door wearing a gorgeous floor-length kimono. It was midnight blue silk and lined with another silk, a lovely deep green, and Marianne fell in love with it. She'd gotten it in Japan, Tiger said, and then seeing that Marianne coveted the robe, she proposed a trade. As it happened, when she was at the Yoors' studio, she'd seen a large tapestry she wanted, the one the Yoors called the *Apocalypse* or *The Adoring of the Golden Calf*.

Marianne was giddy.

Jan asked Marianne quietly, When are you going to wear it?

Marianne didn't care. She wanted the kimono. Then Tiger showed them where she wanted to put the tapestry: on the floor of a raised platform. They were offended that Tiger regarded their tapestry as a carpet, to be walked on and sat upon. So that was the end of that, although in retrospect Marianne realized that Jan had not for one minute had the intention of making such a foolish trade.

TIGER HAD ANOTHER proposal: she wanted to use their studio for a party to introduce her new line of ready-to-wear fashion. Her Pop-influenced designs attracted a prestigious clientele, including Jackie Kennedy, the style setter of the era. It would be good publicity for their tapestries, she said, because everybody would come—the Rockefellers and the Kennedys and the Rothschilds, and all the people from the museums. The Yoors would become famous.

This deal they eagerly agreed to.

Tiger arrived at the studio with a set designer, lighting designer Chip Monck, and a few others in tow to look over the space. They all agreed it was fabulous, perfect. The balcony level, what the Yoors called the hayloft, could be closed off to give the models a place to get dressed. Or what if they built a catwalk running from the hayloft! It could run at a diagonal to that far corner of the studio, and then back again. The models would emerge from the hayloft, step through a door and onto the catwalk and walk zigzagging back and forth over the heads of the spectators. It would be outrageous! At the end of the catwalk, they could step into an enormous birdcage that would lower them to the ground! Oh, and there the models could strip, and under their clothes they would be wearing Tiger's line of bikinis. They could design a beach!

A construction crew arrived and took over the studio. First thing, the loom and the tapestries displayed on the walls had to be moved out of harm's way. Then they began the remodeling. They built the catwalk about twelve feet above the floor, and put up walls around the hayloft and installed a door. And while they were at it they also built a room under the hayloft to store the racks of clothes, and they enlarged the bathroom. Bags of sand were brought in, enough to make a 25-by-25-foot "beach."

The whole thing took a month. The tapestries never went back up on the walls.

On a Monday night in January 1966, Annabert took Lyuba and six-month-old Vanya next door to their friend Mary's apartment. Marianne stood on the sidewalk and watched as hundreds of glamorous people converged on the studio. At one point, she ducked upstairs for a quick peek. "There was a guy," she remembers, "I think he went by the name of Chipmunk, who was the Beatles' manager for lights, for the Beatles or the Rolling Stones or something like that, who was doing all the music and all the lights effects." The place was dark and jammed with bodies, with booming rock-n-roll and strobe lights. She scurried back down to the street. At the sound of a starter pistol firing, the street door was closed to further guests and the show started.

Later, Michael Korda and his wife, Casey, emerged, shaken. This has to stop, he told Marianne. The catwalk was swaying precariously, and there were so many people upstairs dancing that the floor of the studio was in danger of collapsing beneath them. Korda went to the phone booth on the corner and called the police.

After the police had come and cleared everyone out, Marianne watched Tiger and Chip Monck going back and forth, back and forth, bringing out fluorescent pant suits and granny gowns, miniskirts and trench coats, and hanging them on rolling racks on the pitch-dark sidewalk. When they went back inside, people would snatch clothes off the racks and walk away. At the time Marianne was shocked, but she has since reconsidered. "I should have done that, too," she says, "with my beautiful Buddhist robe."

It worked for Tiger Morse: she got the publicity she craved. Bill Cunningham at the *Chicago Tribune* wrote, "It was a cross between a Fellini movie and a nuthouse on the night of a full moon." The *Herald Tribune* crooned, "Tiger Morse's catwalk-sandbox-disco-cage fashion blast Monday night made all the other so-called 'far-out' fashion efforts to date look like square's play." They gleefully described the scene— models dancing down the rickety catwalk over the heads of the nervous mob, their fluorescent clothes throbbing in the black light; another model in bare feet, fishing over the edge, her pole hooked with a hypodermic needle—and the guests: "more than three hundred of New York's most spectacular, kooky creative people." Who was there? The designers Bill Halston and Pauline Trigere, "who did the Frug in a sleeveless white mink dress"; Mr. and Mrs. Andrew Goodman of Bergdorf Goodman's; the model Verushka; Lady Sarah Russell, daughter of the Earl of Marlborough. And of course, the reigning king of Pop, Andy Warhol, and his queen, Edie Sedgwick, who tried to steal the scene by climbing up on the catwalk with the models and doing the watusi.

In the end, though, there was to be no trickle-down for the Yoors, unless one counted the sand that leaked through the floorboards and into the office below. The Yoors were left the next day with their studio in ruins, and they spent weeks dismantling the catwalk and hauling out the sand in buckets, cleaning their tapestries and rehanging them, and restoring their home to its formerly peaceful state.

Tiger Morse, who used to say, "I am living proof that speed doesn't kill," died of an overdose in 1972. "I'm so grateful to Jan that Jan did not let us live that life," says Marianne, reflecting on the fate of Morse and so many in the art crowd. In the fifties, the escape of choice had been booze, in the sixties it was drugs, and no matter what the era, there was always sex. In the fast and loose art world, women were passed around like hors d'oeuvres at a cocktail party.

Marianne still bears some angers toward Jan, but being sheltered from that world isn't one of them. "Jan didn't want us to live that way. And I'm grateful for that, that I didn't have to go through that. We would not have had our life. Jan would not have done all that work. Jackson

Pollock would be in his studio and dribble and drink and get himself killed in a car crash. The other ones would commit suicide . . . We did not live that life. Our life was much more . . ." She pauses, searching for the right words. "We had lots of fun. We were not just little nuns living behind a cloistered wall. Absolutely not. We enjoyed ourselves, we had wonderful moments, we had beautiful music, nature, we did lots and lots of things. But I'm happy that I did not live that life."

31 The Models

Drawing the female form in charcoal was a daily exercise for Jan, and over his career he produced hundreds of figure studies. The charcoal-drawn figures, with their strong lines, were abstractions of femaleness—a single thick curve for a buttock, another for the dip of a lower back—and had the quality of memory and idea rather than actual flesh. Calling to mind the images of Gypsy women that had sustained him when he was in prison, Jan's vision transformed Marianne and all the models who followed her into iconic figures with solid limbs and brown skin, a lush fall of black hair, and dark almonds for eyes. They were, all of them, beautiful. They were life itself.

ON NIGHTS WHEN Jan was working late with his current model, Marianne and their neighbor Mary, whose husband was a night watchman, would keep each other company. One night, Marianne returned home very late to a quiet house. Annabert and the children had long since gone to bed. She opened the door leading to the hayloft and called up—Jan, are you there?—and thought, well, he must have taken the young woman to the bus. She called again, walking upstairs as she did. There was no answer. She reached the top and took one more step before she saw the two of them, lying under a blanket.

She ran downstairs but then, thinking better of it, came back up and threw down an ultimatum: she's out of the house, or I'm out of the house.

With that, she fled the studio. The neighbor's station wagon was parked on the street. She tried the door. It was unlocked, so she climbed inside. She was sobbing and panicked and wondering what to do next. Within five minutes, the front door of their building opened and Jan was

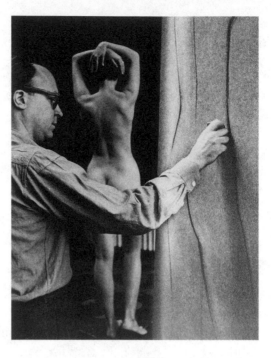

Jan drawing from model, 1962. Courtesy of the Yoors Family Partnership.

letting the model out. After she left, he stood in the doorway, looking left, looking right, waiting. Finally, he went inside and closed the door.

Marianne stayed in the station wagon for what seemed like an hour and cried until she was empty of tears. Jan came back downstairs to the street, and from inside the darkened car she watched him waiting. He had no idea where she was. He went back inside. She climbed out of the station wagon and began to walk. It was perhaps two in the morning, and the long blocks were deserted and quiet, with only a few cabs cruising First Avenue. As she walked, it slowly came to her that she had nowhere to go.

She circled back. Turning onto Forty-Seventh Street, she saw Jan standing again at their front door. Without saying a word, she brushed past him and went upstairs.

Marianne didn't see that model again, though the girl called the house late at night a few times when she was high on LSD and having a bad trip, and Jan would go take care of her. But this girl was beside the point. It wasn't about her, or rather it wasn't about her in particular. There had been others before this one, Marianne realized now; she herself had procured them. If Jan saw a girl at a party or on the street that he wanted for a model, it was always Marianne who approached her. That's my husband, she'd say, and he thinks you're beautiful and would like to paint you. She was good at it, and of course to the young woman it seemed perfectly safe because the wife was doing the asking. In the beginning Marianne hadn't minded, but later on she started minding it very much.

SOMETIME IN THE second half of 1966, an opportunity came from the architect Edward Sövik, who a few years earlier had commissioned the Yoors to create a tapestry for a Lutheran church in Minnesota designed by Sövik's firm.

On behalf of the First International Congress on Religion, Architecture and the Visual Arts, Sövik now commissioned Jan to spend more than half a year traveling around the world and photographing some ninety postwar buildings—primarily churches, synagogues, and temples designed by the leading modern architects—Le Corbusier, Alvar Aalto, Eero Saarinen, Mies van der Rohe, Frank Lloyd Wright, and I. M.

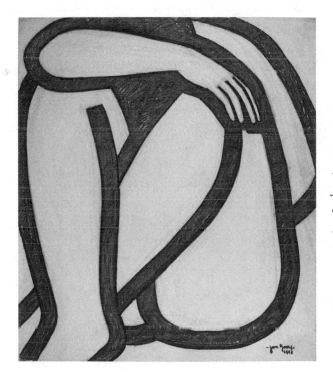

Charcoal on paper, 25.5 × 30 inches, Jan Yoors. Courtesy of the Yoors Family Partnership.

Pei—as well as examples of secular designs by those same architects. The purpose of the congress was to bring together architects, artists, theologians, and leaders from various faiths in order to discuss how architecture and the arts could best express and serve changing social and spiritual needs. An exhibit of the photographs would serve as a visual reference point.

Jan had two young children at home, a solo show of tapestries and photographs opening at the University of Texas Art Museum, and his Gypsy memoir about to come out. He also had a new model, a circumstance that always fired his creativity. Another man might not have been so eager to take off for several months, but for Jan an opportunity to travel around the world was irresistible. He probably would have done it for nothing, but it paid the not-inconsiderable sum of $9,500.

The first and shorter leg of his travels took him to South America for the month of December 1966. He returned to New York for the February release of his book, called simply *The Gypsies*. The reviews were enthusiastic and ubiquitous. Walter Starkie, regarded as the foremost expert on the Rom (and incidentally the man who had helped secure Jan's release from the concentration camp in Spain), contributed his praise at the *New York Times*. Margaret Mead wrote a long and incisive feature for *Redbook* magazine, and dozens upon dozens of reviews appeared across the country.

The book became a surprise hit for Simon & Schuster: in one month, the first printing sold out, the second printing was selling at a brisk clip, and a third had been ordered. Jan appeared on more than thirty television shows, including *Merv Griffin* and *Today*, and only the resumption of his travels at the end of March stopped the publisher from booking more.

Jan was riding high when he headed back out on the road. Rather than a Gypsy wagon, he now traveled by jet and stayed in swanky hotels, though once, while traveling with a hired driver in Uzbekistan, he happened to see a Gypsy caravan of fifty wooden wagons approaching. I'm getting out here, he told the driver, and spent a week traveling around Russia with this *kumpania*.

"It was wonderful," he later told an interviewer. "You might think they would have difficulty getting around in the U.S.S.R., which has internal passports, laws against nomads, and so on. But they managed. Whenever we came to a village, the police would come out. The Gypsies would apologize for having no permits and then say, 'But we are only going to our cousin's wedding. It's not in this village, but the next.' 'Oh, you mean over in Otokino' (or wherever), the police would say, figuring they'd let the authorities there deal with the problem of all these unauthorized people. 'Yes! Otokino! That's it,' the Gypsies would say, and would make a big show of asking directions. And the police would say, 'O.K., move along, then.' They had been traveling for months this way, all across the Soviet Union. The Russians have something of a soft spot in their hearts for Gypsies, after the third vodka, anyway."

Over five months, he logged stops in thirty-eight cities around the world, including Tokyo and Hong Kong, Bangkok, Kathmandu, New Delhi, Kabul, Tashkent, Moscow and Leningrad, and back to Europe— Helsinki and Stockholm and Copenhagen, Dusseldorf and Munich and Frankfurt, Rome and Milan, Zurich and Basel, and on and on. Daily letters went back and forth between Jan and his two wives, Jan describing his adventures, and Annabert and Marianne keeping him abreast with the life he'd left behind.

Your book is still on the bestseller list, Annabert reported, tallying for him the sales and printings and letting him know when one of his interviews was airing. She related the children's activities and told him about visitors to the studio. *Today we had a visit from three of your models.* The next day, two models came. *I made a soufflé*, Annabert wrote.

The new model, a lovely moon-faced Japanese girl named Itsumi, had become a regular visitor. She had been recommended to Jan by the model Marianne had evicted. The two women thought her a bit moody but attributed this to a romantic disappointment: not so long before, Itsumi had followed a man from her home in Japan, a musician who turned out to be married. Marianne and Annabert took her under their wings and were teaching her to weave. Sometimes when she wasn't in school, she stayed the night or the weekend with them. *Itsumi is now so pleasant; she lays in the hammock and sings little songs. She dreams of what she could make. She is full of the tapestry she is going to weave. I regret that she does not want to weave a tapestry of your design. So many of the young girls they want to do their own designs.*

One day, Itsumi was talking with the women and she let slip that Jan had been sick on his travels. He'd made no mention of illness in his letters to them. Annabert's curiosity got the better of her. She went upstairs to where Itsumi slept and found a packet of letters addressed to the girl in Jan's hand.

Shortly after her discovery, Annabert wrote a stunning letter to Jan. A merely forbearing wife might have forgiven him his infidelity, but Annabert went far beyond this. *I love you so much that you love her*, she wrote, *that you want to stop that floating little boat from drifting away and getting destroyed in this life. And that you want to help to give her purpose and a goal in her life. I am happy that you are a creative artist and that you see beauty in a person. How it will grow only you and Itsumi will know*. All she asked was that Jan try to include her and Marianne in his love for the younger woman.

She hadn't shared with Marianne her discovery, but Marianne made it on her own a few days later. Itsumi and another model, Marcia, were visiting, and when Marianne went upstairs to clean up after lunch and put some chopsticks in Itsumi's bag, she saw a letter with Jan's handwriting and under it a whole stack of letters.

She called for Annabert and showed her the incriminating evidence.

Well, didn't you *know*? Annabert asked. Didn't you expect that?

Maybe a part of her had known. Maybe Marianne had hidden the truth from herself. Regardless, she was outraged. Annabert pleaded with her to calm herself and keep her voice down, but when this proved impossible Annabert went downstairs and sent Marcia home, saying that it was just a little sister quarrel. Alone with Itsumi, Annabert explained that they'd seen her letters, and then gently chided her for leaving them lying about where others might happen on them accidentally, though secretly she suspected it was no accident on Itsumi's part.

She understood now, she said, the cause of Itsumi's moodiness. Of course, she must be so confused and fearful, but everything would be all right, Annabert assured her.

And then she led the girl upstairs to smooth things over with Marianne. Somehow, she brokered a peace between the two. Marianne tearfully explained to Itsumi that she wasn't angry with the young woman, that this was between herself and Jan, an avowal that must have genuinely puzzled Itsumi, who believed Marianne to be merely the sister-in-law.

Marianne was desperate to speak with Jan, and that evening she tried to place a long-distance call to his hotel in Kabul. The operator said she would call back when she had the party on the line. Two hours passed before the phone rang. It was the long-distance operator again: she couldn't complete the call because AT&T was unable to locate Kabul.

Marianne would have to content herself with putting pen to paper.

Kik deserves a golden crown, she wrote to Jan some days later. *Every evening there was a long letter from Annabert on my bed. I kept them for you. Last evening, early, Annabert stood before my bed, crying. She said that I should not think on small things but see the greatness of Jan's work. I told her of my feeling that I would never have a child. Jan would not be with me in his heart. Shall I then be only a Mammyjan for other children? And now I cannot call you and I cannot even tell you about my despair. How come I did not see that I was so stupid? Two months before I can talk with you. And then I will never let you go again. I cannot sleep, I feel so miserable without you. And all the time I was talking with Itsumi I didn't know anything.*

We went to the Brooklyn Museum and the Botanical Garden; it was so peaceful. Again she talked with me for hours. I wish that you would say the things that she told me. It would give me so much more confidence and courage. If I don't lose you, if I would be blessed with a child, if we would have the same peace and trust as we have had together for so long, then only the future will tell how everything will grow. Everything is now peaceful in my soul, although I wish I could cry in your arms and ask for lots of reassurance. But I love you and trust you.

Good friends, a couple whose children played with Lyuba and Vanya in the park, volunteered that they needed a nanny; perhaps Itsumi would care to come to Bridgehampton with them for the remainder of the summer? Annabert and Marianne were grateful for the reprieve. Annabert wrote to Jan that Itsumi had not been using her school vacation well. *She had good intentions but there is a strong hand needed. I tried my best, Marianne also. But with the summer and the warm weather she goes outside. She waits for you, but it is a bored waiting—sunbathing, Central Park, the beach, instead of doing something. Marianneke is very sweet, and Kik is also sweet to your models.*

Finally, after a little more than three months, Jan returned to New York on July 5. He was eager to bring Itsumi back to the studio to live with them, but here Annabert put her foot down, gently but firmly. Jan would first have to make things right with Marianne before he brought Itsumi back into their home.

This he did with the promise of a child.

Two weeks after his return, Jan brought his new love back from the Hamptons. He was head over heels, and now there was no need to conceal it. This is not to say that everything was out in the open, however. At least for the time being, he wanted to keep secret from Itsumi that Marianne was more than a sister to him. Presumably, the jig would be up if Marianne got pregnant, but meanwhile he alternated nights sleeping with Annabert and Itsumi, and arranged to come to Marianne's bed only when she was ovulating; then he would slip back to his new love.

32 The Blue Door on Waverly

That fall of 1967, they learned that their lease on the Forty-Seventh Street studio wouldn't be renewed; the building was coming down. (Andy Warhol's Silver Factory met the same fate a short time later.) The Yoors were devastated; they had made this loft their home for eight years, and it was ideally located for Jan, near the UN and the midtown galleries. It was hard to imagine they would find such a magnificent space again.

Marianne scoured the newspapers, searching under "Studios," thinking this must be the section of the Classifieds where artists' lofts were advertised. She wasn't having any luck: when she went to look at the apartments listed, invariably they were all just tiny, single rooms. One day, she accidentally looked under another heading—"Furnished Apartments"—and found something in the Village that seemed like it might be worth a look. They didn't want furniture, but at least it sounded bigger. They made an appointment, and when they got to the address on Waverly Place, just a few steps off Washington Square Park, Marianne caught her breath: it was a handsome granite-faced townhouse with a periwinkle blue door and a Gothic mullioned window in the front. Inside was a huge front room, and passing through that, an even larger room in the back, twenty-five by thirty feet, with high, beamed ceilings, a fireplace, and French doors opening onto a garden. Upstairs were a bedroom and bathroom with skylights, and another set of stairs that took one to the third floor, with two more big bedrooms and another bath.

The house was stuffed with belongings, but the landlady, a second wife who hated the place, was more than happy to jettison the furniture if they didn't want it. She'd even throw in a paint job. The rent was $800 a month, but they felt confident they could afford it. Jan's book was selling well and he was at work on the sequel. The women were busy weaving the first of two large tapestries for a bank in Nashville and had the promise of more commissions lined up behind these. Jan had also been getting occasional work shooting a series of short films of artists at work in their studios, for the prestigious Martha Jackson Gallery. It appeared likely, too, that Martha Jackson would invite him to join her roster of artists.

After nearly twenty years of struggling, the Yoors felt they had finally arrived at a place of security, symbolized by a real home. For the first time since they came to New York, they would have all the little niceties that came with a legal residential apartment, starting with rooms. Bedrooms, one for each of the three women, bathrooms, a big kitchen. They were ecstatic.

WITHIN A FEW weeks of moving, Marianne was pregnant. However, while still in the first trimester, one day she suddenly started bleeding. Panicked, she called out to Jan through the bathroom door.

How much? he wanted to know. A cup? A thimble?

Marianne was hysterical. Buckets, she cried. Buckets.

Her doctor told her to go straight to the hospital. In the taxi, Marianne sobbed and Jan tried to reassure her. Listen, he said, you became pregnant once, you can become pregnant again.

But the baby was still there. The doctor examined her and told her that this was a threatened abortion, but there was still a heartbeat. They kept her overnight, gave her injections, and then sent her home the next morning with strict instructions to go to bed and not to move for the remainder of the pregnancy.

She settled into her spacious, sunlit bedroom on the top floor of their new home with a pile of books. Marianne was constitutionally a worrier, and there were no sonograms, no amniocentesis, no way of knowing if the baby was okay, but inexplicably, she felt serene. She read and looked out the window and watched with joy as her belly expanded. Jan and Annabert and Itsumi fussed over her and brought up special foods. It was the happiest time in her life.

On the morning of October 24, 1968, Marianne went into labor. Annabert, Itsumi, and the children waited excitedly at home, while Jan and Marianne went to the hospital. Natural childbirth, with the father present in the birthing room, was newly the fashion, and so as Marianne pushed through a long and difficult labor, she listened to Jan entertain the doctor and nurses with stories of his life with the Gypsies. When, late that night, she finally delivered the baby, it was Jan who told her its sex.

Een zoontje, Jan said, a son, and then, He looks like a real Yoors.

This is your child, Marianne thought. I want you to be involved with this child. With this child, I have you. She consciously staked a claim, away from the other women and all the other affairs.

Jan named the baby Kore, after his long-gone best friend. Then, so that he might give Kore his last name as well, he divorced Annabert and married Marianne. Although the idea was attributed to Annabert, she was careful to write on the envelope containing the divorce papers a note of clarification for posterity: *Jan and I love each other very much, and this is just so Marianne can marry Jan.*

Marianne claimed that she didn't see the point of getting married. Still, it must have taken a little of the sting out of her former role as the sister. She was now the official wife, and Annabert assumed the role of the sister-in-law. As for Itsumi, when it was necessary to explain her presence, she was identified as an apprentice weaver.

MARIANNE THOUGHT THAT nobody on the outside knew about their life; Annabert was not so naive. How can you be so stupid? she once asked Marianne. Of course, everybody knows what's going on.

Probably the ruse held up, provided others didn't look too closely. A fellow Village artist, Walter Gaudnek, remembers only that Jan lived with two sisters. But those who spent more time around the Yoors began to see cracks in the story.

"For one thing," the former model Marcia McBroom Small remarks, "Annabert and Mammyjan [Marianne] didn't really look much alike."

"At first I bought the wife and sister thing," the dancer Morocco says, "because Annabert had just had a baby. And that was what the relationship seemed. It was only as I noticed the interaction, and while there wasn't much physical demonstration, there was a similarity of attitude and language. If it was a wife and a sister-in-law, there would have been differences. And it wasn't something that was overt and obvious; it was only when I wasn't in the middle of it and I was elsewhere, and I was thinking, Hmm. Hmm. There's a little more here than meets the eye."

"The story as we were allowed to think it," Michael Korda says, "was that Marianne was his sister and Annabert was his wife. That story was maintained, even after Itsumi came along and it no longer quite held together."

For whatever reason, when the two "sisters" switched places, it went unremarked upon, at least to the Yoors directly. Even if people wondered about the setup, it was not the kind of thing you could ask about. It's possible that some wrote off any confusion as just that, their own misunderstanding, but no doubt others guessed at the truth and simply didn't care who was sleeping with whom. After all, this was Greenwich Village.

THE VILLAGE WAS no longer the same neighborhood they'd left in 1959. When the city's docks began to close down in the mid-sixties, the working-class families moved out, stranding the little mom-and-pop shops they had supported. The middle class followed, fleeing to the suburbs to escape a rising tide of crime, corruption, and failing schools. On Mayor Lindsay's first day in office in 1966, the unions shut down the entire city with a transit strike. Under his leadership, the city went from bad to worse: two years later, the teachers' union staged a series of strikes that lasted seven months, and that same year, when the sanitation workers walked off the job, New Yorkers endured streets piled high with stinking, burning garbage. The police instigated slowdowns, and the firefighters threatened similar actions. Even Broadway turned off its lights for three days.

Around the corner from the Yoors, Washington Square Park was overrun by derelicts, addicts, and runaways, and muggings and burglaries had become commonplace. A decade earlier, disaffected suburban kids had flocked to the Village dressed like beatniks; now a new generation wandered the streets costumed in fringe and tie-dye, smoking weed and listening to Jimi Hendrix and Bob Dylan.

In late June 1969, the Stonewall riots erupted a mere two blocks away from the Yoors' studio. For generations the police had routinely raided gay bars, harassing customers and arresting any who were dressed in drag or who didn't provide an ID. That night, the normally passive crowd didn't cooperate, and the police decided to haul them all in. While they waited in line for the extra paddy wagons to arrive, the bar's patrons grew restless. A woman who complained that her handcuffs were too tight was answered with a billy club, and the crowd snapped. Next thing, the crowd was fighting back, first throwing pennies, then beer bottles and then paving stones. Word went out, and they were joined by others in the gay community. Each successive night, the rioting escalated until there were two or three thousand demonstrators blocking traffic on Christopher Street, smashing car windows, setting fires in garbage cans, and yelling pro-gay slogans. Battalions of police in riot gear retaliated with tear gas.

Marianne and Annabert, ensconced behind the two-foot-thick granite walls of 108 Waverly Place, heard not a thing and were so isolated that they only learned of the riot years later.

If the Yoors family was unconventional in its makeup, the household was otherwise a curiously traditional haven in the strung-out heart of late sixties and early seventies Greenwich Village. Michael Korda describes it "as a kind of charmed circle of peace and calm in New York City." He visited often, bringing his young son with him because Jan's family had a soothing effect on the boy. One of the women would serve the men Turkish coffee and little homemade biscuits or cakes, and then Jan and Korda would talk while his son played with the other children. Sun streamed in through the French windows, classical music played on the stereo, and always, Korda recalls, there were at least two enormous tapestries on the looms, and the women in their floor-length skirts clicking away.

"I always felt like I was stepping into the old world," Marcia McBroom remembers, "back to Europe, when I was with them. And it's funny, because whenever I would be there, you could just get lost in that world. You could just not want to leave. It was very seductive, very seductive."

Donna Schwartz, another regular visitor, concurs: "You'd walk in through the kitchen. Somebody would come to the door, usually either Itsumi or Marianne, but someone in an old batik dress and socks, and it always smelled of fresh bread and something brewing. And there was a fire and the old cat sitting in the chair that she didn't ever want to relinquish. And in later years, Kore's iguana. The sense of that house, three women notwithstanding, was very much of a warm, nurturing family atmosphere when you went there. It was in so many ways a refuge from nutty New York going on all around you. You'd open that blue door and the world would disappear. It was calm and it was serene and it was welcoming."

In the front room, Jan drew Itsumi, and inspired by her he began to sculpt again. In the back, Annabert presided over the child-centered household. Like the March family in *Little Women*, they dipped candles and sewed and crafted finger puppets, making each other presents for birthdays and Christmas or saving their pennies to buy the person something special. They hand-painted the kitchen cabinets and embroidered the pillows. At Christmas, they went with their friend Cynthia Mead and her children out to the country to cut down a tree, and then decorated it with paper chains and Mexican eyes of God made from tapestry yarn. To ring in 1973, Itsumi cooked a Japanese dinner over an open fire and they played games, with everyone trying to draw a face while blindfolded and then laughing at the results. A week later, Marianne baked a three kings cake with three beans hidden inside for good luck. The children made crowns, and after dinner they put on a play: Lyuba played Mary; Vanya was Joseph; and Kore, outfitted with his new armor and a homemade tail of red wool, insisted on playing a good devil to protect Mary and Joseph.

On another weekend, Annabert took Vanya and Lyuba for a ride on the Staten Island Ferry and recounted the day in her diary. *The wharf had patches of ice against the wooden beams. The water was all shiny, the sky luminous light Prussian. The Trade Center towers just sparkled with light from all its finished floors and then like stars dots of lights on the unfinished floors. The moon was three quarters. We looked at the fire boat. We stood outside on the back of the ferry. The steam was a cloud of white. The waves speeded past. We went very close to the Statue of Liberty. We saw the lighthouse light going on and off, and black silhouettes of seagulls flying past.*

So it went round the calendar, and round it again, with Annabert recording a steady procession of tapestries going up and then coming down off the looms, the weaving interspersed with school projects and weekend outings to sled or skate in Central Park, and then in the spring to the botanical garden. In the summers, they would go to the beach or load up Cynthia's old station wagon with all the kids in the back and drive out to her little house in the country. After the first of these trips, Jan and Itsumi stayed behind in the city; it was too hectic and noisy for him, and he enjoyed the uninterrupted time with Itsumi. On Sunday evening, everyone would spill back into the house, interrupting each other to tell Pappy and Itsumi stories about their adventures and to show them the treasures they had found, the sand dollars or sunflowers or interesting rocks. In the fall, they took a train back up to the country to see the leaves change, to walk in the woods and through the apple orchards, to drink cider and cut down dried cornstalks and bittersweet branches with which to decorate the house for Halloween.

THOUGH MARIANNE AND Annabert relished their busy domesticity, there was a shadow side. The threefold cord that had bound them so tightly to Jan in the early years had subtly loosened. The three no longer worked closely together—choosing colors for the tapestries, helping Jan with his projects, talking everything over together—and Annabert mourned the lost intimacy of their shared creativity. She couldn't quite put a finger on when or how this had happened—or rather, she could but wouldn't confess it directly, not even to the diary she wrote in every night. It hadn't

Marianne sweeping the sidewalk in front of 108 Waverly Place. Courtesy of the Yoors Family Partnership.

The Blue Door on Waverly

been the babies, she wrote, for they continued to work happily those first three years. Three years, it was a telling slip. That was Lyuba's age when Itsumi came to live with them.

Somehow, she confessed, Jan and Itsumi had taken over their working relationship. As soon as she wrote it, though, she backed away from that mutinous confession. *It was the layout of our house, too—the separate working late in the night, very late. And there became a gap—because the children had to wake up early and go to school.* Recalling that she and Jan had also stopped holding hands on their walks after Itsumi came, she noted that the change had been less noticeable at the time because she now had the hands of their children to hold.

They still did lots of things together, but there wasn't the peaceful harmony that the two women had cherished. Itsumi didn't want to share Jan, and she competed for first place in his affections.

If this change was difficult for Annabert, she had at least made the wrenching adjustment of sharing her husband long ago. When Marianne first came to live with them, Annabert and Jan had constructed a mythology around his infidelity that made it acceptable, even positive. They were a threefold cord, and their union served the higher purpose of Jan's art. Having once reconciled herself to this idea that Jan needed more than one woman, the succession that followed must have felt like part of a deal she had already signed off on. Ironically, though, Marianne, who had formerly been the other woman, had a harder time making the same concession.

Looking back on those years, Marianne makes a confession. "My sweet husband was dedicated to so many women, and I wanted him for myself."

When reminded that she had once denied wanting to be Jan's only wife, she smiles mischievously.

"Then I was lying." She laughs.

After another moment, she says simply, "I never thought about that. I never thought about it. Annabert was there."

33 Survival

In a 1949 letter to Marianne, Jan had laid out rosy predictions for their future. *We will have of course all the money we need and will be able to concentrate totally on our work. No money worries will stand in our way. No upstairs neighbors, downstairs, on the side, only our own studio.* So often over the years, the Yoors seemed on the cusp of realizing this dream.

In the late sixties, the legendary gallery owner Martha Jackson took an interest in Jan. She brokered a big commission for him with the prominent architectural firm of Skidmore, Owings, and Merrill—two large tapestries for the Buffalo headquarters of Marine Midland Bank—and they were discussing the possibility of the gallery representing him. Jan was now known more for his film and photography than for his art, which was a frustration for him, but Jackson could change this; she had already shepherded to fame such artists as Paul Jenkins, Louise Nevelson, Willem de Kooning, Jim Dine, and Joan Mitchell. As part of its commitment, the gallery also typically offered its artists a stipend to free them from any day-to-day financial worries. However, in July 1969 Jackson died unexpectedly at age sixty-two. This was a blow to Jan, for the loss of her friendship as well as her patronage. Two years later, Jan's follow-up memoir, *Crossing*, came out to meet a disappointingly muted reception.

Still, these disappointments were offset by considerable successes. The Yoors were commissioned to design and weave two large tapestries for the lobby of a new steel and glass skyscraper at 1700 Broadway, and there were several tapestries for other buildings. Annabert summed up March 1972 with some quick notes in her diary: they had just finished the second of the tapestries for Marine Midland Bank, and now a man named Richard Roth was thinking he would purchase two tapestries for his brothers. Jan was dreaming of larger quarters and had found a house for sale nearby on Greene Street that would be perfect, with three floors and a huge basement for the studio. *Will it be possible to afford it?* Annabert wondered. *Will the commissions come through? We are in suspense.*

A year later, in March 1973, there was no further mention of buying a house. Annabert was a master of the bright outlook, but uncharacteristically, her optimism faltered. *Several large scale commissions that made us dream of years of security seem to drag or not to materialize. It is frustrating. The commission of four tapestries of 20 X 20 feet for the architect Bernard Shaw in Chicago seems to be almost lost because the building is going to be sold. Still many things are possible, commission-wise. We just have to muddle through, hoping something will come up before we run out of money. Prices go up, tuition fee goes up, up—but with some luck we will manage. Marianne bakes her delicious bread, sometimes raisin bread, sometimes rye and whole wheat. It is most delicious and our home smells so good when the bread is in the oven.*

We are also inviting more people for dinner. In February, Itsumi cooked real Japanese dinner for 30 people—two trustees of the Museum of Modern Art were there, Robert Hughes, the art critic of the New York Times, the architect Abramowitz, James Johnson Sweeney, the Minskovs [sic], etc. Itsumi even barbecued some meat over an open fire. It was very successful. Next Wednesday we have another dinner. Last night Jan, Marianne, and Itsumi were invited for dinner at Mrs. Smith's—a trustee of the Museum of Modern Art. They came home at 2:30 a.m. They again met Robert Hughes and went to his home afterwards.

For every commission or sale, there were many near-misses—the promising contact that went nowhere, the initial interest that fizzled, the deal that fell through—and they would have to rally their spirits and make another push. Some months the Yoors were flush; in others, Annabert quietly sought help. Their parents sent checks to tide them over, and friends came through with timely purchases of art.

In just about any other profession, this might be deemed failing; however, in the arts the measure of success is not financial security. All but a few artists struggle to pay their bills. This is the compact the artist makes with the universe: to create with no guarantee of remuneration, and yet to live always in expectation and hope. It requires nerve, faith, perseverance, and above all the ability to survive disappointment. Whether musicians, visual artists, actors, or writers, it falls out pretty much the same: of the hordes of young hopefuls, only a small handful will ever achieve fame and fortune. Theirs are the names we recognize and whose stories we hear, though even these stories rarely chart a steady upward graph. As for the rest, disillusionment weeds out many early on. They go back home or back to school. They find more sensible means to make their way in the world. Drugs and alcohol take another, disproportionate, cut.

Success, ultimately, is remaining in the game. The Yoors had been at this for twenty-five years now. Better yet, after the first few years, they'd been able to do it without second jobs, a feat made even more impressive by their significant overhead. The scope of Jan's ambition was visible not only in the size of his tapestries but also in the size of his tribe. His dream was of mythic proportions. But like the Gypsies, the Yoors found their joy in the moment, in the journey rather than the destination.

IN AUTUMN 1973, Jan was painting the walls of the studio when the room suddenly blurred. His left eye was hemorrhaging. Two years previously, he had experienced a similar episode, and a specialist had insisted he call

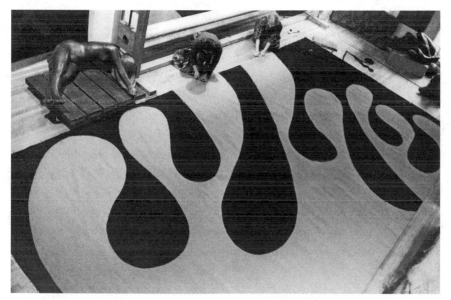

Hemming Red Shape on Black *tapestry in Waverly Place studio, 1970.*
Courtesy of the Yoors Family Partnership.

off his travel plans and get a full work-up, but Jan declined to follow the advice. This time the symptoms were more severe. Reluctantly, he went to a different specialist, one who told him what he wanted to hear, that his vision would gradually clear up. As the weeks passed, though, his eyesight didn't improve.

By their nature hemorrhages are sudden, but this had been years in coming. Traveling with the Rom, working in the Resistance, languishing in prisons: a commonality in all these situations was the absence of medical attention. The medical care available to an artist in the early fifties was only moderately better. Consequently, Jan had long ago cultivated a stoic disregard for his own physical ailments.

However, not too long after Jan first arrived in New York, slowly worsening symptoms had led him to consult a doctor he befriended at a party. Dr. Alton had diagnosed him with diabetes and agreed to treat him in exchange for paintings. Alton never actually tried to collect any art in payment, but this arrangement allowed Jan to be treated for free without feeling indebted. The doctor put Jan on a daily regimen of insulin injections and, presumably, a restricted diet, though it doesn't seem that Jan observed it. At some point, Dr. Alton switched Jan from the insulin to a new drug that could be taken orally, called Orinase. Except for the occasional check-up, Jan was thus able to more or less forget about his disease for years—that is, provided he could overlook the fact that the dosage required to keep his blood sugar stable was creeping up inexorably. By 1973, he was taking sixteen tablets of Orinase a day when the maximum recommended daily dose was three. Jan had been taking the wrong medication for years, but he didn't want to know.

The city of Ghent in Belgium had offered Jan a retrospective in St. Peter's Abbey. Jan was thrilled: they were proposing an exhibit of his work significantly larger than had ever been mounted. It would be a career highlight as well as an artistic homecoming for Jan, whose work hadn't been shown in the country of his birth since he'd left in 1950. He traveled to Ghent in early October 1973 to discuss the plans, and he returned to New York exuberant at the prospect of their tapestries hanging in the beautiful stone hall at the abbey. Amidst all the animated discussion, he mentioned in passing that while there, he had stubbed his toe and it was bothering him.

The toe was infected. Dr. Alton examined Jan, then gave him a solution in which to bathe his foot every night.

Shortly after Jan's return, Richard and Cynthia Mead invited the Yoors to celebrate the Jewish holiday of Sukkot at their home in Connecticut, where they were now living full-time. Richard had built a temporary shelter in the garden made of sticks and roofed with grasses. Inside was a long table lit with candles and heaped with fruits and candies. The *sukkah*, he explained, symbolized the temporary dwellings of the Israelites during the Exodus from Egypt.

The week before, Egypt and Syria had attacked Israeli forces in the Sinai and the Golan Heights, and war had broken out. Even at this very moment, American planes were carrying weapons to Israel. After dinner, they listened to lilting folk songs on the portable stereo. The candles flickered beautifully, and they were glad to be with their friends again, but the mood of the evening was mournful. War had come again, always war and more war. Annabert noted with an ineffable mixture of joy and envy how Cynthia nestled into the nook of Richard's arm. How in love they were. Her own husband was quieter than usual, his expression a mask.

Perhaps an hour after dinner he said he was sorry but they would have to leave early because his foot was bothering him. Annabert knew that the pain must be unendurable for him to admit to it aloud. She was afraid.

For nearly two months, they continued to bathe Jan's foot, but the toe wasn't healing. If anything, it was getting worse. Finally, on the first Saturday in December, Dr. Alton came to the house, took one look at Jan's foot, and told them that Jan had to go to the hospital. If he had suggested this before, they might have ignored him because they couldn't afford it, but there was no longer a choice in the matter.

Marianne asked, Can we go to your hospital?

No. Dr. Alton was firm on this point. In this country, he said, you have to go to the hospital in your neighborhood.

This was untrue, but Alton probably feared being censured by his peers or sued for malpractice. He directed Jan to the emergency room at St. Vincent's, and this was the last they ever saw of the doctor.

Over Annabert's protests, Jan insisted that she and Marianne should go ahead as planned and attend the children's school fair taking place that day. Annabert had worked hard on the fair for weeks, he said. Itsumi could take him to St. Vincent's.

When they returned that evening, the house was dark and empty. Jan was still at the hospital, where he was to remain for four months.

34 The Gypsy King

The toe was gangrenous and too far gone to save, so the doctors at St. Vincent's amputated it. This initiated a terrible sequence of tortures that brought back memories of prison to Jan. He was still in incredible pain and kept asking for more painkillers. At first the doctors thought he just wanted the morphine, but when they finally checked under the bandages, they saw that the infection had spread beyond the toe, and the flesh was putrefying. So they amputated his foot, and when this also proved insufficient they went higher and cut off his leg up to the knee. While under the anesthesia, he had a heart attack and was moved into intensive cardiac care, where for a week he hovered between life and death. The women kept vigil and took turns visiting him for their allotted fifteen minutes every other hour.

One night, when it was Annabert's turn, she sat in the darkened room watching with fascination the small green light on a screen tracing Jan's heartbeat. Jan stirred and began to murmur—he believed himself to be in Korea, a vision prompted by the Korean nurses in their white uniforms who floated quietly about the room, guided by tiny lights on the floor like runway strips. It began to snow, and through the window they could see the Con Edison clock tower, with its beacon of green light pointing up into the heavens. The sight soothed her, and for the first time in months she felt strangely at peace and unafraid.

Jan came out of intensive care, but his ordeal wasn't over. The right leg also began to die. The surgeons put new veins in to try to save it, but when the veins collapsed, this leg, too, had to be amputated to the knee. And then above the knee. Because his doctors were trying to save as much of his legs as they could, Jan endured six surgeries altogether, losing one piece of his body after another. He was also blind in one eye. When Jan was first admitted, a specialist had wanted to try laser beam treatments in the hopes of restoring his vision. It was a new and unproven procedure, though, and Jan's doctor was skeptical. Jan decided no, he had had enough. He was resigned to his fate, believing that he would never leave the hospital. When one of his doctors, shaken by Jan's ongoing tribulations, asked him why he was not cursing God, he replied, What god would I curse?

Jan was hardly more than skin and bones. The women began bringing him nourishing meals from home to build up his strength, and so that he might feel the security of their work continuing Annabert and Itsumi put up a new warp on the loom and started to weave an orange and black abstract to be called "Written in Fire." Meanwhile, Marianne, as the legal wife, was faced with the frightening pile of medical bills. They had no health insurance and no money, but because their income varied so wildly, it wasn't clear whether they qualified for public assistance either.

At the Social Security office, Marianne began to itemize their difficulties to a social worker, when the woman held up her hand and stopped her.

Can you wait just a moment? she asked.

She got up and left the office and when she returned, asked Marianne to follow her to another office where several people were working. She asked Marianne to start her story again at the beginning. As Marianne related Jan's medical odyssey, other women began to gather around the desk. They wept.

Arrangements were made, papers were quietly shuffled and signed, and Medicaid covered all of Jan's hospital bills.

A week before his birthday in April 1974, weighing 102 pounds and equipped with prostheses and a wheelchair, Jan finally came home. He was afraid that the children would be horrified to have their father returned to them without legs, but they accepted it with ease. Kore, then five, returned home from school with two little friends. All three expressed curiosity about the prostheses standing in the corner.

Are they real legs? Can we touch them?

Marianne listened from the kitchen to the boys' questions and Jan's matter-of-fact explanations.

With the help of Vanya and Kore, Itsumi had built a bed for Jan in the dining alcove so that he would not have to heave himself up the steps to reach the women's bedrooms. Later Annabert would move to the couch downstairs so that she might be close to him at all times.

They hadn't told anyone about his illness. Absolutely no one. Jan was insistent. He didn't want visitors coming with their sympathy. He just wanted to get back to work and resume his normal life.

At 3:00 A.M. on that first night home, the phone rang. Annabert answered, and the voice was speaking in Romany, so she carried the phone to Jan. He didn't know the voice, a Gypsy calling from Copenhagen, which had become an international meeting place for Roma.

Vanya, the voice said, addressing Jan by his Gypsy name. We've heard the news. We're coming.

Three weeks later, there was another phone call, again in the middle of the night, this time from Barcelona.

Don't worry, the voice said. We are on the way.

He told Jan that he was one of the sons of another Gypsy, Ruva, whom Jan remembered from his time in Spain thirty years earlier.

Yes, the voice said, the last time we saw you, you had started shaving but we had not.

Jan dimly remembered that Ruva had had small children.

We've been traveling many years in South Africa. Rafi and his *kumpania* are coming from Australia. They will meet us in Montreal and then we will all come to you there.

Three weeks later, he called again to tell Jan they were there: some thirty Rom, men, women, and children. They stayed at a hotel in Coney Island and came to see Jan every day. Marianne, Annabert, and Itsumi roasted whole pigs in the fireplace for them and sometimes they went out—they liked Chinese restaurants—and the whole group would walk over to Chinatown, a procession nearly a block long with Jan in his wheelchair at the head of the parade, like a legendary Gypsy king.

They stayed for three months and then suddenly one day they were gone.

THE GYPSIES HAD come in order to spur Jan back to life, and he returned to that life with a furious zeal, defying his physical weakness. He began planning another book, this one to be about the Roma, from Siberia to Peru, who had survived the concentration camps, showing the ways their culture had changed but continued to thrive.

When, in May 1974, his other eye began to hemorrhage, he agreed to the pioneer laser beam treatments. If he couldn't see, he couldn't make his art, and he had much yet to accomplish. The first treatment at Presbyterian Hospital took only half an hour and improved his vision in that eye immediately. He was sent home with instructions to suspend his rehab and avoid strenuous activity for a month, but at the end of this furlough he again took up the grueling rehabilitation sessions. Every afternoon, Itsumi wheeled him up the street to St. Vincent's Hospital where for two hours he worked to regain his strength and to learn to walk on his new artificial limbs.

The upcoming retrospective scheduled for January 1975 in Belgium gave the Yoors a future to focus on. Though Jan didn't have the strength to sculpt, he continued to draw and paint. They set to work cataloging and photographing all their work for the show, and sank the money from a new tapestry commission into having two of Jan's larger-than-life figures of Itsumi cast in bronze.

Each day was met with a heightened awareness that a person is given only a limited number of days, and that life is almost unbearably poignant. Annabert, always alert to the metaphors provided by nature, wrote, *The trees are now full of green leaves—there is shadow and sun. The linden trees are in bloom and the smell is sweet and overwhelming. The chestnut trees are full of small green fruits. And the park is full of families—and everywhere are handicapped people—old but also young. It is a part of life that is so important, and until now my eyes were closed for it—our work, our life took all my energy. It still does but now there is a greater awareness because of Jan. We have to suffer to become better human beings. I still sometimes have the outcry Why? Why my Jan, my love, why does he have to be physically so hard hit? But it is useless to cry out like this—it hurts more and it does not help.*

The retrospective was the brainchild of their friend Marc Galle, a linguist, professor, and influential politician in the Belgian Socialist Party. He also persuaded the Belgian public television station, VRT, to make a companion documentary on Jan, and in September 1974 the crew arrived in New York to film at the house on Waverly Place. In spite of his efforts, Jan hadn't recovered sufficient strength to walk on the prosthetics and in fact never would; this would be his first time really facing the world from a wheelchair. He did so with his accustomed self-assurance. As he had with countless previous visitors, he took the film crew to meet his friends in Harlem and in Chinatown, and to see the Rom. They went to one of his favorite haunts in the Village, the Feenjon Café on MacDougal Street owned by his friend Manny Dworman, and they listened to the lively Middle Eastern house band, made up of Greek, Arab, Israeli, and Armenian musicians. Back in the studio, Jan sat in a chair, his infirmity hidden by the new legs. Behind him, the three women and his daughter Lyuba worked at the loom, their backs to the camera, their fingers playing the threads like harpists.

Jan talked about the city he loved. "New York is the world in miniature." He paused, thoughtfully. "The whole world is in New York. That's why I made it my home." Uncharacteristically, his delivery seemed pedantic, but the ponderous pace, the long pauses between words disguised his effort to breathe.

> STOP ALL PACKING. EXHIBITION YOORS MAY NOT TAKE PLACE. WILL LET YOU KNOW IN A WEEK.

They received the distressing telegram just before Christmas, from the shipping company in The Hague charged with transporting their work. The exhibit was scheduled to open in only weeks. Jan immediately put in a call to Marc Galle. When Galle got back to him, they learned that the cost of packing all the tapestries and paintings and shipping them by air far exceeded the city of Ghent's budget. Galle worked frantically through the Christmas and New Year holidays, and finally secured an agreement from the minister of transportation to ship the art on military transport planes, and from the minister of culture to pay for the cost of printing the catalog. This left the city of Ghent to cover only the cost of insuring the art. The show was rescheduled to open in February.

When the date finally arrived, the entire family—Jan, Annabert, Marianne, Itsumi, Lyuba, Vanya, and Kore—went to Belgium. In the medieval stone hall of St. Peter's Abbey hung 31 tapestries, 68 paintings, and large numbers of photographs and drawings. The Yoors could see the scope of their lives' work spread out before them, from the first Old Testament designs to sculptures that had been cast only a few months before.

They were entertained lavishly and given a beautiful house to use for the length of their stay. Friends and family came to Ghent, and the Yoors also made trips to Antwerp and to The Hague to visit their parents. Jan went to a big Gypsy funeral and reconnected with Rom in the vicinity, including his sister Keja, whom he had believed to be dead. They remained in Belgium for three months.

35 The Dragon

The summer after the retrospective, Marianne saw a beautiful young Japanese girl in the park. She struck up a conversation, not without effort because the girl spoke hardly any English, and persuaded her to come model for Jan. "I think there was a little touch of evil in me," Marianne confesses. "I think I wanted to introduce Jan and get a little bit of the attention away from Itsumi."

The plan worked. Aiko captivated Jan. Her shy beauty and innocence allowed him pleasant interludes when he forgot his present circumstances, that he was sick and crippled and thirty-five years her senior. He began to draw her figure, telling her his stories as he sketched, and in the reflection of her growing adoration, he felt young and inspired. He took up sculpting again.

Jan finds comfort in the morning visits of Aiko, who is so gentle and cheerful. Her entrance into our life does bring changes. It is almost like a new baby born in a family—yet so different—but it brings change—with change there is extra stress—emotional readjustments necessary in life to keep it flowing instead of stagnant.

Rarely in her diaries was Annabert so evasive. The bald truth was that the tranquility of the house, already strained by Itsumi's arrival six years earlier and then by Jan's illness, was often stretched past the breaking point. It wasn't Aiko's fault—by everyone's account, she was sweet and silent as a little mouse in the corner, and everyone in the family liked her—it was just simply too, too much. Itsumi became increasingly domineering. Annabert retreated for eight and ten hours a day into the lulling rhythm of weaving, and Marianne, who had never forgiven Jan for bringing Itsumi into the house, avoided him altogether.

As for Jan, after breakfast he disappeared into his studio with Aiko and shut the door. In the past, he had been fond of quoting Michelangelo: "O, Lord, grant me to always desire more than I can accomplish." Now that it seemed certain he would be granted his wish, he tried to pack the passions and ambitions of a lifetime into a shortened space. He did scores of charcoal drawings. He made small models for sculptures in wax, clay, and plaster, and instructed Itsumi how to oversee their casting so that they might be finished to his specifications should he not be there to see to it himself. Because painting full-scale color cartoons for the tapestries took too much time, he made small gouaches instead and showed Itsumi how to enlarge them, or he simply made drawings and indicated colors and sizes with notes and snippets of yarn. Though he never discussed it with his wives, he was painfully conscious that he would be leaving his family in financial jeopardy, and this would be their only legacy. He worked himself to his limit every morning and then fell into an exhausted sleep in the afternoons.

On January 31, 1976—Chinese New Year—the Yoors met their friend Wei for lunch at their favorite restaurant in Chinatown. He had reserved the table in the window, and so the nine of them crowded around the little round table and watched the show on the other side of the glass: different colored lions—red and blue and green—dancing down the street, led by clowns and surrounded by their entourages of young men with ceremonial weapons. Drummers ran from storefront to storefront, begging for money and then danced joyously when they received it. Hundreds of firecrackers exploded, and the street filled with smoke and the stinging smell of sulphur. The mood was magical, and after lunch the Yoors children rushed outside to light their own firecrackers and add to the joyous mayhem.

The smoke was too much for Jan. Quietly, Itsumi and Aiko wheeled him out of Mott Street and found a taxi. Marianne and Annabert stayed with the children.

Then came the dragon, mythological symbol of good fortune for those who are worthy. A huge, writhing serpent in green and gold, it was manipulated by fifteen young men dressed in matching sweatshirts and green pants. They twisted and turned the dragon, swinging it around in circles, and the children squealed and screamed in excitement. Heaven and earth exploded in fire and smoke.

THE FOLLOWING EVENING, Jan's breathing was still labored, and his chest felt as though someone were standing on it. His new doctor admitted him into Lenox Hill Hospital and, unsure if Jan had had a small heart attack, kept him in the intensive care unit for five days. He remained in the hospital for another five days of complete rest. Meanwhile, two winter storms had blanketed the city in deep snow. The children were excited by the change in routine, and the next weekend, while Aiko visited Jan, the rest of the family went sledding in Central Park.

Jan came home from the hospital and returned to his work as though nothing had happened. As they always had, the family gathered together at meals. The women encouraged the children to talk about their projects at school and pretended to cheerfulness even when they didn't feel it.

Why be a cloud, Jan would tell the children, when you can be a star?

He acted as their example. I am grateful for my handicaps, he insisted, bringing his hands down with conviction on the sides of his wheelchair. I am grateful for the opportunity to be bound more than ever to my home and close to you all.

As best they could, they tried to be the happy *kumpania* that Jan wanted them to be. Inevitably, though, tensions would spill over. Marianne had all but stopped talking to him, but occasionally she would break her silence to issue sharp little challenges, even in front of guests. Lyuba, now a teenager and testing her independence, also got into disputes with her father. It was the mid-seventies: the other kids in her class were wearing bell-bottoms and makeup, but Jan forbade it and insisted she stay in long skirts and braids. While he admired his daughter's spirit, Jan was unused to being challenged, and the challenges were coming now from all sides. Frustrated by his failing health and in pain more often than he let on, Jan was no longer the master of his temper. Annabert confided to Marianne one morning that she had heard a commotion coming from Itsumi and Jan's room the night before. She had snuck up to the door, put her ear to it, and listened to them fight.

Even Annabert, who had never in her life found fault with Jan, took her turn. When he talked to the children about the prospect that he and Aiko would go sledding with them come winter, she felt angry that he would even talk this way. *My fear*, she wrote later, *became this black shaggy cat that kept creeping in through different doors. I worried about Aiko,*

I worried about almost everything. I did not love you less, schat, *but I was angry at your taking up a task that seemed too much.*

One night they fought bitterly. At the height of their dispute, he shook his wheelchair so hard that he accidentally fell forward and onto the floor, screaming. Annabert ran upstairs, leaving him as he was on the floor. She just couldn't cope anymore, but it was a momentary lapse of love that she regretted for the rest of her life.

Still, there were other moments when they came together again with the old deep tenderness that had seemed lost. One afternoon, Annabert was at the loom weaving and a song came on the radio, the Moroccan-Israeli singer Jo Amar singing a favorite of hers and Jan's. "Lulu be my own. You are my heart, my hope, my life, my little one." She began to cry silently, and Jan came over to her and put his hand on her shoulder. She leaned into his breast and wept and felt as though they were one again, as though all the pain they had endured was nothing compared to the love they had for one another.

36 Thanksgiving

November 24, 1977

It was a brisk morning, but when the sun came out from behind the clouds it warmed the upturned faces of the crowd gathered behind wooden barricades along the parade route, all looking north in anticipation. Here came the giant white Astronaut Snoopy balloon, like a white cloud drifting alongside the apartment towers lining Central Park West. Behind Snoopy, the star of the hit musical *Annie* waved from the Big Apple float. Big Bird and the cast of *Sesame Street* waved from another. Then Smokey Bear cast a long shadow over the avenue, and behind him floated two other longtime favorites, Bullwinkle and Underdog, each giant balloon lashed to the earth by its team of handlers in their matching jumpsuits. Even as one marching band disappeared from view, leaving behind only a distant thump of drums, the swelling theme song from the new movie *Star Wars* announced the approach of the next band. Clowns ran down the avenue, shaking hands and giving out balloons. A forty-foot dragon with slowly flapping wings roared from the back of the new *Hobbit* float. And then came a new balloon and an instant crowd favorite, sixty-three feet of green: Kermit the Frog, his spindly legs pulling in invisible breezes. By the time the rear of the parade approached, with the Rockettes in their red Christmas costumes and Santa on his sleigh, the day had become unseasonably warm, and people were unzipping their parkas and doffing scarves and mittens.

After the parade, Annabert and Marianne and the assorted children—Vanya and Kore had brought along friends—went into the park, exhilarated by the festivities and happy to be moving. It was a glorious Indian summer day. As she watched the children playing, Marianne thought they should have a picnic. She found a phone booth and called home to suggest that

Jan, Itsumi, and Aiko get a taxi and meet them. No, Jan said, he was a bit too tired to go out. He'd been working all morning and was just about to have some lunch and then take a nap. She told him they'd be home by three and then she would cook a big goose dinner to celebrate the day.

A few minutes before they got home, Jan awoke from his nap, sat up, and then collapsed, felled by a massive coronary. When the family came through the front door, he was lying unconscious on the low bed in the studio, his head cradled in Aiko's lap. The two Japanese women had called his doctor and then for an ambulance, but the doctor was out of town and the ambulance hadn't come. Marianne ran to the phone and dialed 911, only to learn that the ambulance had been dispatched to the wrong address and was sitting in front of the hotel across the street. In minutes, paramedics arrived and were working over Jan's naked body, giving him mouth-to-mouth resuscitation and then electric shocks, trying to revive him. Though Marianne had immediately whisked Kore out of the room, the two older children watched in horror.

At five o'clock, the paramedics gently lifted up Jan's body onto a stretcher and carried it out to the street and into the back of the ambulance. Marianne and Itsumi climbed into the back with him, and the paramedics closed the doors.

Though his body remained on life support for another day, Jan was gone from the world. He was fifty-five.

THE DAY AFTER his death, Marianne ran into a friend, who was upset to see her out on the street with a pushcart.

What are you doing? the woman asked, and Marianne replied, Well, I have to shop.

From her childhood and the war, she remembered the severe necessities surrounding death and survival. One has to eat. One has to put one foot in front of the other and carry on. They had $500 left in the bank and a small weekly income from looking after a friend's baby. It wouldn't be nearly enough, and there were no commissions in the pipeline. She didn't feel she could afford the luxury of mourning, not with others depending on her.

She found work shopping for and preparing a weekly luncheon for sixty at a woman's club. The other days of the week, she cleaned apartments in the neighborhood, and on Sunday mornings a doctor's office. Monday was her co-op day. Before Jan died, Marianne had started a co-op to supply her family and eleven others with fresh fruits and vegetables. She picked up the weekly order from a wholesale market in the Bronx and sorted it into boxes to be picked up. Whatever time was left she spent at the loom. She figured she would have the rest of her life to sort out her feelings.

Annabert had a harder time accepting that they were on their own now. For nearly forty-three years Jan had been the focus of her life, and she couldn't conceive of how to go forward without him. The religion of her childhood told her that she would see him again in another life, and she clung to that hope. They had been apart for long stretches before. After the week they first met, when she was seven, she hadn't seen him again for twelve years; they were reunited for a few short days and then he was gone again. Even after they were married, Jan had frequently gone off on trips lasting weeks and even months. Perhaps this was simply another long journey, and at the end they would be reunited.

Faced with his absence, Annabert did what she had always done in the past when he was away: she began to write to him. In her diary, she went over the last days leading up to his death, turning them over in her mind like faceted jewels, seeing now what she had neglected to notice in real time. She recalled the dream he had shared with her perhaps two nights before he died. With her by his side, he was walking through a castle belonging to him. Art filled all the halls and rooms, the most beautiful art through all the ages, from cave paintings and ancient bronzes to rugs and illuminations and jewelry. Everything beautiful that he had seen during his life, all of it was in this castle. There were endless halls. And as he walked, he showed her one room after another. He had woken up, he told her, suffused with great joy and a deep feeling of fulfillment.

The day after Jan's dream and the evening before Thanksgiving, they'd had dinner guests, the Belgian ambassador and his wife. They were sitting at the long red table, surrounded by their family and friends, and there was some small dispute in the kitchen between Marianne and Itsumi, which Annabert attended to. When she returned to the room, Jan was looking at her. *I looked at you, and you looked at me—In that look we stood face to face, holding our life and our dreams between us. Fathomless sorrow flowed from your eyes. Indeed they were as the scientists describe the black hole in which a whole star, a world, has been pulled by an incredible magnetism into itself. At that moment you must have seen your own end. You said farewell to me.*

In the diaries, she also voiced questions and sought reassurance. What had he meant when he said it would be better for the women after he died? This she answered for herself: now there would be less competition between them. *Yet I did well during the years we were together, didn't I—I too sometimes wanted you more for myself, but most of the time I was very, very satisfied and happy with your happiness—and being together like a family, with all its shared joys.*

Then, when the empty echo of her words on the page became too unbearably lonely, she answered her voice with his, writing the words she longed to hear from him.

Janneke . . .

"I am in you, Kik—the dreams you had will become stronger and stronger because the essence of our life was love. As always, hold me for a while in your arms, and start the day. I love you, mouse—"

—Jan

Annabert was resolute in her belief that his *kumpania* must continue on. Jan had loved them all and envisioned them as a family; so long as they stayed together he was, in a sense, still among them. Besides, there were more than a hundred designs yet to weave.

She took upon herself the task that had formerly been Jan's, to solicit commissions, showings, and sales of his work. She was far too much of an introvert to actually go out to openings, galleries, and cocktail parties, or to charm potential clients. Instead, she wrote letters, hundreds of them, to anyone and everyone she could think of: architects, collectors, museum directors and gallery owners, friends, acquaintances and strangers alike. In these letters, she extolled Jan's genius and asked for help. And then, because she was not officially Jan's widow, she signed the letters with Marianne's name. When they sold two large tapestries, they reinvested some of the profits into printing gorgeous color catalogs, and she mailed these out as well.

The spring after Jan's death, Marianne was in midtown and on a whim went over to the lobby at 1700 Broadway where two of Jan's big tapestries hung. She was appalled: the tapestries had been dry cleaned and then poorly stretched. One was smudged and hanging upside down. She called Jerry Weinstein, the developer who had originally purchased them, and asked if she and Annabert could take them down to clean and press them. As they talked, he volunteered to host an exhibition of tapestries in Jan's honor, there in the lobby. He wanted to do it soon, though, at the end of that month.

Through sheer will and dogged energy, the women made it happen. Marianne contacted James Johnson Sweeney, the former director of the Guggenheim and a longtime supporter, and he signed on as a cosponsor. Then they printed up and sent out invitations. All four women wove madly for the intervening weeks to finish three more small new tapestries. In her diary, Annabert described to Jan their plans, how she was trying to think like him when making decisions.

On May 25, 1978, friends and collectors showed up for the exhibition, some flying in to be there. Hundreds of people they didn't know came as well, and in her diary that evening, Annabert told Jan all about it, and then drew a little map of the installation, detailing where each tapestry was hung. It had been a wonderful success, reminiscent of the parties they had hosted at the Forty-Seventh Street studio. *Oh Lieveke*, she wrote, *I see your beaming face—we did well—and you are proud of us. . . . Really, it was your celebration. May something good come from it.*

JAN'S LIFE HAD been like a tightrope act, the daring artist walking a rope suspended high up in the air, working without a net and balancing four spinning plates to boot. That it had ever worked at all was amazing. But the plates cannot keep spinning of their volition, and in the end the studio couldn't continue as a going concern for long, without the artist. It was only right, too, that Itsumi and Aiko should eventually leave to find their own husbands, their own lives.

The children grew up and went out into the world to make their own families. Annabert and Marianne remained in the house on Waverly Place, where they returned to one of the things they did best, mothering the babies and young children lucky enough to be entrusted to their care.

For nearly twenty-five years, the sons and daughters of actors and brokers were delivered every morning to the blue door on Waverly Place and entered that circle of peace where time stopped. Soup was on the stove, bread was in the oven, and two silver-haired Dutch grandmothers in long dresses were ready to read stories aloud, teach the children songs, and perhaps help them make something pretty from leftover yarn.

In a sense, the two friends had come full circle to a time before Jan, back to the early thirties when together they had pushed their doll carriage in a quiet, flowered suburb of The Hague. Back then, they had dreamed ordinary dreams: a husband for each, children, a house with a garden. Their lives had turned out to be anything but ordinary, and in place of simplicity and security they had been given the complicated blessings of great passion and art. Looking around, each of them sometimes envied the women they knew who were growing old with husbands. Still, each had the other, a lifelong companion and comfort not often given to other widows. When asked if she had ever considered leaving after Jan died, Marianne doesn't hesitate. "Oh, I couldn't leave Annabert."

After thirty years with Jan, they carried on together for another thirty years without him. However, Jan remained entwined so tightly in their lives that death could not entirely separate the three. When Kore suggested to his mother that she find a gentleman companion, if only to keep her company at the opera, Marianne found that she couldn't imagine any man in her life but Jan. For all their past difficulties, when she closed her eyes it was always him that she saw.

Like the little frog in the milk pail, Annabert continued to weave and to send out her letters, keeping Jan's memory alive. From that faith and perseverance came exhibitions of his work: at the Natural Academy of Sciences in Washington, D.C.; at the Pratt Institute, and the legendary Clocktower Gallery in Tribeca; at the Museum of Natural History in New York; at Duke University and Cleveland State University; at galleries in East Hampton, New York, and Summit, New Jersey, and as far away as Australia. In 1996, Marianne carried two tapestries folded into suitcases to the Biennale of Contemporary Tapestries in St. Petersburg, Russia.

And of course, at home, all around them in the studio remained the glorious physical evidence of their lives together and the dream the three of them had shared.

In 1999 the owner decided to sell 108 Waverly Place, and in spite of a grassroots effort that included articles in the *New York Times*, Marianne and Annabert were forced out of the home where they had lived and raised their children for thirty-one years. The same night they were served with the eviction papers, Annabert fell and broke her knee. When she came out of the hospital, it was almost like day and night. Her memory had been deteriorating subtly for some time, but suddenly she was a different person, distracted and absent. The doctor diagnosed her with Alzheimer's disease.

In their new studio—smaller but only a few blocks from the old one—Kore set up the loom and they put up threads for another large abstract tapestry, but it was more than Annabert could manage. Instead, she returned to the series of small biblical designs that Jan had first designed in the forties. For long hours at a time she would sit contentedly at the loom, her fingers going through the motions of weaving, almost of their own accord.

Marianne, Annabert, and Jan, at the loom. Courtesy of the Yoors Family Partnership.

Annabert died on June 27, 2010, and was buried next to Jan at the cemetery for writers and artists in East Hampton, New York.

I DREAMT THAT Jan had returned; he was still ill. We had just moved to another large loft, one unbroken space, still empty except at the entrance was a cozy, small room with an arched door. Somewhere in the large space was a platform bed. Jan lay on it, and Marianne lay next to him. I sat on the other side. Then Jan spoke and said that he would like to ask Itsumi to come back to us, and to give the small room to her. I took Jan's hand and pleaded: "Can we not stay like we are? We have it so good together. Can we not stop here?" There was an overwhelming feeling of wanting that moment of us three together to linger on. And Jan was not angry. He gently looked at me and shook his head. In my heart, in my deepest heart, I knew that I wanted to give him what he desired. I did not say anything and woke up. Still half asleep, thinking "I cannot make Jan sad." But this is almost as if that was not the issue of my dream. It was just the nostalgic feeling: Could we three not remain as we are? As we had been: a threefold cord?

Marianne (standing) and Annabert (foreground) with tapestries in the Forty-Seventh Street studio. Courtesy of the Yoors Family Partnership.

Naples, Florida, 2015

I pick up Marianne and Kore from the Staybridge Suites. This is one of several firsts for Marianne: in her eighty-eight years, she has never stayed in a hotel. And never set foot in Florida. It's all new, but she is captivated in particular by the foliage. For two days now, we have been harvesting air plants and variously shaped leaves for her to take back home and press into the ceramic plates and vases that she creates in her Thursday afternoon pottery workshops.

We've come to this wealthy Gulf Coast town for another first. Though the tapestries and photos are undergoing a revival of interest and have been shown with increasing frequency in Paris, Brussels, Amsterdam, and New York, this is the first American museum retrospective of Jan Yoors' work since his death thirty-eight years ago.

Kore was up until midnight last night to help the museum staff finish hanging the show. When he arrived, about a third of the tapestries, uncrated and unfurled from their massive rollers, were still strewn on the gallery floors, and some of the ones already up on the walls needed adjusting along the top edge so that they would drape more evenly. Kore chuckles when he tells me that at one point he asked someone to locate a vacuum cleaner. The usual method that conservators use to clean these tapestries involves cotton swabs, but necessity called for other measures, so as the staff watched—their training, not to mention insurance protocols, prevented them from participating in this sacrilege—Kore ran the vacuum hose over an expanse of wool, removing dust that had accumulated in storage. Some of these tapestries have not been seen for years.

Together with the museum director, we take the elevator to the second floor. Entering the first gallery, I am literally brought up short by the tapestry *Written in Fire*. At twenty-four feet long, it spans nearly the entire length of the wall—an aggressive, swirling Sanskrit of vibrant orange on black that calls to mind the energy of urban wall murals. I've seen photos of it, but now the familiar image explodes around me like a galaxy, and I experience the shock of seeing something familiar transformed before my eyes.

Over the years spent researching the Yoors, I have looked at hundreds of photographs, but I'm conscious now that, with four or five exceptions, I have never seen the physical tapestries. The full power of them does not reproduce. It's not simply a question of scale, though that's certainly part of what makes them so commanding. They are as big as Eugeen Yoors' stained glass windows, sized to overwhelm and inspire awe. The color, too, contains stained glass's depth and intensity, with gradations of dye lot, texture, and shadow that reproduced images can't convey. Finally, they are three-dimensional and weighty, exuding the tactile sensuality of the handmade. My fingertips itch with the desire to reach out and touch them, but since we are in a museum I refrain. (I notice later that Marianne shows no such compunction. When a visitor asks her how they tied off the threads, she reaches over, lifts the corner of a tapestry from the wall and flips its back side up so we can see the white linen warp.)

The nine galleries display several dozen photographs, two sculptures, a half dozen charcoal nudes, thirty small gouaches—the "Biblicals" that were Jan's earliest designs—and glass cases containing sketches and ephemera, letters, false passports, and so forth. However, the stars of the show are the twenty-two tapestries. Here is *The Fishermen*, the Yoors' first commissioned design, rejected by Rubin Rabinowitz because— what did he say, that it was perhaps too powerful? I remember thinking at the time that this might be a euphemistic reference to the bare-chested and brown-skinned men, but I see now that he was speaking directly. The tapestry—taller than most men and fifteen feet long—radiates such energy in its lines that it practically surges from left to right, and with its intense reds and violets it *is* far too assertive for a suburban dining room. How could one possibly sit in its presence and chat about local politics and golf scores, fork up a bite of roast beef or chicken salad, and remark on the weather?

On an adjacent wall hangs *Roots*, woven in 1958. Though strictly speaking it's not an abstract—the web of ruddy lines on a black ground looks recognizably like the thick and gnarled roots of a tree—it marks

Jan's shift away from the narrative iconography of his father's work. From this point on, the designs move increasingly toward the abstract. In the next room, for instance, is a striking piece titled *Jungle*. Nothing in the design is pictorial, and yet its sinuous vertical shapes, the incredible deepness of the black, and the cobalt blue like welder's flames convey the velvety, claustrophobic *feel* of a jungle.

These organic forms and the limited palette of two or three colors, always including that bottomless black, became Jan's most recognizable motif, a motif that culminated at the end of his life in the *Tantra* series. Seven are displayed here. I'm standing in front of *Yellow Tantra*, the design chosen to represent Jan's work on a Belgian stamp issued this past fall. And here is one of the earliest of the series, *Noh Pine*, designed in 1973 and woven a few years after his death. In Noh theater, a pine tree is painted on the back wall of the stage to symbolize the conduit by which the Noh dramas were passed from heaven down to mankind. Inspiration came through the tree. This turns out to be true for the *Tantras* as well. The designs began as leaves taken from the Yoors' Greenwich Village garden. (I'm reminded of Marianne's leaves pressed between paper in the trunk of my car.) Jan made negatives or shadows of the leaves imprinted on photo-sensitive paper, cropped the images, and then blew them up to the point where they transmuted from recognizable forms to pure design or idea. He then transferred the design and applied color, often using the same technique—cut-out paper—that Matisse used at the end of his life when he, too, was coping with impaired vision. For both artists, though, failing eyesight doesn't begin to explain the dynamism of their last works.

Marianne has come up to stand beside me. She tells me she has found a mistake in one of the tapestries, a single stitch flaw that she had never noticed before.

"Which is your favorite?" she asks.

For reasons that I can't articulate I walk over to *Purple Tantra*. Eight by ten feet, it's a composition of curves and angles that, because it uses only dark magenta and black, retains the mood of the original negative. But then in the upper-right quadrant, a small cutout of fluorescent orange pierces the darkness like a shard of atomic light. It looks like the mystery of creation made visible.

Definitions of the word *tantra* vary, but according to the Buddhist scholar Alexander Berzin, the Sanskrit word means the warp of a loom or the strands of a braid. Others translate it as a verb, "to weave." It is both verb and noun: a practice as well as a doctrine of enlightenment that recognizes the oneness of everything. Spirit, body, and the material world around us—all are woven together into one. It is an apt title for these tapestries, which distill organic forms into pure spirit and color, a burst of uncomplicated joy. Faced with his own mortality and the agonies of a failing body, Jan embraced a vision that celebrated being in the world.

We walk through the galleries one more time, admiring the work of a lifetime. Marianne is happy, smiling. In the end, we circle back to the entrance and the tapestry *Written in Fire*. This is the design the women chose to put up on the loom after Jan first went into the hospital more than forty years ago, as a pledge that the work would continue in his absence.

Their work was finished long ago, the last tapestry cut down off the loom. And their individual lives have begun to recede into myth. Still, dreams can survive the dreamer, or what is art?

Marianne Yoors at Baker Museum, Naples, Florida, 2015. Photo by author.

It is what is unseen in a person or a drawing that makes
them interesting.
—JAN YOORS

Upon first reading Jan's accounts of his adventures in his memoirs, *The
Gypsies* and *Crossing*, I was incredulous. These are amazing and entertaining stories, but one doesn't have to be much of a cynic to consider the
possibility that the boy who concocted fantastical adventures for himself
in his childhood letters to Annabert might grow up and invent a heroic
role for himself in the Resistance, and might even make up travels with
the Gypsies. Who would be the wiser? After all, it's hard to imagine two
sets of circumstances more immune to fact-checking.

However, when I spoke with Michael Korda, the editor of the memoirs, he expressed complete confidence in the veracity of Jan's accounts.
He believed that Jan withheld things—it was part of his character to keep
secrets—but according to Korda, everything Jan *did* reveal subsequently
checked out when Korda went looking for corroboration.

When I asked Marianne directly if all of this could really be true—the
torture, the escapes—she wasn't offended. "His body told the story,"
she answered simply. "His whole back was whip lashes. And there were
two big scars on the bones here." She pointed to her clavicle. "That, you
don't make up."

However, there is far more evidence than Jan's physical scars. The desk
that Kore built in their studio holds binders cataloging correspondence
and ephemera ranging from newspaper articles to official documents.
Included are the 120 photos that Jan took of the Gypsies in the thirties
with his Brownie camera; letters and postmarked envelopes addressed
to him and forwarded to various locations around Europe, including a

prison in Belgium; and a handful of passports and identity cards with Jan's photo identifying him variously as Jan Yoors of Antwerp, Jean Baptiste Jansenns of Brussels, and Henri Vercamerton, born in Nice.

For all this documentation, though, it's difficult to verify his actual whereabouts during much of the war. This, of course, was the point of many of the documents: to provide a convincing alibi. For instance, he was registered as a student in a sculpture course at the National School of Architecture and Decorative Arts in Brussels during the academic year of 1941–42, but how much he was actually in attendance is open to question. A friend whom he first met at this school said that Jan came and went. The leader of Jan's old Boy Scout troop in Antwerp said the same thing and surmised that Jan's sporadic involvement with the Scouts provided a good cover. When the Gestapo imprisoned Jan in 1943, a professor of linguistics and ethnology at the University of Ghent, Franz Olbrechts, wrote to the head of the military government that Jan was an etymology student there and that his presence with the Gypsies had simply been fieldwork. In fact, Jan was never registered at that university.

Whether due to the habits of an oral storyteller or those of a former operative, Jan himself was maddeningly vague in his memoirs about places, dates, and names. A little sleuthing turned up, again and again, corroboration for his stories, but it also turned up fresh mysteries.

There is, for instance, the matter of his work in the Resistance with Betsie Hollants.

Betsie Hollants was honored in 1950 by the Jewish community of Belgium for saving Jews during the war and was added posthumously to the list of the Righteous Among the Nations at Yad Vashem, the Holocaust memorial in Israel that honors martyrs and heroes. She acknowledged that she had worked in the Resistance and that she'd been arrested and imprisoned during the occupation. However, she herself kept no record of her underground work: during the war, she acquired the habit of destroying letters after she'd read them, and for the rest of her long life she wrote everything on small scraps of paper so they could be eaten if necessary. For the most part she kept her own counsel, believing she had only done her duty as a Christian. At the end of her life, when her great-nephew, Jan van Impee, asked her about the war, she would only smile like the Mona Lisa and say, "Oh, the adventures we had!"

Clearly, she and Jan worked together. She was the one who first arranged an introduction to Professor Olbrechts, who would go on to vouch falsely that Jan was a student. And in all likelihood Betsie engineered the meeting between Jan and Monsieur Henri. A Resistance network in Paris code-named Jade Amicol was made up largely of other politically active Catholics who reported directly to MI-6 in England. Their safe house and the place where MI-6 agents made radio contact and received secret mail was a convent, the Sisters of the Holy Agony, a few blocks up Rue de la Santé from the Sisters of St. Joseph de Cluny where Jan stayed and which would later become the Paris headquarters for the escape line he created. Could it be mere coincidence that Jan chose to stay at this convent when he first went to Paris, or was he directed there for a purpose by his mother's friend? And, for that matter, who first tipped off Monsieur Henri that Jan Yoors was traveling with the Rom? Who could know this but a close family friend?

Apparently, Jan himself never knew the answers to all these questions. Years later, he tried to explain how he could be so in the dark. "You see, to me the main feeling of secret service work is mistiness, the illogic. When I do read about it, which is very rarely, how logical, how rational, how well-organized the whole thing sounds . . . when you read it. And when you live it, it is not. You see, for example, many times I was sent on specific missions to a place I had never been before, given a complete itinerary with a full map illustrating the houses, the streets, everything, and going on location and recognizing the place with a strange, misty feeling. Recognizing a place you have never been to. This whole first part to me was that: reliving a thing I have never lived before. Almost a dream quality. You know there is something behind it, you knew there is a reason for it, but you don't know what it is. As in a dream, maybe you read too late or you ate potato salad: you know there is a reason why this thing occurred, but you can't analyze it. And from then on, I was so wrapped up in this whole thing that the whys were fairly unimportant."

Did Jan embellish or conflate here and there for the good of the story? Yes. For instance, he reported conversations he would be unlikely to have remembered verbatim years later. From one interview to the next, details sometimes changed. One of the escapees who was with him on that last trip over the Pyrenees later said that his account was exaggerated. Still, the larger point holds: Jan led this group of escapees over the mountains and out of occupied Europe.

I am a novelist, but in the end I decided that to fictionalize the Yoors' story would undercut the very thing that first attracted me to it. To the best of my knowledge, it is bizarrely, improbably, and wonderfully true.

ACKNOWLEDGMENTS

Eight years ago, my friend Mitchell Kaplan and I were talking in his Coral Gables, Florida, bookstore, Books & Books. "I've got your next book," he said. Authors hear this a lot, and it's never, ever true. Except this time. My heartfelt thanks to him, and to his sister Susan Kaplan, for introducing me to the Yoors and setting me upon this long and rewarding journey.

This book simply could not have happened without the enthusiastic and generous collaboration of Marianne Yoors and her son, Kore Yoors. Marianne sat with me for well over a hundred hours, sharing her stories, answering even my most prying questions, and patiently transcribing letters and diary entries from Dutch. Kore Yoors provided me with access to the Yoors Family Archives and helped me track down the information and people necessary to the writing of this book. They have been beside me every step of the way.

My thanks to friends, family, and colleagues of the Yoors who also shared their stories: Carolina Varga Dinicu (aka Morocco), Kathy Komaroff Goodman, Michael Korda, Marcia McBroom Small, Cynthia Mead, the late Rubin Rabinowitz, Phyllis Stevens, Dorothy Schwartz, and Vanya Yoors.

For research information, I'm indebted to Jean van Impe, at the Leuven University Library, Leuven, Belgium; to Gary Kleinman, University of Miami; to Ken Hartmann; Dan Wakefield; Dr. Ron Rosenthal; and Vanya Yoors.

Thanks to Marci Calabretta Cancio-Bello and Jennifer Maritza McCauley, research assistants, for transcribing audio interviews. And to Beatrice Thornton and Rem Koh De for additional translations.

My colleagues and friends at Florida International University read the earliest version of the manuscript and offered helpful advice and continued moral support over the ensuing years. Thank you to Lynne Barrett,

John Dufresne, Meri-Jane Rochelson, Les Standiford, and Julie Wade. I'm also grateful to my friends who beta tested the book and whose smart feedback made it more user-friendly: Dawn Davies, Jennifer Cody Epstein, Angie Griffin, James W. Hall, Mitchell Kaplan, Kate Kremer, Dan Kremer, Kathleen Tyau, and Cynthia White. I'm lucky to rest in the circle of such talented and loving people.

Gianna Francesca Mosser and the editorial board at Northwestern University Press have my deep gratitude for taking a chance on a story that doesn't fit neatly into the usual boxes. Many thanks also to the talented team at Northwestern University Press who transformed the manuscript into a book and sent it out into the world: Anne E. Gendler, Maggie Grossman, JD Wilson, Greta Bennion, Paul Mendelson, and Marianne Jankowski.

Close to the heart of whatever I write is my husband and in-house editor, Clifford Paul Fetters. Thank you, my love, for your brilliant insights, your steady patience, and your belief in this, and in us.

1. *Pingola*

3   "A child will forever remember . . .": Annabert Yoors' 1989 diary, undated entry. Annabert van Wettum kept diaries for most of her life, thirty-eight volumes of which are preserved in the archives of the Yoors Family Partnership. Jan Yoors gave a number of interviews over the course of his life and published two memoirs of his wartime experiences. Together with the recollections of Marianne Yoors, collected in more than a hundred hours of recorded interviews, and the correspondence and ephemera in the Yoors Family papers, these form the bulk of source material for this narrative.

4   Her first morning at Zonnehuis . . . : In a video interview conducted late in Annabert's life by Susan Kaplan, Annabert discussed this first meeting. Jan Yoors and his sister, Bixie, had been invited to stay at the mansion by their "Aunt" Lena. The mansion was where the disabled children were housed, and Aunt Lena worked there as a nurse.

6   "Dear Jan": Annabert van Wettum to Jan Yoors, Oct. 3, 1935. Except as noted, all letters are from the Yoors Family Archives in New York and were translated from the Dutch by Marianne Yoors.

7   "Dear Annabert": Jan Yoors to Annabert van Wettum, Dec. 18, 1935.

2. *The Gypsies*

11   "I was probably 6 . . .": Undated notes made by Jan Yoors in preparation for his memoirs. Translated from the French by Beatrice Thornton.

12   "who were ethereal, mythical, and above all imaginary . . .": Yoors, *Crossing*, 8.

12   *Rom*—Nanosh pointed proudly . . . : In using the word "Rom," rather than "Roma," I have followed Jan Yoors' convention, as well as his

spelling of "Gaje," rather than the variant "Gadje." He uses the terms "Gypsy" and "Rom" interchangeably, and I have followed suit here as well.

13   "I just stayed . . .": Jan Yoors, WBAI Radio, New York, 1966. The story of Jan's first encounter with the Gypsies is recounted in numerous radio and print interviews and appears in his memoirs *The Gypsies* and *Crossing*. Minor details change from one telling to the next, but the larger narrative is consistent.

13   The tribe he had joined . . . : The Roma are believed to have originated in India. There are five Romani tribes, corresponding to the Indian caste system. According to Jan, the Lowara corresponded to the Indian Brahmins. "Among the Gypsies, they are the lawmakers, the judges. Then you have the Tshurara, the warriors. Then you have the tradespeople, the Macvaya; you have the craftsmen, the Kalderash, and then you have the outcasts, who are the musicians, the dancers, entertainers, the Sinti. And these last are the sedentary gypsies." (Jan Yoors in a recorded interview with Andrew St. George for *Argosy* magazine, Yoors Family Archives.)

14   "Joining and splitting . . .": Jan Yoors, WBAI Radio. In Jan's memoirs relating his travels with the Rom, there is a striking absence of the cornerstones of most travel accounts: place names and dates. He later told an interviewer that he traveled with the Gypsies mostly in the Balkans, but everywhere from Turkey to Poland; however, in the memoirs themselves there is not a single name of a town or a country. When it was convenient, they might pretend to be from one place or another, to be Hungarian or Spanish or Russian if it suited their purposes in the moment, but they regarded borders and nationalities as another senseless invention of the Gaje, and these held no more meaning for the Rom than they do for the rest of creation, for birds and animals, for mountains or rivers.

14   "It was something we never talked about . . .": Yoors, WBAI Radio

15   "I was drawn to the Gypsies . . .": Yoors, *Crossing*, 10.

3. The Belgian Bohemians

17   Jan's mother, Magda . . . : Magda Yoors-Peeters, in *Een Vlaming in New-York*, 1975.

18 "Something fell from my eyes . . .": Magda Yoors-Peeters, "Daring to Be Human," 258–59.

19 "And if we cannot be found . . .": Elizabeth Hollants to Eugene Yoors, Feb. 25, 1932. Postcard sent from Antwerp Central Station. KADOC Archives, Leuven University, Leuven, Belgium. Translated from the Dutch.

19 "Dear Woega . . .": Annabert van Wettum to Jan Yoors, undated.

19 "Dearest Chikita . . .": Jan Yoors to Annabert van Wettum, undated.

20 In their defense . . . : Yoors, WBAI Radio.

22 "Dearest Chikita . . .": Jan Yoors to Annabert van Wettum, April 12, 1937.

4. The Best Friend

27 Marianne Citroen and Annabert van Wettum: I have regularized the spelling of the two women's names throughout. In the earliest letters and documents, Annabert's name is more often spelled Annebert and Marianne's name is spelled Marian. Later, the spellings changed.

29 Scheveningen: The name of this town is one of the most difficult words for a non-native Dutch speaker to pronounce. Consequently, it was used as a password for Resistance fighters during the war. Even Germans who might otherwise manage a passable Dutch accent would be tripped up by the word.

31 Her friend Gerdie: In a video interview with Susan Kaplan, Annabert says of her childhood friends: "We had another girl—Gerdie—we were three. And we would fight together. We were just girls that liked each other."

31 Looking back on the aftermath of her mother's death, Marianne says, "I think I was just a little box, locked up, all my emotions locked. Maybe that's why I'm so emotional now, all that years of keeping your emotions in and not showing emotions. But that was 1939, and children were kept away. And because you are kept away—that's what I'm thinking now—you don't internally grow. You're numb inside because nothing is awakening. . . . Don't you think you grow differently? I think there was a plug on top of me: nothing drained, nothing grew." (Interview with author, June 6, 2011.)

33 The chaotic nature of the paratroop landings: Germany's plan had been to bomb the three airfields around The Hague, grounding the few Dutch military planes there and knocking out defenses. Paratroops would then land, seize the airfields, and secure them before the next wave of planes arrived, those carrying air-transport troops. It is a commonplace that the military strategies of generals bear little relation to the actual experience of war on the ground, and the attack on The Hague was no exception. Everything went wrong. The paratroopers were dropped too far apart from each other or too far from the airfields. They were not able to secure Ypenberg airfield in time, so Dutch machine gunners were firing on the incoming transport planes. Worse, the airfield was full of burning Dutch planes, and the Junkers circled futilely and ended up landing wherever they could put down, in dunes and meadows. At Valenkenberg airfield, things went according to plan in that the airfield was captured, but because it was still under construction, the grass strips wouldn't bear the weight of heavy planes and were quickly rendered useless by mired transports. The attack on the third airfield, Ochenberg, failed because only thirty-six paratroopers were dropped within range (Amersfoort and Kamphius, *May 1940*, chap. 5)

34 The bombing of Rotterdam: Amersfoort and Kamphius, *May 1940*, chap. 5.

35 In our early conversations, Marianne did not recall much of that first year. Her story tended to elide from one traumatic event to the next. She said that her father had taken her out of the liberal Waldorf school because he knew that the Germans would close it, that after May 10 she didn't go back to school, and it must have been then that he found a private teacher for her. But then she remembered that this wasn't true; the tutor had come later. She had first attended another school, operated by the same director who ran the boarding school to which her brothers were sent. It is likely that she was removed from these schools because her father was Jewish.

35 Joseph Emanuel Kalker: b. Eindhoven, Oct. 8, 1900—d. Auschwitz, October 1943.

36 Henri Citroen goes into hiding: Citroen's business got a *verwalter*—a German "administrator"—who took over in March 1941. This may mark the time when Henri Citroen went into hiding.

36   One of the contentious questions in Holocaust studies . . . : The Netherlands had no history of Jewish persecution; on the other hand, the Dutch were rigorous in keeping Jews out of Holland until the Inquisition brought Sephardic Jews from Spain.

37   "The Jews for us are not Dutchmen . . .": Artur Seyss-Inquart, translated by Carmelo Lisciotto, "Deportation from the Netherlands," Holocaust and Education Research Team, 2007, http://www.holocaust researchproject.org/nazioccupation/holland/netherdeports.html.

38   "A gazillion questions of extraordinary delicacy": Joseph Goebbels, translated by Nathan Stoltzfus and printed in Appendix 4, p. 235 of *Protest in Hitler's "National Community": Popular Unrest and the Nazi Response.*, ed. Nathan Stoltfus and Birgit Maier Katkin (New York: Berghahn, 2015). Goebbels's diary can be found at "Die Tagebücher von Joseph Goebbels," https://www.degruyter.com/view/db/tjgo.

38   Dutch Jews required to register: van der Zee, *The Hunger Winter*, 126.

42   The Kalkers' daughter, Marion, survived the war, and she and Marianne reunited in The Hague in November 2011, after a separation of almost seventy years. Marion Kalker was able to fill in some of the story: that her parents had been paid handsomely by Henri Citroen to take in Marianne as a boarder when he went into hiding. They had given Marianne their bedroom and moved into a small ground floor room off the garden. The family went into hiding in August 1942.

6. The Operative

43   The mass exodus: In his memoir *Crossing*, Jan presents this journey as one he made with Pulika and his Roma family—most probably an artistic liberty taken in the interest of simplifying a convoluted story and keeping it focused on the Gypsies. However, Marianne is adamant that he was with his birth family, and the scant independent evidence supports her version.

44   Evacuation over the Channel: Joos Florquin, "Trouentenhoflaan 24, Berchem-Antwerpen," ed. Davidsfonds, Leuven, *Ten Huiz Van . . . 1 (tweede druk)* (Bruges: Orion–Desclée De Brouwer, 1971), 318. In this interview, Eugeen Yoors verified that he and his family witnessed the massive British military evacuation at Dunkirk. Over the course of

eight days, from May 26 to June 4, 1940, 338,000 Allied soldiers were rescued off the beaches by military transport ships as well as a flotilla of small civilian boats and carried across the English Channel to safety. Eugeen, Magda, and Bixie Yoors were among them.

45 Convent across the street from the infamous La Santé Prison: This location was identified by Annabert van Wettum in her 1947 diary, as the place where she and Jan stayed after the war. "Now I sit in the window sill of an old house, opposite the prison La Santé. Here were the nuns with Mother Superior who broke from the Catholic church and started a Christian community. Jan brought here the boys he had to bring to Spain." There is, in the present day, a convent, the Sisters of St. Joseph de Cluny, located opposite the prison. However, to confuse matters, the convent more famously associated with the Resistance movement, whose mother superior hid escaping soldiers and Jews, is located further down the Rue de la Santé.

46 The Resistance: The word "Resistance" suggests a unified movement, which was not the case, and certainly not in the early days after May 10. Even later, though, what has become known variously as the Underground, the Resistance, or the Maquis was made up of great numbers of unconnected small cells.

48 "Dear Woega . . .": Annabert van Wettum to Jan Yoors, undated.

49 Pulika advising Jan: Yoors, *Crossing*, 52–54.

50 Story about Tonkin: Yoors, *Crossing*, 77–78.

50–51 Drill and real encounter with German dragnet: Yoors, *Crossing*, 80, 82.

7. Rom Underground

53 "So you see, my days are filled . . .": Jan Yoors to Annabert van Wettum, Feb. 7, 1942.

55 Scabies ruse: Jan Yoors, interview with St. George.

55 German boxcar sabotage story: St. George, "The Wild Goose," 78.

55 "Sense of fierce exultation . . .": Yoors, *Crossing*, 129.

56 Frog story: Jan Yoors, interview with St. George.

57 "Here among the Rom . . .": Jan Yoors to Elizabeth Hollants, Nov. 24, 1942, translated by Remko Caprio.

61   Begijnenstraat Prison: Jan never named in print the prison or its location, but letters in the Yoors Family Partnership archives, dated or postmarked from March 6 to June 25, 1943, are addressed to and from him at the prison:

> Kriegs wehrmachtgefangnis Geforngnis
> Cel 105 (later 86) Konto No. 7322
> Begijnenstraat
> Antwerpen

61   "A clear and strong vision of a long line of Gypsy wagons": Yoors, *Crossing*, 147.

63   Jan became like Scheherazade: Many years later, in New York, he would become famous for his storytelling and was known to hold forth for hours at a time to a rapt audience.

63   Jan talking about his torture: Hochschild, "A Gypsy for Our Time."

64   "The trouble with Germans . . .": St. George, "The Wild Goose," 80.

65   "Dear Woega . . .": Annabert van Wettum to Jan Yoors, postmarked 1943.

9. The Sardine Letters

69   "Bixie has sent them via the Red Cross . . .": Elizabeth Hollants to Jan Yoors, June 18, 1943.

70   Connections with Swedes in the Red Cross: Jan Yoors, in interview with St. George.

70   "The first sentences from Moeky . . .": Jan Yoors to Elizabeth Hollants, June 22, 1943.

72   "Still as happy and healthy as before": Jan Yoors to Annabert van Wettum, July 20, 1943.

10. Death and the Gardener

77   Transport trains from Westerbork: Jewish Virtual Library, http://www.jewishvirtuallibrary.org/jsource/Holocaust/Westerbork.html.

78   6,035 people were employed at Westerbork: Holocaust Research Project, http://www.holocaustresearchproject.org/othercamps/westerbork .html.

78   "Voluntary" sterilization in May 1943: Presser, *Ashes in the Wind*, 195. Although Dr. Presser doesn't cite Henri Citroen individually, the dates of Citroen's stay at Westerbork and his subsequent sterilization line up. Given his status as the spouse of a non-Jew, I have extrapolated that he was among this group.

11. The Hunger Winter

84   Railway strike: van der Zee, *The Hunger Winter*, 28.

86   New Year's V-2: van der Zee, *The Hunger Winter*, 185.

87   Cats and dogs disappeared from the streets: van der Zee, *The Hunger Winter*.

87   Caloric rations at end of war: Lowe, *Savage Continent*, 37

12. The Wild Goose

89   The story of leading a group of escapees over the Pyrenees during a snowstorm is one that Jan told innumerable times, to friends and reporters as well as in his memoir *Crossing*. I have synthesized from several sources but have relied in the main on his memoir, as well as the story written about the trip by Andrew St. George for *Argosy* magazine. Both of these accounts are clearly dramatized for their audiences. However, there is independent corroboration of the incident from one of the nineteen persons who made this trip with Jan: Paul Peeters. Peeters' unpublished recollections are in the keeping of his daughter, Karen Polak, of the Anne Frank House in Amsterdam.

89   He was young, slender, and almost effeminate-looking: Jan Yoors, interview with St. George.

90   Escorting to safety more than two hundred people: This figure comes from Annabert Yoors' diaries.

95   Strange Ice Age creatures come back to life: Jan Yoors, *Crossing*, 203–4.

96   This was not yet liberation: Jan Yoors, interview with St. George.

97   "Dearest Annabert . . .": Jan Yoors to Annabert van Wettum, Nov. 18, 1943.

13. Annabert's War

99   "All his letters were taken open . . .": Annabert Yoors, video interview with Susan Kaplan.

99   "[It] vibrated in the atmosphere . . .": Ibid.

99   The Nazis closed the Vrige School: Ibid.

100   "I was really scared . . .": Annabert van Wettum to Jan Yoors, undated, but context suggests late 1941.

100   "I hope you are not very angry . . .": Jan Yoors to Annabert van Wettum, June 25, 1942.

100   Voorschoten Lane: The van Wettums' address was Van Voorschotenlaan 12.

100   "Did you ever receive . . .": Annabert van Wettum to Jan Yoors, March 11, 1943.

101   In her next letter: Annabert van Wettum to Jan Yoors, postmarked 1943, only the year is visible, but the context of the letter suggests spring.

101   "Dearest Annabert . . .": Jan Yoors to Annabert van Wettum, July 20, 1943.

101   "Now something else, Jan . . .": Annabert van Wettum to Jan Yoors, Dec. 8, 1943.

102   "Dear Annabert: Jan requests . . .": Elizabeth Hollants to Annabert van Wettum, Dec. 22, 1943.

103   "I'm so happy that you wrote . . .": Annabert van Wettum to Elizabeth Hollants, Jan. 14, 1944.

104   "I find it so difficult . . .": Ibid.

104   "They are so sweet . . .": Annabert van Wettum to Jan Yoors, April 22, 1944.

105   The German soldiers next door to Zonnehuis: Annabert Yoors, video interview with Susan Kaplan.

106   Hitler's eugenics program: http://www.jewishvirtuallibrary.org/jsource/Holocaust/disabled.html.

106–7 Incident with SS officer: Annabert Yoors, video interview with Susan Kaplan.

107 300,000 "divers" in hiding: van der Zee, *The Hunger Winter*.

107 "Omie's dear angry Gotthard": Annabert van Wettum's diary, winter 1944–45.

107 "Dearest Annabert": Jan Yoors to Annabert van Wettum, Feb. 4, 1944.

14. The Ghosts

109–10 Celebration still risky: Rijkmuseum Timeline, https://www.rijks museum.nl/en/rijksstudio/timeline-dutch-history/liberation.

110 Rounding up collaborators: For all the humiliations visited upon collaborators, in Holland revenge was acted upon less violently than in other occupied countries: 100 collaborators were killed there during and following the liberation, compared with 265 in Belgium, 9,000 in France, and the worst, somewhere between 12,000 and 20,000 in Italy (Lowe, *Savage Continent*, 150).

110 Auschwitz-Birkenau transport: Citroen and Starzynska, *Auschwitz-Oscwięçim*. Hans Citroen is Henri's grandson. On the transport that carried Henri Citroen, Anne Frank, and her family were 498 men, 442 women, and 79 children. They arrived at Birkenau on the 5th. After selection, there remained 258 men, 212 women, and no children.

111 The Citroen family photo album is in the Yoors Family Partnership archive, albeit in fragile pieces.

113 Bombing of Britain, Coventry: Lowe, *Savage Continent*, 6.

113 The Citroens' 1945 Christmas dinner menu, written and illustrated by Marianne, is also in the family's archive.

114 The *Porajmos*: Karen Polak, "Teaching about the Genocide of the Roma and Sinti during the Holocaust: Chances and Challenges in Europe Today," *Intercultural Education* 24, no. 1–2 (2013): 79–92.

15. Pingola Redux

117 "Oh isn't it beautiful . . .": Annabert van Wettum to Jan Yoors, June 13, 1945.

117–18 Jan and Annabert's reunion: recounted in Annabert Yoors' 1982 diary, undated entry.

118 "I was a different person": Ibid.

118 According to the immigration stamps on Jan's passport (#12709), he left Spain on March 1, 1944, and arrived in London on April 18, 1944.

119 "There was the moonlight-filled night . . .": Annabert Yoors' 1982 diary, undated entry.

119 Jan stationed with Belgian Army: After he arrived in England, Jan Yoors joined the Belgian Brigade Piron and served from April 18, 1944, to June 20, 1946. He was demobilized in December 1945 to do postgraduate work at London University. (His military I.D. card is in the Yoors Family Partnership Archives.)

119 "The V-day is past . . .": Jan Yoors to Annabert van Wettum, Aug. 15, 1945.

16. Christ on the Mountainside

122 Alfred Zimmern: Sir Alfred Ekhard Zimmern was a historian and political scientist, and a founder of both UNESCO and the League of Nations Society. He was nominated for a Nobel Peace Prize in 1947. In a letter to Annabert, dated October 22, 1945, Jan mentions in passing that he had meant to go visit Lord and Lady Zimmern that evening but was too down.

122 The Gypsy Lore Society: Jan Yoors was a frequent contributor to the *Journal of the Gypsy Lore Society*.

123 "I don't want to acknowledge . . .": Jan Yoors to Annabert van Wettum, Oct. 22, 1945.

124 "We have to build a new world . . .": Annabert Yoors' 1978 diary, undated entry.

124 Annabert's "pilgrimage" with Jan: recounted in her 1946 diary, undated entry.

125 Marie-Madeleine Davy was involved in the Resistance from the beginning in November 1940, and was very active in helping to hide and transport French persons under threat, as well as British and American pilots shot down over French territory. In 1945 she received the prestigious Croix de Guerre medal, as well as decorations from British, Belgian, and American authorities.

126 Viewing the wreckage of the Battle of the Bulge: Forty years later, in her 1985 diary, Annabert recalled this as a pivotal moment in her and Jan's life, when he described his artistic vision to her. "You visioned [*sic*] there a life dedicated to art. . . . And thus was our life—a vision seen—a vision partly realized."

127 Letter from Gypsy girl: In the archive of the Yoors Family Partnership, there is an undated letter written from Jan to Annabert that says only this: "A large scar on my arm but deep secrets. A scar from Weinela, deep, deep in me. I will tell only you and that sorrow will help us.—Putzi." Marianne believes that Weinela was a Sinti girl with whom Jan was involved during the war. However, Jan's secret is safe: there is no other evidence or information, nothing to explain these tantalizing tidbits.

17. The Other Girl

Marianne Yoors told all the stories in this chapter to the author in a series of interviews.

18. The Apocalypse Tapestry

133 *Masterpieces of French Tapestry*: Arts Council of Great Britain, *Masterpieces of French Tapestry: An Exhibition Held at the Victoria and Albert Museum* (catalog), 1947.

133 A year to weave a single square foot: Jeppson, "Death and Rebirth of a Noble Art."

19. Betwixt and Between

137 "Don't forget, we came out. . . .": Marianne Yoors, in Drake, "Tied in the Wool," 154.

137 Jan's moods: Over forty years later, Annabert reflected on the beginning of their life together. "He needed me—And I had no idea of the hidden psychological wounds the brutality of war had inflicted. . . . It is only now and I am over 60 years old that I begin to understand the dark forces that were at play in the personality, or character, of my so

deeply loved husband. And my heart weeps—I was so young, so foolish, so ignorant." (Annabert Yoors' 1989 diary)

137   "Where is Putzi? . . .": Jan Yoors' diary, August 28, 1945.

139   Whatever Jan wanted: "Even thirty years ago," Marianne said in a 2011 interview, "I would say to Annabert, 'How could you do it?' And she said, 'Jan needed you. I could not take it; I could not take all his emotions, what he needed.'" (Interview with author, July 11, 2011)

141   Marianne entered the mix: "I came right into that as an open book," Marianne explains. "Whoever would have gotten hold of me then would have . . . if the Dalai Lama had met me or if I had gone to California, I would have followed any guru, any master, and Jan became my master." (Interview with author, March 14, 2011)

143   "A gap between ordered worlds . . .": Victor Turner, *The Ritual Process* (New York: Cornell University Press, 1977), 95.

20. A New Family

145   "Marianne came to live with us . . .": Annabert Yoors to Vanya Yoors, undated.

146   "Kneeling next to that little baby . . .": Annabert Yoors' diary, Sept. 2, 1971.

147   "Oh my angel . . .": Annabert Yoors to Jan Yoors, August 15, 1948.

147   "Another long day . . .": Marianne Citroen to Jan Yoors, August 22, 1948, translated by Remko Caprio.

148   "Worked today . . .": Annabert Yoors to Jan Yoors, undated, but from context, August 1948.

149   "But this is the same old egoism . . .": Marianne Citroen to Annabert and Jan Yoors, March 6, 1949.

21. A Threefold Cord

151   The exhibition for which they were preparing was the Eighth Annual Exhibition of Catholic Art, at the Royal Institute of British Architects in London, which ran from Jan. 19 to Feb. 5, 1949. Yoors' tapestry *The Miraculous Draught of Fishes* was listed for sale in the catalog for 350 pounds.

153   "This morning I talked to Lidi . . .": Marianne Citroen to Annabert and Jan Yoors, undated.

153   "My dearest sweet Marianneke . . .": Jan Yoors to Marianne Citroen, May 6, 1949.

155   "Oh silly ones . . .": Marianne Citroen to Annabert and Jan Yoors, dated only as "Jan's feast day." The Feast Day of Saint John is June 24.

155   "Two are better than one . . .": Ecclesiastes 4:9–12, King James Bible.

155   Biblical role-playing: Marianne is as embarrassed by the evidence in the letters of their youthful zealotry as she once was by their sexual frankness. She has little patience for her twenty-two-year-old self. "We were still . . . very romantic, very holier than thou." She shakes her head dismissively. "We knew everything better, we were going to save the world. We were so good, and Jan was such a hero." (Interview with author, July 23, 2013)

22. The New World

159   "After a long, boring trip . . .": Annabert Yoors to Josephine and Louis (surname unknown), July 2, 1951.

159   In the Yoors Family Partnership archive is an affidavit written by Annabert Yoors and dated June 18, 1950, in which she states her approval of her husband's intent to move to New York City. She also asserts that he is now living in Montreal.

159   The Yoors' first address in New York City was at 5 West Sixteenth Street.

160   "In the city you see. . . .": Annabert Yoors to Josephine and Louis (surname unknown), July 2, 1951.

160   "For ten cents . . .": Ibid.

160   "Special air coolers . . .": Ibid.

160   Meeting the Gypsies at the Staten Island Ferry: recounted by Marianne Yoors, interview with author, March 12, 2011.

161   John Reed, "A Day in Bohemia, or Life among the Artists" (written in 1902 and privately printed, 1913).

161   96 Fifth Avenue: Other artist-tenants in the building included William Zorach, Jack Levine, and Leon Nicholas Kalas.

162   Balducci: Ma and Pop Balducci prospered with the changing demo-
graphics of the Village; in the 1970s, they moved their business across
the avenue and expanded it into a famous icon of luxury, a gourmet
market where Villagers could pick up a tin of goose liver pate or sam-
ple the latest gastronomic import, buffalo mozzarella or blood oranges
or salted licorice. Forty years later, that store is gone, too. In the tiny
storefront on Greenwich Avenue where the Yoors used to buy spoiled
fruit for a nickel, a florist now sells orchids for $150.

163   Party with the Rom: Phyllis Stephens, interview with author, May 15,
2014.

163–64 "The moment you can't up and leave . . .": Yoors, Boston Radio
interview.

23. Faux Boho

165   "Our generation in the fifties . . .": Wakefield, *New York in the Fifties*,
121.

165   Postwar American culture: Strausbaugh, *The Village*, 228.

165   "A man with a beard . . .": John Cheever, "The Wrysons," *New Yorker*,
Sept. 13, 1958, 38.

166   "What I couldn't see back in the fifties . . .": Wakefield, *New York in the
Fifties*, 180.

166   Abstract Expressionists and New York School: Strausbaugh, *The Village*, 244.

166   "I allow no nostalgia . . .": Wetzsteon, *Republic of Dreams*, 541.

168   Organizing benefit for Romany Marie: from Annabert Yoors' diary
entries, March–June, 1955.

168   *New Yorker* piece: Henry Hope Reed and Geoffrey T. Hellman, The
"Gypsiana," Talk of the Town, *New Yorker*, Oct. 27, 1951, 26.

168   "Tapestries Made by Gypsy Prince," *New York Times*, Dec. 9, 1956.

169   "In our young hands and minds": Annabert Yoors' diary, May 1978.

24. Rubie

171   "One day he called up . . .". Rubin Rabinowitz, interview with author,
Aug. 18, 2011. All quotations of Rabinowitz are from this interview.

25. A Lesson in Weaving

175   "The teamwork demanded . . ." Jan Yoors, typed and undated artist statement, later quoted in Cynthia Hoy's documentary *Jan Yoors*, 1987.

175   Herter Looms: Hunter, *Tapestries*, 207–15.

175   "[Jan] is the only person . . .": Nobuko Kajatani, quoted in Drake, "Tied in the Wool," 155.

176   There's this sense that this thing is conceived . . .": Robert Hughes, in *Een Vlaming in New-York*, 1975.

177   Jan and the Paternaya Brothers: Annabert Yoors, in *Jan Yoors*.

178   "Do you know how to darn . . .": Marianne Yoors, interview with author, Jan. 8, 2011.

179   "After the tapestry is unrolled . . .": Marianne Yoors, interview with author, March 13, 2011.

26. The Patrons

182   Posthumous success of *Let Us Now Praise Famous Men*, Strausbaugh, *The Village*, 197.

182   Dinner with Jackson Pollock and Lee Krasner: recounted in Annabert Yoors' diary, May 14, 1955.

184   El Charro, on Charles Street in the West Village, was a hip new Spanish-Mexican restaurant in 1955; it closed in March 2016.

184   Dorothy Miller: Lindsay Pollock, "Mama MoMA," *New York*, Nov. 3, 2003.

184   Holger Cahill: As Marianne relates it, Holger Cahill was very impressed with the charcoal drawings and told Jan that if he became director of the Brooklyn Museum he would give Jan an exhibition there. Unfortunately, his health was in decline and he died a few years later.

185   Art versus craft: One of the first notices in New York of Jan's work had articulated the problem well. At the end of 1951 Betty Pepis, the *New York Times Magazine*'s design writer, wrote an article called "One of a Kind" showcasing original objets d'art in ceramics and textiles. These various pieces—Jan's *Knight of Nadara* tapestry among

them—offered the homemaker or interior designer a way to offset the impersonality of modern furnishings. However, her praise came with a caution. "Because objects which fall in this category lie somewhere in a no-man's land between art and the crafts, there can be no precedent for judging them and each must reflect the individual's own taste." In other words, these *objets* lacked the imprimatur of Art. Still, Pepis breezily concluded, "one might be tempted to splurge a Christmas check."

186 Story about Trujillo tapestry: Rubin Rabinowitz, interview with author, Aug. 18, 2011; recounted by Marianne Yoors, interview with author, March 26, 2014.

187 Jim Thompson's Thaibok Fabrics, Ltd., became a place on the map when their silks were used for the Broadway production of *The King and I*, and later for the film, which won the 1956 Academy Award for costume design. Thompson was credited with almost single-handedly saving the Thai silk industry. During the war, he had served as an operative and founded the OSS office in Bangkok—yet another of the many connections Jan made with fellow operatives. In 1967 Thompson disappeared from the Cameron Highlands in Malaysia, and despite a huge search of the region, was never found.

187 "Our big exhibition . . .": Jan Yoors to Eugeen and Magda Peeters Yoors, Feb. 25, 1956, translated from the French by Beatrice Thornton.

188 "It is unbelievable . . .": Annabert Yoors' diary, Jan. 7, 1957.

27. The Family of Man

189 "What amazes me . . .": Robert Hughes, in *Een Vlaming in New-York*, 1975.

189 "We are seeking photographs . . .": Edward Steichen, quoted in Bill Jay, "The Family of Man: A Reappraisal of 'The Greatest Exhibition of All Time,'" *Insight*, Bristol Workshops in Photography, Rhode Island, Number 1, 1989.

190 "It's fantastic . . .": Annabert Yoors' diary, Feb. 26, 1955.

190 270,000 viewers: Jay, "The Family of Man," 3.

190 Catalog sales: Ibid.

191 "Jan is in his thinking, quiet period . . .": Annabert Yoors' diary, May 4, 1955.

191 On the Yoors' list of monthly expenses for September 1955, Anna-bert recorded $15 to Frederick Max (first secretary to the UN's French ambassador) for a camera.

191 "Jan finished his 'Blue Fire'": Annabert Yoors' diary, Feb. 19, 1957. This tapestry was subsequently titled *Primeval Night*.

191 "For me, tapestry is an epic format . . .": Jan Yoors, in *Een Vlaming in New-York*, 1975.

192 Buildings in the Village being torn down: Strausbaugh, *The Village*, 343.

192 Their new address was 329 E. Forty-Seventh Street. Their initial rent was $300 a month. When they renewed the lease in September, it went up to $450.

192 Fashion shoot: "The Tapestry Sweater," *Look*, Aug. 30, 1960.

192 Dizzy Gillespie performed at the Yoors' studio on March 22, 1962.

194 "Jan had parties like that . . .": Rubin Rabinowitz, interview with author, Aug. 18, 2011

194 Mead meets and then models for Yoors: Cynthia Mead, interview with author, June 6, 2012.

195 Daddy Grace: Born Marcelino Manuel da Graça, Daddy Grace was the founder and first bishop of the African American church called the United House of Prayer for All People in Harlem. Jan later shot a sequence for the film *Only One New York* at this church.

196 "This is the pleasure . . .": Jan Yoors, WBAI Radio.

197 "There is a notable humanity . . .": Kathy Komaroff Goodman, inter-view with author, July 30, 2014.

28. Only One New York

200 Jeanyee and Wei Wong: Jan's first job in America, gotten through Betsie Hollants, was for the Catholic publisher Sheed & Ward. He illustrated several book covers for them. It was here that he met Jeanyee, who worked there as a calligrapher.

200 Nigerian voodoo practitioners: According to the production notes for the film, Gaisseau was at first thrown out, but then allowed to return when he showed a tattoo he'd received from a similar sect in Africa.

200 "There was an all-night beauty parlor . . .": Morocco, aka Carolina Varga Dinicu, interview with author, June 8, 2014.

201   Rabbi Menachem Mendel Schneerson and Jan: "Jan never met a stranger, okay? Whoever you were, you had something of interest for him. Now most people don't know that Jan was very friendly with the Rabbi called Menachem Mendel Schneerson, the Lubavitcher Rebbe. . . . One of the reasons, of course, was that Jan spoke French and the Rebbe spoke French because he's a graduate of the Sorbonne in electrical engineering. So they could talk to each other, and they liked each other." Rubin Rabinovitch, interview with author, Aug. 18, 2011.

201   Bobover Grand Rebbe Shlomo Halberstam: "Jan and Pierre went this evening to another wonder rabbi, a Hasidic Jew. A fantastic man, with a brown silk cattan with flowerwork in it. . . . A beautiful fine face. He showed his own private papers from during the war, when he was a secret agent trying to help the Polish Jews escape. He had his beard shaven off, with a fake name. His whole family died in Auschwitz. After the interview, they went to visit his wife and seven children. They ate cake and they saw a film of a girl that had polio that the rabbi had married out." Annabert Yoors' diary, Jan. 28, 1963.

202   "I admit I wouldn't want . . .": Jan Yoors, WBAI Radio.

29. Baby Book

205   "The warm little head . . .": Annabert Yoors' diary, June 14, 1964.

205   "Mammie and Pappie want . . .": Ibid.

206   "Marianne loves our baby . . .": Annabert Yoors' 1964 diary, undated entry.

206   "Mammie duck . . . Mammie rat . . .": Ibid.

206   "Today our baby . . .": Annabert Yoors' diary, Aug. 30, 1964.

208   *Only One New York* reviews: "The fine, fresh, tingling documentary that Mr. Gaisseau has compiled, assisted by Jan Yoors and Jean Hamon, imaginatively explores the more picturesque and obscure ethnical byways of a giant metropolis that seldom sees them—or bothers to" (Thompson, "New Film"). "Their cinematography is perfection" (Crist, "Love Poem").

208   "A heartbreak because of the realities . . .": Jan Yoors, typewritten letter, with handwritten annotation: "Jan Yoors' last letter before his death—in 1977."

209   "I think close to five thousand . . .": Jan Yoors, WBAI Radio.

209   "They like to speak . . .": Ibid.

210   "I want to evoke . . .": Yoors, *The Gypsies*, 13.

30. Tiger and Chipmunk

211   Michael Korda says that Yoors took him to the Factory for the first time.

212   Tiger and the kimono story: recounted by Marianne Yoors, interview with author, June 12, 2014.

212   Chip Monck (born Edward Herbert Beresford Monck) got his start doing lighting at the Village Gate and went on to do the lights for the Monterey Pop Festival and concerts for the Rolling Stones, the Byrds, and Crosby, Stills, and Nash. He served as master of ceremonies at the Woodstock Festival in 1969.

213   "There was a guy . . .": Marianne Yoors, interview with author, June 12, 2014.

214   "I should have done that, too . . .": Ibid.

214   "More than three hundred of New York's . . .": Rice, "Tiger Gives a Blast."

214   "Who did the Frug . . .": Cunningham, "Fluorescent Fashions," B2.

214   "I'm so grateful to Jan . . .": Marianne Yoors, interview with author, June 12, 2014.

214   "Jan didn't want . . .": Ibid.

31. The Models

219   Tapestry for a Lutheran church: *Sheep Going to the Well*, the 30-foot-long tapestry commissioned for the Shepherd of the Hills Lutheran Church in Edina, Minnesota, and completed in 1962, still hangs behind the altar.

220   Two reviews for *The Gypsies*: "An exciting first hand impression of life in a Gypsy camp forever on the move . . . a most valuable and original contribution to Gypsy scholarship" (Starkie, "Forever on the Heath"); "absolutely delightful" (Mead, "Margaret Mead Reviews").

220   "It was wonderful . . .": Jan Yoors, quoted in Hochschild, "A Gypsy for Our Time."

221   "Your book is still on . . .": Annabert Yoors and Marianne Citroen to Jan Yoors, April 12, 1967.

221   "Today we had a visit . . .": Annabert Yoors to Jan Yoors, April 26, 1967.

221   "I made a soufflé . . .": Annabert Yoors to Jan Yoors, April 27, 1967.

221   The new model, Itsumi: Itsumi is a pseudonym.

221   "Itsumi is now so pleasant . . .": Annabert Yoors to Jan Yoors, April 27, 1967.

222   "I love you so much . . .": Annabert Yoors to Jan Yoors, May 9, 1967.

223   "Kik deserves a golden crown . . .": Marianne Citroen to Jan Yoors, undated.

223   "She had good intentions . . .": Annabert Yoors to Jan Yoors, June 14, 1967.

32. The Blue Door on Waverly

225   "Marianne caught her breath": Any persons unacquainted with New York real estate may simply substitute in their imagination the thrill of winning the lottery.

226   Short films for Martha Jackson Gallery: The only one of these films I've been able to find is *The Ivory Knife: Paul Jenkins at Work*, for which Jan did the still photography.

227   Walter Gaudnek, interview with author, Aug. 1, 2014.

227   Marcia McBroom Small, interview with author, July 22, 2014.

227   "Morocco," aka Carolina Varga Dinicu, interview with author, June 12, 2014.

228   Michael Korda, interview with author, Sept. 24, 2011.

228   Working class leaves the Village: Strausbaugh, *The Village*, 448.

228   New York City strikes: Strausbaugh, *The Village*, 450.

229   "as a kind of charmed circle of peace . . .": Michael Korda, interview with author, Aug. 4, 2011.

229   "I always felt . . .": Marcia McBroom Small, interview with author, July 22, 2014.

229   "You'd walk in through the kitchen . . .": Donna Schwartz, interview with author, Feb. 12, 2014.

230   "The wharf had patches of ice . . .": Annabert Yoors' diary, January 1973.

232   "It was the layout of our house . . .": Annabert Yoors' 1978 diary, undated entry.

232   "My sweet husband . . .": Marianne Yoors, interview with author, June 24, 2011.

33. Survival

233   "We will have of course all the money . . .": Jan Yoors to Marianne Citroen, May 4, 1949.

233   The two tapestries commissioned for the lobby of the Marine Midland Bank in Buffalo were titled *Negev 1* and *Negev 2*. They were each 7'5" by 22'6" and had undulating black-and-white shapes on a gold-colored ground. They were inspired by aerial photographs of the Negev Desert in Israel that Jan took on his travels.

233   Jan better known for film and photography: Kathy Komaroff Goodman, interview with author, July 30, 2014. Goodman was Martha Jackson's assistant and the coordinator of the gallery's Red Parrot Films.

234   "Will it be possible . . .": Annabert Yoors' 1972 diary, undated entry.

234   "Several large scale commissions . . .": Annabert Yoors' 1973 diary, undated entry.

234   "The architect Abramowitz, James Johnson Sweeney, the Minskovs, etc.": Max Abramowitz's best-known design is perhaps Avery Fisher Hall in New York. James Johnson Sweeney was director of the Guggenheim Museum from 1952 to 1960, and was formerly the curator of modern art for the Metropolitan Museum of Art. The Minskovs [*sic*] were most probably Dorothy and Myron Minskoff, who visited the Yoors studio on other occasions. Myron Minskoff, a real estate executive, oversaw the design and construction of the Broadway theater that bears his name.

236   Dr. Alton's name has been changed by the author. It appears that Jan's doctor may have been negligent in his treatment of Jan, but all of the parties are now dead and the medical records destroyed, so I am

relying on the memories of Jan's friends and family. Given the subjective nature of such testimony, it would be unjust to use the doctor's actual name.

236   Jan's diabetes: In his memoir *Crossing*, he makes a few oblique references to injections, of particular note when they are crossing the Pyrenees: "I burned with fever and realized that for quite a while I had not taken the daily injection upon which I depended. The sealed glass phials, each containing a single day's dose, had frozen in their container and I did not dare use them anymore. I left the container behind, breaking yet another bond with the past" (202). He later said that he was injecting quinine, which some recent research suggests can cause diabetes. It's also possible he was injecting insulin or an insulin substitute. Dr. Gary Kleinman, executive director of medical development at the University of Miami's Diabetes Research Institute, suggested in a 2013 interview with the author that it's possible Yoors had Type 1½, a recently identified variation of the disease.

237   Sukkot at the Meads: recounted in Annabert Yoors' diary, June 22, 1974.

34. *The Gypsy King*

239   A night in Jan's hospital room: recounted in Annabert Yoors' diary, June 22, 1974.

240   At the Social Security office: recounted by Marianne Yoors, interviews with author, March 13, 2011, and Aug. 13, 2014.

241   Visit from the Roma: summarized from Hochschild, "A Gypsy for Our Time."

241   Unfortunately, Jan's book about the Roma survivors never got beyond the planning stages.

242   "The trees are now full . . .": Annabert Yoors' diary, June 22, 1974.

242   The documentary on Jan is titled *Een Vlaming in New-York*, or *A Fleming in New York*.

243   "New York is the world in miniature . . .": Jan Yoors, in *Een Vlaming in New-York*.

243   Insuring the art: Lloyd's of London insured the transport of 31 tapestries and 68 paintings for $129,040.

243 *Jan Yoors Retrospective*, Ghent Cultural Center in St. Peters Abbey, Belgium. The show ran from Feb. 22 to March 16, 1975.

35. The Dragon

245 "I think there was a little touch of evil . . .": Marianne Yoors, interview with author, March 16, 2011.

245 Aiko is a pseudonym.

245 "Jan finds comfort . . .": Annabert Yoors' diary, Dec. 28, 1976.

246 Chinese New Year: recounted in Annabert Yoors' diary, Jan. 31, 1977. "It was breathtakingly exuberant—Magic come real—all hearts felt strong, ready to conquer anything, fearless of death, enjoying life to the utmost. It was just so fantastic."

247 "I am grateful for my handicaps . . .": quoted in Annabert Yoors' 1980 diary, entry undated.

247 "My fear became this black shaggy cat . . .": Annabert Yoors' 1978 diary, entry undated.

248 Song on the radio: recounted in Annabert Yoors' 1980 diary, entry undated.

36. Thanksgiving

249 1977 Macy's Thanksgiving Day Parade: Grippo and Hoskins, *Macy's Thanksgiving Day Parade*.

251 Jan's dream: recounted in Annabert Yoors' diary, January 1985.

251 "I looked at you . . .": Ibid.

252 "Yet I did well during the years . . .": Annabert Yoors' 1975–78 diary, entry undated.

253 "Oh Lieveke, I see your beaming face . . .": Annabert Yoors' diary, June 15, 1978.

254 "Oh, I couldn't leave Annabert": Marianne Yoors, interview with author, June 24, 2011.

254 Natural Academy of Sciences, Washington, D.C., *Tapestries by Jan Yoors*, April 8, 1980, opening.

254 Pratt Institute, Brooklyn, N.Y., *Contemporary Tapestry*, Oct. 7–Nov. 7, 1980.

254   Clocktower Gallery: March 7, 1979, opening. This was an alternative arts space founded in 1972 in Tribeca at the top of a landmarked McKim, Mead & White building. In 2013 the city sold the building to be turned into luxury condos.

254   Museum of Natural History, New York City, *Jan Yoors, Gypsies*, 1986.

254   Duke University, Durham, N.C., *Jan Yoors, Contemporary Tapestries*, Sept. 25–Oct. 6, 1983.

254   Cleveland State University, Cleveland, Ohio, *The Yoors Tapestries*, May 11–June 9, 2001.

254   East Hampton, N.Y., Lizan Tops Gallery, *Tapestries and Drawings by Jan Yoors*, Nov. 21–Dec. 30, 1998.

254   Summit, N.J., Kent Place Gallery, *Tapestries and Sculptures of Jan Yoors*, Oct. 7–Nov. 8, 1991.

254   Melbourne, Australia, Westpac Gallery, *Tapestry Symposium*, May 6–26, 1988.

254   St. Petersburg, Russia, State Academy of Art and Design, 1996.

255   Articles in the *New York Times*: Robert Lipsyte, "Coping: Three into Two Did Go," *New York Times*, June 7, 1998; Robert Lipsyte, "Coping: The Thanks from Three Tables," *New York Times*, Nov. 29, 1998.

256   After Jackson Pollock was buried at the Green River Cemetery in East Hampton, it became an unofficial cemetery for writers and artists. In addition to Pollock and Lee Krasner, other notable residents include Frank O'Hara, Alan Pakula, Jean Stafford, Ad Reinhardt, Elaine de Kooning, and Charles Gwathmey.

256   "I dreamt that Jan had returned . . .": Annabert Yoors' diary, July 2, 1980.

Afterword

257   Naples, Florida, Artis-Naples, Baker Museum, *Jan Yoors: A Retrospective*, May 16–July 26 and Sept. 5–Oct. 11, 2015.

262   Definition of tantra: Alexander Berzin, "The Meaning of Tantra," Berzin Archives, https://studybuddhism.com/en/advanced-studies/vajrayana/tantra-theory/making-sense-of-tantra/the-meaning-of-tantra.

263   "It is what is unseen . . .": Jan Yoors, in Drake, "Tied in the Wool,"
154.

Amersfoort, Herman, and Piet Kamphius, eds. *May 1940: The Battle for the Netherlands*. Leiden, Neth.: Brill, 2010.

Arts Council of Great Britain. *Masterpieces of French Tapestry: An Exhibition Held at the Victoria and Albert Museum* (catalog), 1947.

Citroen, Hans, and Barbara Starzynska. *Auschwitz-Oscwięçim: The Hidden City in the East*. Rotterdam: Post Editions, 2012.

Coles, Harry L., and Albert K. Weinberg. *United States Army in WW2 Special Studies. Civil Affairs: Soldiers Become Governors*. Washington, D.C.: Center of Military History, United States Army, 1992.

Comenas, Gary. "Andy Warhol Chronology." http://www.warholstars.org/chron/contents.html.

Crist, Judith. "Love Poem on Film of Our City." *New York Herald Tribune*, Oct. 1, 1964.

Cunningham, Bill. "Fluorescent Fashions." *Chicago Tribune*, Jan. 31, 1966, B2.

Deflem, Mathieu. "Ritual, Anti-Structure, and Religion: A Discussion of Victor Turner's Processual Symbolic Analysis." *Journal for the Scientific Study of Religion*, no. 30 (1991): 1–25.

Drake, Cathryn. "Tied in the Wool." *Metropolis*, June 2001, 136–39, 154–55.

Dunmall, Giovanna. "Double Exposure: Photography's Biggest Ever Show Comes Back to Life." *The Guardian.com*, July 5, 2013.

Een Vlaming in New-York, directed by Jos van Schoor. Brussels: VRT, 1975. Film.

Goodlet, Sean C., ed. "The Tapestries of the Apocalypse (Château d'Angers)." The On-Line Sourcebook, 2001. http://sourcebook.fitchburgstate.edu/history/apocalypse.html

Grippo, Robert M., and Christopher Hoskins. *Macy's Thanksgiving Day Parade*. Mt. Pleasant, S.C.: Arcadia, 2004.

Harden, Blaine. "Grand Rabbi Shlomo Halberstam, 92, Is Dead." *New York Times*, Aug. 3, 2000.

Hedgepath, Sonja Maria, and Rochelle G. Saidel, eds. *Sexual Violence against Jewish Women during the Holocaust*, 164–66. Lebanon, N.H.: University Press of New England (Brandeis University Press), 2010.

Hochschild, Adam. "A Gypsy for Our Time." In *Finding the Trapdoor: Essays, Portraits, Travels*. Syracuse University Press, 1997.

Howells, Tom, ed. *Tapestry: A Woven Narrative*. London: Black Dog, 2012.

Hunter, George Leland. *Tapestries: Their Origins, History, and Renaissance.* New York: John Lane, 1912.

Hurska, Jane. "Tapestries: One of the Many Lives of Jan Yoors." *RWA* magazine, Spring 2012.

Jan Yoors, directed by Cynthia Hoy. New York: NYU Tisch School of the Arts, 1983. Thesis film, video.

Jarry, Madeleine. "French Tapestry Today." *The Bulletin of the Needle and Bobbin Club*, no. 54 (1971). https://www.cs.arizona.edu/patterns/weaving/articles/nb71_tp1.pdf.

Jay, Bill. "The Family of Man: A Reappraisal of 'The Greatest Exhibition of All Time.'" In *Insight*, Bristol Workshops in Photography, Rhode Island, no. 1 (1989).

Jeppson, Lawrence. "Death and Rebirth of a Noble Art." *Nauvoo Times:* True to the Faith. Nov. 5, 2012. http://www.nauvootimes.com.

Kerr, David, and A. Bdiri. "Quinine-Associated Hypoglycaemia Causing Diabetes." *Diabetic Medicine*, no. 25 (2008): 241–42.

Lipsyte, Robert. "Coping: Three into Two Did Go." *New York Times*, June 7, 1998.

Lowe, Keith. *Savage Continent: Europe in the Aftermath of World War II*. New York: St. Martin's, 2012.

Mead, Margaret. "Margaret Mead Reviews." *Redbook*, September 1967, 52, 54–58.

McKnight, Floyd. *Rudolf Steiner and Anthroposophy*. New York: Anthroposophical Society in America, 1967.

Mikhman, Dan. *Belgium and the Holocaust: Jews, Belgians, Germans*. Jerusalem: Daf-Noy, 1998.

Moffat, Charles. "Andy Warhol, Pop Artist." *The Art History Archive*, November 2007. http://www.arthistoryarchive.com/arthistory/popart/Andy-Warhol.html.

Only One New York, directed by Jean-Pierre Gaisseau. Burbank, Calif.: Embassy Pictures, 1964. Film.

Pepis, Betty. "One of a Kind." *New York Times*, Dec. 3, 1951, 24–25.

Polak, Karen. "Teaching about the Genocide of the Roma and Sinti during the Holocaust: Chances and Challenges in Europe Today." *Intercultural Education* 24, no. 1–2 (2013): 79–92.

Pollock, Lindsay. "Mama MoMA." *New York*, Nov. 3, 2003.

Presser, Jacob. *Ashes in the Wind: The Destruction of Dutch Jewry*. London: Souvenir, 2010.

Reed, Henry Hope, and Geoffrey T. Hellman. "Gypsiana." Talk of the Town, *New Yorker*, October 27, 1951

Reed, John. "The Day in Bohemia, or Life among the Artists" (poem). New York: Hillacre Bookhouse, 1913.

Reymenants, Geraldine. "'La Bergère d'un immense troupeau d'âmes': Betsie Hollants' leven in dienst van katholieken, joden en vrouwen." *Brood & Rozen: Tijdschrift voor de geschiedenis van sociale bewegingen*, no. 3 (2003): 48–63.

Rice, Don. "Tiger Gives a Blast." *New York Herald Tribune*, Jan. 31, 1960.

St. George, Andrew. "The Wild Goose." *Argosy*. November 1956.

Sandeen, Eric. *Picturing an Exhibition: The Family of Man and 1950s America*. Albuquerque: University of New Mexico Press, 1995.

Starkie, Walter. "Forever on the Heath." *New York Times*, March 3, 1967, 294, 316.

Steichen, Edward. *The Family of Man*. New York: Museum of Modern Art: Distributed by Harry N. Abrams, 1986.

Stoltzfus, Nathan. Florida State University home page. http://history.fsu.edu/person/nathan-stoltzfus.

Stoodley, Sheila Gibson. "Dream Weavers." *Art & Antiques*, Sept. 25, 2009.

Stourton, Edward. *Cruel Crossing: Escaping Hitler across the Pyrenees*. London: Doubleday UK, 2013.

Stout, Robert Joe. *The Blood of the Serpent: Mexican Lives*. New York: Algora, 2003.

Strausbaugh, John. *The Village: 400 Years of Beats and Bohemians, Radicals and Rogues: A History of Greenwich Village*. New York: HarperCollins, 2013.

Thompson, Howard. "New Film Draws Portrait of City." *New York Times*, Aug. 14, 1964, 14.

Thornton, Beatrice V. "Bohemian Rhapsody." *Modern Magazine*, Summer 2010.

————. "Reconsidering *Metaphors*: A Photographic Essay on Religious Architecture." Unpublished, 2014.

Turner, Victor. "Betwixt and Between: The Liminal Period in *Rites des Passage*." *The Proceedings of the American Ethnological Society, Symposium on the Study of New Approaches to Religion* (1964): 4–20.

Van der Zee, Henri A. *The Hunger Winter: Occupied Holland, 1944–45*. Lincoln, Neb.: University of Nebraska Press, 1982.

Van Galen Last, Dick, and Rolf Wolfswinkel. *Anne Frank and After*. Amsterdam: Amsterdam University Press, 1996.

Van Gennep, Arnold. *The Rites of Passage*. Translated by Monika V. Vizedom and Gabrielle L. Caffee. Chicago: University of Chicago Press, 1960.

Wakefield, Dan. *New York in the Fifties*. New York: Houghton Mifflin, 1992.

Weaving Two Worlds: Jan Yoors, 1922–1977, directed by David E. Lackey. New York: Whirlwind Creative, 2008. DVD.

"Westerbork Transit Camp." Holocaust Education & Archive Research Team, 2007. http://www.holocaustresearchproject.org/othercamps/westerbork.html.

"Westerbork Transit Camp: History and Overview." Jewish Virtual Library. American Israeli Cooperative Enterprise. http://www.jewishvirtuallibrary.org/jsource/Holocaust/Westerbork.html.

Wetzsteon, Ross. *Republic of Dreams: Greenwich Village: The American Bohemia 1900–1960*. New York: Simon and Schuster, 2002.

White, N. J., D. A. Warrell, P. Chanthavanich, S. Looareesuwan, M. J. Warrell, S. Krishna, D. H. Williamson, and R. C. Turner. "Severe Hypoglycemia and Hyperinsulinemia in Falciparum Malaria." *The New England Journal of Medicine*, no. 309 (1983): 61–66.

Yoors, Annabert. Unpublished video interview by Susan Kaplan. Archives of Yoors Family Partnership.

Yoors, Annabert, and Marianne Yoors. Unpublished audio interview by Susan Kaplan. Archives of Yoors Family Partnership.

Yoors, Jan. *Crossing: A Journal of Survival and Resistance in World War II*. New York: Simon and Schuster, 1971. Prospect Heights, Ill.: Waveland, reissued 1988.

————. *The Gypsies*. New York: Simon and Schuster, 1967. Prospect Heights, Ill.: Waveland, reissued 1987.

————. Interview by Andrew St. George. Unpublished audio recording. Archives of Yoors Family Partnership.

————. WBAI Radio, New York, 1966. Interview.

Yoors, Jan (photographs), and Charles Samuel (text). *Only One New York.* New York: Simon and Schuster, 1965.

Yoors-Peeters, Magda. "Daring to Be Human." In *Peace Is the Way: Writings on Nonviolence from the Fellowship of Reconciliation*, edited by Walter Wink. Maryknoll, N.Y.: Orbis Books, 2000.